THE
CROSSROAD

THE
CROSSROAD
Mark Donaldson, VC

MACMILLAN
Pan Macmillan Australia

First published 2013 in Macmillan by Pan Macmillan Australia Pty Limited
1 Market Street, Sydney

Reprinted 2013 (three times)

Cataloguing-in-Publication entry is available
from the National Library of Australia
http://catalogue.nla.gov.au

9781742612287 (hardback)
9781743519103 (paperback)

Typeset in 13.5/15pt Bembo by Post Pre-press Group
Printed in Australia by McPherson's Printing Group

Papers used by Pan Macmillan Australia Pty Ltd are natural, recyclable products made
from wood grown in sustainable forests. The manufacturing processes conform to the
environmental regulations of the country of origin.

This is dedicated to my family by choice,
my family by blood and
my family who I've fought alongside.
And to anyone who thinks it isn't possible to become
something bigger or better.
It is.

PROLOGUE

I don't want this to sound like anything other than what it was. Not romanticised and breathless like a Hollywood movie, and not matter-of-fact either, as if I'm too much of a hard man to feel anything.

My memories of combat sit between those poles. I was highly aware of everything going on around me. I was concentrating on doing my job, which is often just a matter of doing one thing properly, then the next thing properly, and staying in the moment. But that's not to say I didn't feel the same emotions any normal person would when the bullets and grenades were whirring so close that I could feel them before I heard them. I won't pretend I wasn't shitting myself, but in my job it's all about not letting those feelings get the better of you.

The day I'm talking about, 2 September 2008, would change my life and in some ways come to define who I am. I respect how history and myth build up around events and lend them importance, but I can also clearly remember how it was from my point of view, and that's the story I'll tell: a contact I was in, alongside my mates, fighting to survive. It's true that every soldier is, at these moments, fighting his own personal war.

I was on my third trip to Afghanistan with 3 Squadron, Special Air Service Regiment (SASR or SAS); the names of the operators have been changed to protect those members still serving in the SAS. I had only been in the SASR for four years, and was still a trooper, equivalent to a private in the regular army. My first two trips had been, for the most part, frustratingly lacking in action. Like my mates in the Regiment, I was keyed up for battle and craving that ultimate test of our professionalism.

During that third trip, the tempo of our tasks in Uruzgan province had risen steeply. In July, we'd lost one of the Regiment's signallers, Sean McCarthy, to an improvised explosive device (IED), which had become the Taliban's favoured major tactical threat. In August, I'd been in a vehicle that hit an IED, the explosion throwing me several metres into the air then dropping me onto the ground via the bonnet of the vehicle. When an American Black Hawk helicopter came to pick up the wounded, it had crashed almost on top of us. I'll get to these incidents later. Suffice to say, there'd been a bit going on.

At the end of August, we went up to Forward Operating Base (FOB) Anaconda, named after the big battle in 2002 when the Americans and their allies, including Australian SAS soldiers, had taken a hammering from Al Qaeda but emerged to secure many of their objectives. I'd read books about Anaconda and heard about it even before I joined the Regiment. The story, about recovering from a disastrous situation and surviving despite being horribly outnumbered by the enemy, had inspired me by redefining what 'success' could mean from a soldier's point of view.

The land there, in the east of Uruzgan, is mostly open rocky desert marked out by spectacular jagged mountains and valleys with bands of vegetation, the 'green belt', near the watercourses where the Afghans have their crops, live-stock and villages. Even up in the desolate higher ground, though, one thing you learn in Afghanistan is that you're never alone. No matter how isolated and barren the land, there's always someone out there.

FOB Anaconda was a small base manned by American Special Forces Green Berets working with and training the Afghan Security Forces. Earlier that summer, we'd captured the Taliban commander of Uruzgan province, an achieve-ment that was always tempered by the fact that as soon as one head was removed, another immediately grew in its place. The second night we were at Anaconda, we received a tip-off that this new commander was at a compound in the area. We walked all night through the green belt, but when we got to the compound it was empty, apart from a couple of women and kids. Either he'd slipped us, or the intelligence was wrong or slow in reaching us, which was pretty standard at that time.

This was the first of a series of jobs with the basic aim of sticking our finger into the hornet's nest and seeing what we could stir up. Unable to get Chinook or Black Hawk helicopters to take us back to the Australian base at Tarin Kowt, we asked the Americans how we could help.

They said there was a valley to the east, called Ana Kalay, where they were constantly getting attacked. When they'd ventured up there, they'd also heard a lot of enemy talk on the Taliban's ICOM network (ICOM is a brand of two-way radio), an indicator of heavy hostile activity.

I knew this valley. On my first trip in 2006, I'd been there and seen Afghan National Army (ANA) checkpoints and compounds. But by 2008, the ANA had been unable to hold these points and had backed away towards the west. The eastern end of the valley was now a virtual no-go zone – it had gone from what we call 'permissive' to 'non-permissive' – which was an eye-opener to me. In two years, things had got much worse for us as the enemy had reorganised and rearmed.

The general plan was for the Americans to set themselves as bait for ambushes. SAS patrols would walk out into the valley at night, pick our way through the hills, and set up at points where we figured an ambush would take place. The next day the Americans would come driving up through the green belt, the enemy would concentrate behind the cover of trees and buildings to get them on their return trip, and we'd be ready to take the enemy out.

It worked like a dream, at first. The Americans drove up in convoy, and the interpreter – or 'terp' – we'd have in the patrols listened to a radio and passed on the ICOM chatter, giving us an insight into the enemy's movements. After the Americans went through, the Talibs responded to their orders and poured down from the east and into a position near the green belt to attack the US vehicle patrol. Everything went to plan, and we were able to take out thirteen enemy fighters and two cars.

Our morale was perky and the Americans, as usual, were stoked after getting into a contact. They had a different way of thinking. We approached contacts with, we hoped, calm professionalism, whereas the Americans got very amped up. They were incredibly brave, willing to take a risk to get a reward, but much more exuberant about the whole thing than we were. It had been a perfect ambush in that environment, and back at the FOB the Americans were high-fiving and whooping. We were just quietly pleased with having carried out another job in a professional way.

We spent the night at the FOB and again asked the Americans what we could do while we waited for our helo transport out. The Americans told us no one had been able to get past a certain point in the Ana Kalay Valley, an old white building that used to be a school. The Talibs' view was that once any coalition troops went past that school, we were fair game. We suggested something similar to the previous job: send patrols up the night before, get them to walk around and set up, and then send a vehicle convoy out as bait.

This time our patrol, India 4, would be part of the bait. Other SAS patrols went out on foot on the night of 1 September to take the 12-kilometre trek into the valley and mountains, and we loaded up the cars on the morning of the 2nd. We had Barry, from one of the other patrols, with us in India 4 because he'd had an attack of gastro and couldn't walk far. One of our troopers, Louis, got cut away to the walking team – luckily for him, as it turned out.

As we were loading the vehicles, the 2IC of our patrol, Bruce, was giving me shit. This was the first time I'd been in a vehicle since being blown up in August, and he was saying, 'Damn, we're gunna hit an IED before we even get up there,' like I had a hex on me. Humour was our way of dealing with things. Bruce took photos of his legs before leaving, as he always did, so he could look at them later and say, 'That was the last time I saw my legs.' I joined in, passing him the camera, saying, 'You sure you don't want to take another shot?'

We drove in a five-vehicle convoy into the rising sun, a mixture of almost forty Australians, Americans and Afghans. We were in Humvees, as wide as a tank but lower, with a dual cabin and a trayback set-up, like a ute. Each Hummer had a gunner in the turret and another in the tray. One car had a US explosive-detection dog (EDD) and his handler,

'Rod' Rodriguez, and masses of gear and ammunition. We ragged out the Americans pretty mercilessly for packing for each trip as if they were going to the Battle of the Bulge. It would turn out to be fortunate for all of us that they'd packed so much ammo.

It was extremely quiet on the ICOM, even more than usual for an early morning. In my experience, quiet is often an indicator of impending combat. We were also going very slowly, driving off to the side of the road on a dry creek bed to avoid the IEDs we suspected would be on the road. Our engineers and their dogs were out to the sides of the vehicles, minesweeping, while the Afghan engineers were at the front. They were impressive: they had a nose for a mine, and would often just stroll up, poke with a stick and find one, whereas we had a lot of technology to help us out.

Our convoy's role as bait seemed to be working. We could see lots of women and children leaving the area, as always when something was about to happen. The ICOM sparked up. A Taliban commander's voice was revving up his fighters saying, 'We should attack them, we should attack them! How dare they come this far up the valley? We're not doing anything about it!'

The Green Berets cleared a village at the eastern end of the valley. We saw about seven Taliban fighters 'squirting', or taking off up to the hills, and another SAS patrol shot them all, a clan leader and his cronies, as they ran straight into the waiting patrol. It was too far away for our patrol to join in. I had the shits and said to the boys, 'This is bullshit. Nothing ever happens to our patrol.'

By mid-afternoon, we were preparing to go back to the FOB. The ICOM traffic suggested that enemy fighters were getting ready for us to turn around and come back past the green belt. Some of us thought this was too risky, and our patrol commander (PC), Adam, said to his American counterpart, 'Let's wait till night. We know we've got the advantage in moving at night. We have NVGs [night-vision goggles] and they don't, or if they do it's only going to be one or two sets.'

The Americans were adamant about getting back before nightfall. They said their Afghan drivers didn't like being out at night, and their boss wanted them back. We had the option of either helping them out or cutting them away and going up into the mountains to link up with our other patrols to walk back at night. But it's not good for coalition relations if you say, 'You guys fend for yourselves, we're outta here.' So we jumped in with them and started the drive back at about three o'clock. I remember drinking some water – it would be the last for a while.

Our patrol was in the last of the five Hummers. We drove through one area where the Talibs had said on the ICOM they were going to ambush us, and they hadn't. It wasn't unusual for them to talk big but take no action. There was just one farmer out there ploughing his field.

We went through a shallow pass, some 4.5 kilometres from Anaconda. The terrain was undulating enough to slow the cars as we came over a knoll. The cars edged forward until all five were on the forward-facing slope.

Ours was the last car through, and the moment we emerged, the air erupted. Rounds and rocket-propelled grenades (RPGs) were zinging past the cars. Guys in our convoy were yelling, and the cars were moving around into a defensive formation. Rounds were kicking up the dust all around us. The attack was coming from two points ahead of us and two to the southern flanks, in the green belt about 300 metres away, but it was hard to pinpoint exactly where they were.

We had a rough plan for what to do when it was 'action on'. My job was to get an 84-millimetre rocket-launcher, push out to a flank and return fire. I had a heightened awareness, with my adrenaline going, but didn't feel that I, or the situation around me, was out of control. In training, I'd seen guys losing control, going crazy, and later being unable to recall anything they'd done. In my mind, everything that happened that day is clear.

Soon we got word of our first casualty. One of the Americans, Joe, had been hit, a round passing through his arm while he was setting up a 60-millimetre mortar. Taking maximum care of our wounded was a priority for us, and probably something that made Afghanistan different from many previous wars Australians had been involved in (possibly besides Vietnam), where casualties were pushed back behind the lines and the momentum of the battle maintained. Here, a casualty was something we would deal with immediately, calling for an aeromedical evacuation (AME) by helicopter if possible. No one would be left behind. It's a subtle but significant change in the approach to warfare.

Joe was put into a car to be taken care of by a medic. It was far too dangerous for an AME, even if it had been necessary for him. Rounds were still coming at us: I remember seeing shrapnel bounce off a car, whizzing and tumbling along next to it, still spinning in the dirt beside me.

With the rocket I managed to seemingly nullify one Taliban position, but it was impossible to tell how many more of the enemy were firing at us. As a scout for the patrol, my job was to find out where they were and shoot back, while reporting information up the chain through the 2IC, Bruce. But it had become pretty clear that we were caught in an ambush of some size.

After that opening assault, which went for about twenty minutes, things went into a brief lull before it was on again. A volley cut straight through our patrol, four or five of the bullets coming between me and my patrolmate Taylor, who was only a couple of metres away. We realised this firing was coming from behind us, on the high ground to the north. This was the moment we understood we were surrounded – including from above – obviously at a major disadvantage, and being driven towards an open killing ground to the west.

We felt really exposed at that point. Fortunately, one of the American JTACs (joint terminal attack controllers, who call in air strikes) had got an F-18 jet overhead, and it gave us some breathing space by coming through with a couple of gun runs to the north, putting rounds from its 30-millimetre cannon onto the fighters there. The JTAC, who was in one of the Hummers with a stack of communications technology, must have given the pilot a good 'talk-on', describing the target, because those rounds caused the enemy to back off for about ten minutes.

Despite increasing casualties, the Americans were still insisting on trying to get back to Anaconda. We kept trying to persuade them to wait till night. Another gun run from the jets gave us some more relief, but it only quietened the enemy for a few minutes. The shooting returned more heavily, from the green belt. About a kilometre thick, the green belt had plenty of cornfields, trees and buildings for the enemy to hide in.

Our car was giving us cover, but was also the enemy's target. Whichever side we hid on, we'd receive incoming fire from that flank. When we switched, we'd cop it from there. Five of us were racing from side to side, huddling in and trying to get some rounds off, but we were mainly on the receiving end. Every car was getting covered in buzzing hornets, and RPGs were flying across the bonnet.

I ran towards the northern side of the vehicle and jumped into the tray, taking a few deep breaths as it started crawling towards the FOB. Bursts of incoming rounds were still alternating from the north and south. On the back of the Hummer beside me an American was on the 240 Bravo, a 7.62-calibre machine gun, firing wildly, everywhere.

I looked up to the north and could see this enemy position behind a sangar, or a rock wall that they'd built for cover, with holes they could put their barrels through. I put the American onto that target. 'Left a bit . . . Left a bit . . . You're on.'

He fired, which only brought heaps of rounds our way, pinging off the car. He was ducking and weaving, though in that situation it pretty much doesn't matter what you do, either your number is up or it's not. Then someone yelled out a target indication to the south. As I turned, I could see a Talib pop up in the longer grass in the green belt with an RPG-launcher on his shoulder. I shouted, 'RPG!' I got a couple of shots off, but the enemy managed to get a rocket away. *Whoosh* – you could feel the power of the rocket pushing the air out of the way. The enemy fighter dropped.

Our group started taking a few hits. Adam, the patrol commander, was shot through the wrist. Barry was hit in both legs, and then Eric, our JTAC, who was talking to some Apaches to assist, caught a round through his ribcage. A few of us who were uninjured pushed away from our car and lay in a ditch. All Bruce and I had for cover were two small rocks, about the size of footballs, stacked on top of each other to create what passed for a wall. Rounds were zooming over our heads. Bruce, who was now leading the patrol, was doing an awesome job, telling us where to look and what to report on, asking how much ammo we had and giving us orders. It's a big thing in a contact having someone talking to you who exudes calm. For myself, I felt I was able to control the fear and stay lucid.

In the ditch, Bruce and I had a chat. There was an abandoned compound about 50 metres away on the edge of the green belt. We talked about making a strongpoint there and pushing into the green. He said, 'They might come out and try to surround us, but at least we'd have the cover of that building.'

I said, 'I don't think the Yanks will want to do that. We could cut them loose and do it ourselves, but then we'd be on our own in this valley trying to fight until night-time.'

There was a chance of getting more air support from some Dutch Apache helicopters, but when they were called in by the JTAC they decided not to attack. I'll get to that in detail later. For now, all that needs to be said is that when the Apaches flew away we realised we were on our own. If we were going to get out of this it would have to be without further air support.

Again, we were limited in our actions by our responsibilities to the whole convoy. Meanwhile, the medics stabilised Barry and Eric and wanted to move Barry into our car. I ran around to help get him out, but the front car took off at speed and left me in the open. I tried to get alongside it, but a shower of rounds came at me as I was in the open.

I managed to make it to the relative safety of the next vehicle in the packet. Bruce and Taylor were beside it. The car in front was copping a heap of rounds. I remember seeing a lot of RPGs coming onto them. One bounced off the bonnet and the other went under the car and blew up. There was a big burst of dust and at first I thought they'd hit an IED. *Fuck, we're going to have a mobility kill.* A mobility kill, or a disabled vehicle, could change everything for the worse. We'd have to rally around this car, put up a section defence, transfer all the people and gear out of it, and consolidate two cars into one. *If we take a mobility kill*, I thought, *we're in the shit.* As if we weren't already.

The car was all right, but we were taking more casualties. I said to Bruce, 'They've got this spot dialled in.' The Talibs had their guns and RPG launchers set for that exact distance. 'I'm going to run through that position and take cover there.' I pointed to a rock about the size of a coffee table. 'The cars are what's drawing the RPG fire,' I said. If we ran out, we might be able to divert the fire for long enough to get our car through.

Bruce said, 'Righto,' and ran into the open beside me.

I remember hearing one RPG being fired off. We dived behind that rock and watched the car go through. No RPGs were shot at it, but we'd nearly been knocked off. I joked to Bruce, 'That probably wasn't such a good idea.'

For the next kilometre, Bruce, Taylor and I basically ran around and around our car as it drove along, firing back as much as we could. We were drake-shooting across the likely enemy positions, raking them with fire, but it was depleting our ammunition. I'd gone through all six of the magazines I'd brought with me – there were thirty rounds per mag – but I still needed more, and picked up extra from the back of the car.

It was a pretty hairy period, maybe the most intense of the whole ambush. We'd be three seconds on one side of the car, with rounds banging in around us. We'd run around the vehicle to escape, and the rounds chased us. Once we got to the other side, we'd have five seconds' breathing space to locate the enemy and shoot back before the rounds would come in from *that* side.

At one point I felt a round come really close behind, like someone had ripped my pants. I later realised that this was exactly what had happened: a round had gone through my pants without touching me. Soldiers have a complicated relationship with the idea of luck: obviously you train in order to minimise the impact of luck and maximise your control over a situation. Some believe more in luck than others. I'm one who trains extremely seriously to improve my odds, but I'm also under no illusion about how decisive luck can be.

I saw some enemy fighters breaking from one building to another, took some shots at them, and was changing my magazine when the strangest thing happened. Everything around me felt like it closed in and went quiet. I was shooting my weapon but couldn't hear it. I felt odd, and kind of numb.

Soon I figured out what had taken place. The .50-calibre machine gun in the turret of the vehicle was only a foot above my head and the percussion of that, three or four rounds at a time, had dulled my senses. My ears were ringing and I felt deaf. Now I was getting a shock every time it fired, due to the percussive effect of the weapon.

Once I got myself together, I took some more cracks at the fighters in the buildings on the edge of the green belt. I could feel rounds hitting the metal of the car just beside me. I felt even more exposed than earlier, more or less a sitting duck. The metal was flaking, bits flying off and hitting my cheek. I had to run around again to the other side.

By now the ambush had been going on, the enemy rolling along beside us, for more than two hours. But we were getting towards the end of the valley. About two kilometres from the FOB, the ridge line squeezed in from the north and formed a choke point. It was another dangerous spot, but possibly the last before we could accelerate towards safety. The sun, setting in the west, was shining into our eyes but we could see the cars in front copping a fair bit of fire, as were we.

A bullet hit Taylor in the head; it caused a serious graze but he was still alive. It's all luck, in the end. We were inching closer to our escape, but the fight was a long way from over. The car in front of us was having a really bad time, and as it came through that choke point, an RPG went off in airburst right above it. The grenade sent shrapnel down, and the force of the blast threw at least two people out. One was an Afghan interpreter, who'd basically had half his face taken off by shrapnel, and another was a dog-handling engineer, David.

Our car veered off to the flank and was overtaking the position where the other car had been hit. Freakishly, the vehicle was still able to move and had laboured forward. As we went past them, I saw the EDD labrador, Sarbi, running around like crazy. Her handler, David, got up and dusted himself off, but Sarbi took off towards the buildings in the green belt. Famously, she'd turn up again a year later.

I also saw the Afghan terp lying face-down in the dust. These terps took enormous risks just by working with us. If the Taliban knew their identities, their families would be threatened and their lives wouldn't be worth living. I didn't know the guy well, but he was part of our convoy and when someone's injured you don't make distinctions.

I yelled to Bruce, 'I'm going to get that bloke.'

Bruce looked at the terp, who wasn't moving.

The convoy was grinding towards the end of the valley and what seemed like safety. In probably 500 metres, we'd be all right. We were now about 80 metres ahead of the terp.

I said again to Bruce, 'I'm going to grab this guy.'

He shook his head. 'Nup, don't worry about him, let the other cars pick him up.'

But we knew the condition of the car nearest us, and for all we knew the other vehicles might have been getting hit just as badly. I remember looking at Bruce, and looking back at the terp. A lot of fire was still coming in, hitting the ground around us. I said nothing.

And then I took off.

*

There are times in life when you reach a crossroad without realising it. That day, in Afghanistan, I'd unknowingly reached such a point, and a voice in my head told me to take a particular path. If I'd made a different decision, chosen another path, then my life wouldn't have turned out the way it has, and whether that's for better or for worse I still don't know. But that voice told me to take off, and what happened next became a bigger thing than me. It gained a symbolism that seems heavier than one individual can carry. For the Australian Army, it would turn into a badly needed 'good news' story. It brought me the Victoria Cross, an honour I only really began to understand when I saw how much it meant to other people, from senior military officers, the Queen and political leaders to people who came up to me in the street in Australia and overseas with tears in their eyes. To my mates in the Regiment, it was just a small part of one of many important jobs we did together in Afghanistan. To that interpreter, it meant the difference between life and death. But there's a flipside. To Bruce, it's still the stupidest thing he's ever seen in battle. And to my wife, Emma, it's not a pleasant memory. It's the day when, in her mind, I could just as easily have not come home.

At the bottom of it, whether it was brave or dumb or both, whatever combination it was of my professionalism and luck that got me through, it was what it was. A crossroad I didn't know I'd arrived at, and a voice in my head that told me to run back and pick up that terp. And what I get asked – what I ask myself, without going anywhere near really knowing the answer – is where that voice came from.

ONE

I was in the SAS for a few years before I realised that a lot of us had hardship or some big trauma in our backgrounds. One guy had seen his father murder his mother when he was six years old. Another saw his girlfriend die in a car accident. It makes a certain sense that big things like this, if they don't kill you, can shape you into a person who wants to take on the particular challenges of life as an elite soldier.

How I became that person is a complicated story. A lot of it comes from my mum and dad – what they gave me, and what happened to them when I was a teenager. I don't feel like I'm a victim in life, and don't want to make too much of how a couple of terrible events shaped my character. I'm more than just the product of what happened to Mum and Dad, and my childhood had a whole lot more happiness than tragedy. But at the same time, I can't run away from it, and I can't say for sure that losing my parents didn't play a big part in producing that voice that told me, one day in Afghanistan, to get to my feet and do something they would be proud of.

*

There are military families, and there are families with soldiers in them. Ours was definitely the second type. We had men, uncles and great-uncles down to my own father, who'd joined the military and fought in wars going back to World War I. But that didn't mean we had medals on the walls and photographs and memorabilia and evenings of sitting by the fireside hearing stories of wartime hero-ics. In fact, we didn't even go to Anzac Day marches. Men in our family were soldiers by temperament, but being a soldier didn't define them. If you weren't aware of their histories, you wouldn't have known they'd ever been in uniform.

Some of them never got to be returned servicemen. My mum's uncle Bernie, a commando in the Australian infantry, was killed in Borneo in 1945. Three weeks before the ceasefire, he died of his wounds. Another of Mum's uncles also died in that war, after going to Britain and joining the RAF. My dad's father, Luke, had migrated to Australia from Scotland in the 1920s but decided to go back home when World War II broke out. His ship was sunk in the Mediterranean by a German torpedo, but he survived and went to work as a fitter and turner in a munitions factory outside Edinburgh. He and my grandmother Prue came back to Australia after the war and moved to Griffith, in southern New South Wales, where Luke set up an aircraft parts and car repairs workshop. Their eldest son, my uncle Ross, would be in the RAAF for twelve years, making electronics components at the Williamtown base near Newcastle. It's a pretty strong military heritage, but I didn't hear much about it growing up, and at the centre of that silence was my father, Greg.

Luke and Prue had three sons by the end of the 1940s: Ross, Ian and Greg, who was born in 1947. Luke developed problems with his health after a lifetime working in factories, and in 1950 they moved to Nambucca Heads on the north coast of New South Wales for a quieter and healthier lifestyle. Dad was a wiry, freckly redhead, and as the baby of the family seems to have been a favourite of his father's. Dad was a lot closer to Luke than he was to Prue, and spent a lot of time following his old man around. He was only eight when Luke died from a heart attack at the age of forty-seven, and it must have been a shocking blow. The family didn't know how to tell him, and he was sent away to stay with friends for a few days without having it explained. He only found out his father had died when he saw a funeral notice in a window in Nambucca.

It doesn't surprise me when I hear that Dad was a rebellious kid; Uncle Ross says I'm cut from the same cloth, both physically and in temperament. To see photos of Dad, I almost feel like I'm seeing a version of myself.

After his father died, Dad spent most of his time with his mates, and didn't pay much attention to the academic side of his schooling. He left Macksville High School at fifteen and went straight to work as an apprentice butcher for Oldham's, a meat company based in Newcastle. As the 1960s went by he honed his butchering skills, put down roots in the Hunter Valley and began to look out for a girl.

*

Mum's father, Fred Smee, was a welder at the BHP steelworks when he met Kathleen Hurley in the 1940s. Her father,

William, was a wharf worker and a local sporting identity, part of the rugby league, cricket and athletics scene in the Mayfield area, where a lot of wharfies and steelworkers lived. Fred and Kathleen had four children: Margaret, Carol, Kenny and Bernadette.

Like any family, they had diverse personalities, and a few cracks opened up when Kathleen died at fifty. Bernadette, the youngest, already had something in common with Greg Donaldson up the coast: she was only a twelve-year-old when her mother died, and at first she wasn't told. Fred told the elder three kids but couldn't face up to telling Bernadette, the baby, leaving it to the others.

After Kathleen died, they managed to get by for a while, sharing the housework and cooking: Margaret grew up never knowing how to make custard, because that was Kenny's job, and likewise Kenny didn't have a clue about gravy.

Losing her mother really rocked Mum's world. From a stable traditional nuclear family, they soon began to break up. Margaret and Carol both got married, and in what must have been a big shake-up for Mum, Fred remarried. Joan, his new wife, was very jealous and wouldn't let Mum spend the time she needed with her only parent. Before long Kenny had moved out as well, so Mum was alone with Fred and Joan in a house where she often felt unwelcome.

She was a bright girl though, and cracked on with it, playing netball and learning to drive a Mini Minor. She left school early, wanting independence, and worked as a hairdresser before getting a job as a secretary at Oldham's Meats, where one of the butchers started to show an interest in her.

I'd have a clearer picture of Mum and Dad as young adults if they were still around. As you do with your parents, you don't credit them with much of a life when you're growing up. You're too tied up in yourself. It was after I lost them that I asked a lot of questions of my aunts and uncles and began to get to know Greg and Bernadette a bit better.

I can imagine Dad being pretty quiet but determined about courting Mum, and I imagine her as also being quiet, but lively and fun for him to be around. By around 1969 they were an item, and probably thinking about marriage. But Dad had been in the workforce for a few years by then, and he had an adventurous streak that no doubt wasn't quite ready to be domesticated. In 1970, a mixture of fate and that spirit came together to delay any future plans and play a role in shaping the man Dad was to become.

Since reintroducing conscription for the Vietnam War, the Australian Government had been sending thousands of kids a year into the army and up to the conflict. Dad's number came up in the ballot, but rather than being a conscript he wanted to take matters into his own hands, so he entered the army as a volunteer instead. There were financial benefits in volunteering, but knowing Dad, I bet something of his contrary nature was coming through.

Up to that point, Dad hadn't told his family about Bernadette, and it was only when Ross and his wife, Val, came down to Sydney Airport to see Greg off that they realised the cute little strawberry-blonde shedding a quiet tear was his girlfriend – or, as they found out, pretty much his fiancée.

Mum kept working at Oldham's, and then in the records department of the Mater Hospital at Waratah, while Dad was in Vietnam. He went for one tour from 1970 to 1971, working as a loadmaster/rigger for the Chinook helicopters, the military workhorse I would come to know very well. But I wouldn't learn about them from Dad. He never talked to me in any detail about Vietnam, and from what I know he didn't share much of it with Mum either. He told Ross about resupplying the CIA up in the north, and about being shit-scared when he witnessed a death from friendly fire. An Australian soldier took a grenade and his self-loading rifle into a mess tent, threw the grenade and let rip with the gun. He'd just walked past Dad and said hello seconds before he breached that tent. Dad was one of the first on the scene to assist.

He was badly shaken up by some of the horrific things he'd seen. One bloke, he said, had had to be 'hosed out of his cockpit'. Later, Dad would also be scared about another after-effect of Vietnam. He believed he'd been exposed to Agent Orange, the defoliant that, among other things, could cause genetic defects in the children of those who'd ingested it. The Americans dropped it in a mist from above, to kill off vegetation and deprive the Viet Cong of cover, for ten years from 1961 to 1971, only stopping the year after Dad's tour.

There are funny stories though as well, like one I've been told about when he was on piquet – this is when soldiers are maintaining a watch for the enemy so they can provide an early warning of any threat. He and the guy he was with heard a rustling and grunting in the bushes late at night. They knew it was a bush pig sow and her piglets. For whatever reason Dad wanted a piglet, so he jumped the wire in the middle of the night and tried to chase one down. Apparently he got it, but was chased back to the relative safety of the pit by the squealing and raging sow.

Family members said that when he came back, he was a changed man. He didn't look for recognition, but he was pissed off that Vietnam veterans were not honoured with a homecoming and, more than that, were spat at and abused on the streets. He wasn't any great anti-communist ideologue, but he thought that a man who'd served his country deserved better. Mum's sister Margaret, who always got on very well with him, found him to be short-tempered and sometimes agitated after he came back, traits she'd never seen in him beforehand. The one thing they couldn't do to Greg now was creep up on him from behind or give him any kind of surprise: he might swing around and throw a punch.

One thing that hadn't changed was his commitment to Bernadette, and they got married in 1972 at St Columban's in Mayfield. It was a Catholic wedding, but Greg was proud of his Scottish Presbyterian background, and they had bag-pipers in tartan kilts to celebrate that side. He'd bring this influence to bear a few years later in naming me Mark Gregor Strang, strong Scottish names.

Mum and Dad went to Papua New Guinea for their honeymoon and had five years together before my brother, Brent, was born. After Vietnam, Dad retrained as a meat inspector, Mum kept working as a secretary, and they saw a lot of Margaret and her husband Ken, their three kids Kay, Tony and Christine, Mum's brother Kenny, and also Ross and Val, who'd moved to Sydney and had three kids of their own, Christine, Fiona and Brodie.

For holidays they went to Lake Macquarie to the south and Tanilba Bay to the north of Newcastle. Mum would like to kick back and relax, while Dad was up early every day to go out fishing, waterskiing, snorkelling, scuba diving or trail bike riding. He was very fit and was often found under his car. He couldn't sit still, and seemed at his happiest if he was outside fixing or building stuff or going on one of his expeditions. He was highly strung and quick-tempered, but his siblings and their partners knew they could get a laugh by taking the piss out of him. They just had to make sure they picked the right moment.

TWO

I was born on 2 April 1979 at the Mater Hospital in Waratah, where Mum had been working in the records department. I don't know if Dad was there. Brent was a two-year-old, so the old man might have been with him at home, which at that point was a rented house in Waratah on Christo Road, basically next door to the hospital.

The first house I remember was one we called 'the farm', though it wasn't really a farm, just acreage on the fringe of Denman at Sandy Hollow near Muswellbrook. One of my earliest memories of that place is seeing our dog Angie's tail sweeping back and forth through the grass paddocks as she was chasing rabbits and rodents. Dad used to go hunting out there with her. There were mountains beyond the house, and I have a fond memory of tagging along with Dad into the scrub, Angie going ahead and sniffing out the prey before Dad would whistle her to come back and take a shot. He kept a couple of guns, and even a bow and arrow. Sometimes he'd let us come, and we'd do our best to keep up with his slouch hat moving through the bush. Mum didn't like him having the guns around, though, especially as Brent and I got older. We knew where he kept them and were quite interested, but at some point Mum persuaded him to get rid of them.

Before long we moved into Denman town proper. The XPT used to race past on the train track just behind us, which might not have been a great selling point for adults but as kids we and our friends loved it. The yard was a bit of an adventure playground. We had a swing set and a big paddock of long grass, where Brent and I built an intricate tunnel system and played with Angie, whose dried white poos had the added advantage of exploding spectacularly when we kicked them. Scotty and Michael Pritchard, sons of the milkman and rugby league teammates of ours at the Denman Devils, would play war games in the long grass with us. Scotty and Michael always used to fight, just like we did, and eventually we sorted ourselves into warring factions, the two youngest against the two oldest. They turned into big pitched battles, and sometimes all the kids from the neighbourhood joined in.

We were always excited to come home because Mum was there with some hot Milo, keen to listen to the amazing things we'd been up to. If it was rainy, she'd have a favourite meal or some hot soup to dish out and let us watch *Wide World of Sport*, before it became all about horse racing. One of the great things about Mum was, she genuinely cared about our adventures, no matter how real or imaginary they were.

Brent and I were always following Dad around the Denman place, getting into everything. He built a rotunda and a barbecue by hand, and all we wanted to do was be involved. He had a practicality you don't often see, and a can-do approach that I now recognise as soldierly, even if he didn't see himself as part of the military set. He looked after all his tools and equipment meticulously, and had some of them for years and years. Everything was looked after. Nothing got thrown out if it was broken – and often it wasn't broken for long because he found a way to fix it.

One of the most striking things about Dad, looking back, was that he wore his khaki army shirts, with the pockets and epaulettes, whenever he was working at home or going out fishing or camping. He always wore his slouch hat from Vietnam. There aren't many photos of him in his later years when he doesn't have that slouch hat on. If you listened to what he said – or didn't say – he was anti-army, anti-RSL, anti-Anzac Day and all that went with it, because of his Vietnam experience. But if you looked at what he did, there were telltale signs that he had a soldier's nature through and through, and was proud of it as well.

Unfortunately, his fastidious soldier's nature added up to a short fuse when Brent and I were trying to help, and my instinct for pushing things to the limit put us on a collision course.

We were always covered in mud, with the hose out, mucking around in the dirt, making a big mess of his garden. If we weren't helping him the way he wanted, he'd tell us to do something else. Generally by that time we'd have the shits with him, so we'd wander off and make trouble for him. We would climb up a pine tree and drop down onto his beloved Kingswood, which drove him crazy. Once, a mate and I went into the scrapyard next door to play with the kangaroos that hung out there, but ended up finding some old engine batteries and tipping out the sulphuric acid to get the marbles from inside them. Dad had a distinctive whistle when he was upset – loud and sharp. Sure enough, when I heard that whistle I realised we were in trouble, but I was so excited that we had these marbles I kept on playing. Dad came upon us with steam pouring out of his ears. He took me home and gave me a whipping with an electric cord or a wooden spoon, I don't remember, whatever was within reach.

At the end of a typical day, we'd come into the house for dinner covered in grass stains and mud, all itchy from the overgrown fields, eyes watering, grass through our hair. We sat down as a family every night. Mum and Dad were pretty firm and traditional on this. Dad set the four-seat table in the kitchen and Mum always cooked. Brent and I had to be sitting down and waiting. I was particular about having my Mickey Mouse plate and fork and spoon and knife, just so. If I didn't have them, there'd be problems. For some reason, as soon as we sat down, Brent and I would swap our knives and forks into the opposite hands, left and right instead of right and left. We still do. I don't know why we do it, because Mum and Dad didn't.

Dinner was always a home-cooked meal, usually steak or lamb cutlets with vegies. Dad brought home whole carcasses from the abattoir, chopped them up and put them in the deep freezer, and from an early age I was familiar with the sights and smells of butchering fresh meat. When the food was ready, Dad would come in and sit, the last one at the table. We didn't have the TV on. Dinner was a pretty straightforward affair, Mum and Dad doing the talking while our job was to eat what was in front of us. If you didn't eat everything on your plate, you couldn't get dessert or even leave the table. Brent was fussy about vegetables, so there were plenty of stand-offs.

The softness in our life came from Mum. She was our constant, always there. She was a gentle instructor, keener than Dad on helping us enjoy learning new things. I remember going to swimming lessons with her in Denman when I was only three or four. Mum wasn't a good swimmer – she was comfortable wading in the water but didn't like sticking her head under – so she made a point of us learning at the public pool where family friends ran swimming classes. I hated it the first time but soon got the hang of it. It was an example of how Mum's softer approach got results.

If Dad yelled at us, we ran to Mum. Or to be honest, it was mainly me that Dad was yelling at. Brent had Mum's easygoing nature and didn't rise to the bait when Dad started getting worked up. I, on the other hand, was desperate to be involved, and, being younger, tended to get in Dad's way. It was a case of two similar temperaments butting heads, even when I was little. I had a bit of a temper, and when I was in trouble I'd go into a big sulk. There are quite a few photos of me with my bottom lip sticking out, obviously having just been scolded: a nice Christmas photo of all the kids in the family, except Mark.

If I wasn't trying to get into Dad's business, I'd be following Brent around. I remember being constantly afraid of missing out. It's something I've had all my life, even in the SAS in war zones, where I have a reputation for making a pest of myself in a command area trying to find out what's coming up next and how I can get involved. I just hate the idea that action and excitement are happening elsewhere. As a kid, if I was sent to bed early, I'd stay awake so I could hear what else was going on. When Brent wanted to go riding his bike up the street with his friends and I was told I was too young to join them, I blew up. Dad would say, gruffly, 'Get over it,' but Mum had another approach. 'Come here, come play out the back. We can do something much better.'

We could piss Mum off as well. Like Brent, she had a longer fuse, but once it was lit it could go off. She hated it when Brent and I were fighting, and would give us the whole 'When your father gets home he'll hear about this' routine. It didn't matter who was at fault; we got equal punishment. She didn't like it when we ran off during the day without telling her where we were going. As long as we were home by five o'clock in the afternoon it was okay, but if we missed that, she'd really let us know.

Being adventurous and mischievous boys, we couldn't help giving her a rough time. If we were out at the big department stores, we'd take off and hide under the clothes racks, to collect the coloured tags or to jump out and scare each other. She didn't like losing sight of us, but it was too tempting in those big exciting places. Once, I remember coming out from a clothes rack to discover that Brent and Mum weren't there any more. I went to the counter in tears. 'I've lost my mum, I've lost my mum!' She was anxious too at first, but once she and Brent had found me she had to laugh.

Mum remained a practising Catholic and on Sundays made sure we all went to church. In Denman it was a social thing: the parents would get together after church for a barbecue. It was hard for Brent and me to take church too seriously, though. It was all about taking your bit of bread and getting told everything you were doing wrong. When we got a bit older, Dad stopped going. He was pretty anti-religion, and if Jehovah's Witnesses came to the house he would chase them away. Mum made a last big effort to get him to stick with church, but eventually he flat-out refused. That gave Brent and me the green light to do like-wise. I thought, *If Dad's not going, I'm not going.* Soon Mum's attendance began to peter out too.

The withdrawal from regular churchgoing happened at Dorrigo, where we moved when I was seven or eight. Dad had got a job as a meat inspector up in the north of New South Wales, and he liked the idea of being further out in the bush, where he could work on a house and explore the rivers and forests, and take trips down to the beaches. Our lives really broadened out in Dorrigo. We stayed in a caravan park on the first night, then rented a few houses, and finally moved to acreage Mum and Dad bought. Working on his own house and garden long-term was the ideal project for the old man.

Unlike the home jobs, where he was a bit tense about getting us involved, he was always happy to take Brent and me on adventures: climbing rocks, trekking up mountain trails, camping, fishing and swimming. Those were the happiest times for us, and would be at the core of my drive to be in the SAS. I always wanted to find an outdoor skill I could improve. When we were still in Denman, Dad would take us down to the Hunter River to swim while he went fishing. He'd float an air mattress for us and we'd drift down the river till he picked us up. Or Mum would look after us. Once I fell off and got caught in a whirlpool. I thought, *I'm going under here!* Eventually I got pulled out, but it was a wake-up call. My response to these things from the start was not to be afraid of the river, just to make sure I got better at swimming.

Being further out in the bush also gave Dad more opportunities to hunt rabbits and foxes. He taught me how to trap rabbits using the old style bear-traps that are now banned. I've always associated being in the outdoors with the adrenaline rush of hunting, or combating dangerous creatures or just being on an adventure. I didn't realise it at the time, but it was another piece in the puzzle that was turning me into a soldier.

We could have done with a gun when I was about ten and had a run-in with a red-bellied black snake. It wasn't my first time. Back in Denman, when I was only two or three, I'd found a black snake on the concrete slab the house's metal poles stood on. I grabbed it by the tail and swung it around. Dad came down and warned me to stop. The snake was dead – he'd already shot it – but he didn't like me so enthusiastically taking on a dangerous reptile as a playmate. I was certainly cured of any liking for snakes when I came home from primary school alone one day in Dorrigo. I went to the toilet, which was off the back of the patio under a covered walkway. We kept the keys to the house in the toilet. I went in and sat down, then heard this hissing. *That's weird.* I looked for the keys by my feet and saw a six-foot red-bellied black snake cocked and ready to strike. The keys were there, but I wasn't going to reach for them. My heart was racing. I waited and waited, and one centimetre at a time eased the door open. The snake reared up. I thought, *I've got to go NOW or it'll bite me.* I dived off the toilet and through the doorway, and then kicked the door shut behind me. I broke into the house through one of the windows and called Mum at work. 'There's a snake in the toilet and I can't get the keys out!' Dad was away, so she sent one of his mates from the abattoir. He came quickly and grabbed Dad's long-handled rotary edger. We opened the toilet door. The snake was still there, looking pretty pissed off. Dad's mate hooked the snake out with the edger and chopped its head off with a shovel.

Soldiering is not just about defeating an adversary; most of the time, it's about using your imagination and often slim resources to build things. Another of Dad's hobbies that had a soldierly edge was his ham radio. Soon after we moved to Dorrigo, he installed a whopping great antenna. He didn't know how to do it; he just read a book and cracked on. He dug a hole for a telegraph pole and got some mates to help him sink the pole with the radio's metal mast attached to the top. He ran the cable into the house and set up the receiver in the hallway. His technical skills were amazing. At one point he bought some electronic components from

America to expand the radio's bandwidth, and had to send Uncle Ross to get them out of Customs after they were impounded as contraband.

His radio was an early form of social media when I think about it. After dinner, he'd pick up all sorts of stuff. He listened to passenger-jet pilots talking to each other. Brent and I would go and sit with him and ask, 'What's this all about?' Dad told us to just sit quietly and listen, and not press the talk button. He mostly preferred listening in to the jet pilots, but also made friends with other ham-radio operators in America. He told some friends in Arizona that Brent and I were into basketball and football, and they sent us a box with an American flag and an Arizona state flag and all this merchandising from the Chicago Bulls, the San Francisco 49ers and the Miami Dolphins, which we thought was the bee's knees.

Although he didn't talk about it, Dad took a lot of pride in his work. He was a real by-the-book kind of person; even though he had a strong sense of independence, he saw the importance of rules. I have an early memory from back in Denman. We went to the Hunter River, which was flooding, and there was a huge crowd, fifty to eighty people, watching this bloke who was trapped in a tree out in the middle. The Westpac Rescue Helicopter came and winched him out. I remember Dad explaining how that guy was an idiot because he'd tried to swim across the river; he hadn't done what he was told. The rescue made quite an impression on me.

As a meat inspector, Dad was known as a stickler for standards, even to his own detriment. When he found out that some inspectors were turning a blind eye to contaminated carcasses, he blew the whistle. He also stepped in when some meatworkers were killing sick goats to harvest their gallstones, which could be sold to traditional

Chinese medicine practitioners. Being such a strict by-the-book operator didn't win the old man any friends at work, and there were times when he felt quite isolated.

He didn't bring those dramas home, but a couple of times he took Brent and me to the abattoir. I was really excited to see it all happen. He showed us the process – 'This is where the cows, sheep and goats come, this is where they're killed' – and seemed happy to get us involved. He was allowed to bring home a couple of live lambs from the abattoir and fatten them in our paddock. We were counting the days to the weekend when he'd kill them and cut them up for the freezer so we'd have lamb for the next six months.

When the day came, I was adamant about helping him. Brent was not so keen; I think he may have been away playing rugby. I had to hold the lamb's neck back while Dad cut its throat.

'You sure you want to see this? There'll be a lot of blood.'

'Yeah, I want to see how it's done.'

It trembled in my arms as it bled out. I helped him carry it over to the shed. He had a chain strung up from the roof with an S-hook, on which he hung it up and skinned it.

'Now stand under it,' he said, 'and put your arms out.'

I didn't know what was going on. Earlier in the day he'd got me to dig a hole near the shed. I'd asked what the hole was for. 'You'll find out later,' he said.

Now he was working inside the sheep up to his elbows while I had my arms around it.

'Are you ready?'

'Yeah,' I said, not having any idea what I was ready for.

'Righto, catch this.'

All the guts came out – the stomach, the intestines, the liver, the bladder. The smell hit me in a wave. I was gagging, just thinking, *Don't vomit, don't vomit.*

He pointed to a bulging sac of grey gizzards and said, 'Whatever you do, don't pop that.' It was the bile duct, which, if it broke, could poison everything around it.

Dry-retching, I dragged this heavy mass of stinking internal organs towards the hole, telling myself, *Don't vomit, don't vomit, you have to show him you can do this without messing it up.*

I got it there and kept myself in one piece. When I came back to him he said, 'Righto, let's do the other one.'

I enjoyed the next one more, I'll admit, and fresh lamb was the best meat you could have. Looking back on it, even though it was gross and confronting, it was one of my treasured moments with Dad, and set me up well for some of the stomach-turning things I've had to do in my professional life. He and I bonded over blood and guts. I remember one week in later years, when I was fourteen, when Mum and Brent were away somewhere and Dad and I had to look after ourselves. He'd leave for work early and I had free rein in the kitchen, making myself Milo sandwiches to take to school. One night, the old man announced that he was cooking.

'What are we having?'

'You'll find out. Don't ask, just eat it, see how you go, and we'll talk about it after.'

He fried some kind of meat in the pan and put it down in front of me. I thought, *What the fuck is this?* I sat and ate it with him. Then I asked what it was.

He pointed to each bit. 'That was heart, that was kidney, that was lungs.'

I thought he could have told me beforehand, but it was good. And it was good to be doing something like this with him, just the two of us.

It's only when I sit down and think back over these events that I understand how they were more than just isolated moments in a fairly typical country childhood. At the time, they were little spikes of love and enjoyment in what was often a pretty fiery relationship with the old man. Later, when I lost him, I would treasure these memories all the more for the fact that we could never do such things together again. But even later still, having seen what I've seen in Afghanistan, I wonder if all the elements of these episodes – the confrontation with bleeding flesh, the need to overcome my revulsion, the motivation to win Dad's approval and be a man in front of him – were part of a pattern, all leading to the particular kind of person and soldier I am now. It's impossible to say how important childhood experiences are in determining your future, but that association of pleasure and achievement with acts when I had to fight my disgust and fear must have helped me do some of the things I've had to do in war.

As kids, there was one big, communally approved outlet for our warlike instincts, and Brent and I were both into our sport: basketball, cricket, rugby league and union, swimming, soccer, whatever was going. It was always Mum, not Dad, who got up at the crack of dawn for long drives to other North Coast towns to soccer or rugby. She was happy to drive us, cheer for us, provide the half-time oranges or take home all the jerseys to wash for next week's game. They're things you take for granted as a kid, and I'm conscious now of the need to remind my kids of how much their mum does for them. There's never a bad time to say thanks to your mum.

Brent was much more talented than me, as well as being older, but I was a determined bugger and was desperate to match him. He'd get me to come out into the yard to play cricket, where he'd bat as Steve Waugh and I'd be the cannon fodder bowling at him all day as he smashed me around. All I did was chase the ball and get angrier. Eventually I'd crack the shits and chuck the ball at him and we'd have a fight. Brent soon realised that if he wanted to keep me playing, he'd have to let me get him out. It didn't matter; the games usually ended up in a fight anyway.

We had a basketball ring the old man built, which we used a lot, but Brent was taller and better at that too. We also played one-on-one rugby, which I'd play grudgingly again because he'd smash me.

I looked up to Brent more than anyone else, as little brothers do. He was happy to play together at home, but in public he didn't want his little brother in his team, and eventually, instead of trying to mimic and compete with him in everything, I decided I wanted to be my own person. He was such a good rugby league player, I got into soccer to be different. But although I was so competitive with him, he was my hero and role model. I was always fighting kids at school in what I thought was a noble defence of Brent's reputation. Generally the conflict went along the lines of, 'My big brother's better than your big brother!' and it'd be on. One day I was fighting with an older kid about who was a better rugby five-eighth, him or my brother. Brent got up me for causing him dramas.

I said, 'But you're heaps better.'

He said, 'It doesn't matter. The guys are coming up to me at lunchtime and having a go at me about my hothead little brother.'

*

Holidays involved long car trips, and Dad's determination and hunger for adventure had to be balanced by Mum's calming hand. On the first day of a holiday, he was up at four in the morning, packing the car, hustling everyone along. We'd be still rubbing the sleep out of our eyes when he'd say, 'Have your toilet stop now, that's it, no stopping on the road.' He didn't even want to eat, he was in such a hurry to go, but Mum managed to stall him for a few minutes so we could have some breakfast.

When we got going, he was a competitive driver, always having to be first in the overtaking lane. He liked to drive fast, never letting anyone pass him, desperate to get in front of a truck before the road narrowed to one lane. In the back, Brent and I would soon be fighting over the imaginary line demarcating our space.

'You put your hand over it!'

'No I didn't, *you* did!'

Dad reached back to smack us, before Mum told him, 'Come on, concentrate on the driving.'

Three hours into the drive, after we'd had our poppers and some apples and sandwiches, the cry would go out.

'I need to go to the toilet!'

After all the work he'd done overtaking cars, having to stop for a toilet break drove Dad insane. He'd ignore us or urge us to hold it in, until Mum persuaded him that he had to be humane or risk an accident on the back seat.

Any chance I got to prove myself to him, even on holidays, I took it. We did a big drive to Victoria once and went hiking up Mount Buffalo. Brent and Mum ran out of gas some way from the peak, but Dad said, 'I've come this far, I want to see what it's like at the top.' I followed him, and we left the others behind. One holiday I remember was particularly special, because it was just Dad and me for two weeks, during the school term. I was about nine or ten and he had to drive to South Australia to see an old friend of his from the Newcastle butchery. We went fishing in Adelaide, and Dad's mate showed us where the Indy cars went and drove us on the track. I loved my cars, saved my coin to buy *Wheels* magazine and pinned posters of V8s and super cars on my wall, but even better than indulging this love was spending all that time alone with Dad. He let me get away with things I couldn't do at home, like taking our seatbelts off. Crossing the desert in New South Wales, I read a book and lay across the back seat. At a servo, I could get an ice-cream or a treat. Normally it was 'No, nothing, you can never get anything from a servo.' On this trip, everything was allowed.

He was terse and stern so often, the exceptions are what stick in the mind. At one Christmas party, at a friend's place on a lake, Dad went waterskiing, and we watched him zip around on the two skis. Then he dropped one off and started single-skiing. Then he dropped that one too and went bare-foot. It was amazing to see the old man showing the talent he had. When he came back in, he was so happy and joyful with his friends, and Mum was having a laugh too. There are photos of us all clowning around and Dad's poking his tongue out while Brent's sticking his middle finger up. It was one of the rare times we saw Dad really let go. Now that I'm a father, I can understand how stressful it can be, but as a parent I think Mum's influence on me has come out more. I don't get worked up over little things like Dad did. He was such a clean freak, he'd go nuts if we smudged a window he'd cleaned or a floor he'd polished. I'm much more easygoing. And as a soldier, I don't get wound up over small matters like obsessively keeping every piece of equipment sparkling and well organised. I think I take after Mum in being a bit more pragmatic.

But Mum did like keeping things tidy, sometimes to a comical degree. On our Easter holiday camping trips, it was Mum who made sure the eating, cooking and sleeping areas were always in order. Dad, Brent and I would go off fishing for hours and when we came back to the campsite it would be immaculate. One time we came back to find the tent all zipped up and Mum sitting on a fold-out camp chair under the tarp with a big stick, looking intently towards a large gum tree. She told us she'd been taking a nap in the tent, only to wake and see a large goanna next to her. She'd jumped up and ran out of the tent, knocking the camp table and food all over the place, and charged around whacking the reptile with this stick until it had scuttled up the gum tree. It was funny enough hearing that she'd scared the goanna up a tree; hilarious that while warding it off she'd still re-ordered the camp to the way it was when we'd left.

Where we really saw Mum and Dad at their most relaxed was on family holidays visiting Uncle Ross and Auntie Val at Lake Macquarie or Sydney, or Auntie Margaret and Uncle Ken at their holiday house at Tanilba Bay. Those holidays were the highlight of the year. When we arrived, we'd go bananas. Was Uncle Ken's boat there? If the trailer was standing empty next to the shed, the boat was already out. The first thing was to run through the Nancarrows' yard – they had a couple of kids our age – to the access road to see the bay. Angie would follow us. We tiptoed through the bindies to get to the buffalo grass, racing each other. We got to the water and threw jellyfish at each other, feeling our feet in the sand. It was awesome, that anticipation of hitting the salt water and seeing our cousins. Kay and Tony would be windsurfing, and Christine, who was much closer in age to us, would already have rounded up some friends to play with. Being the youngest, I was as usual running myself ragged trying to keep up with everyone. My cousins teased me a bit about my red hair. The family was full of redheads, but in that generation I was the only one. They said it gave me a temper, which only made me angrier. Actually, it was my tough wavy curls that bugged me more than the colour. I spent a lot of time trying to straighten it, even running my head along the hallway carpet, which gave Auntie Margaret no end of amusement.

When I joined the SAS, we could choose between three modes of insertion: by water, air or land. I think I owe the origins of my choice to be a 'watery' to those days at Tanilba. Every day was an adventure. We'd crowd around Dad and Uncle Ken: 'Where are we going today?' It would be swimming in the rivers and estuaries, or up to the oyster leases at Karuah. Uncle Ken had a four- or five-metre runabout, and fishing with him was so relaxed compared with Dad. When it was just us and him, he'd have to set up our lines and cut us free from snags or untangle our messes, and never get to relax and fish himself. At Tanilba, Dad was so much calmer, even Mum came. When the fishing got slow, we had competitions to hold our breath and dive under the boat, which was also powerful enough to take us waterskiing.

Our aunts, uncles and cousins had such close relationships because Mum and Dad were partly estranged from their surviving parents. As kids, this only dawned on us gradually. We didn't notice anything unusual in the fact that we hardly ever saw our Grandma Prue, even though she lived only a short distance away at Nambucca. Dad had never fully got over his father's death, and never patched things up with Grandma Prue. She had a lot of gentleman friends after she became a widow, and Dad reckoned she'd chased him out of the house when they were there. Either because he didn't trust her or he wanted to pay her back, he wouldn't let us stay overnight at her house.

To compensate, Dad would go out of his way to make sure we saw our maternal grandfather, Fred. He was old and bald and lots of fun when he could be alone with us. The train ran by his house in the semi-industrial part of Mayfield, and we loved going there. We'd be shy at first, then treat it as our own house. We knew where the lollies were. We'd go into the shed with him and he'd show us how to use the tools. He had some old scooters in the shed and we'd tear off on them. But this relationship was problematic too. Eventually, if we were having too much fun, it would be brought to an end when Joan came out to send him off on an errand or to take us shopping. She wasn't mean, she just didn't want us getting too close to him.

It was only when we were teenagers that Mum explained how Joan wasn't her mother. She didn't let on how cruel Joan had been to her, but in her subtle way she was letting us know that if we weren't getting to know our grandfather as well as other kids knew theirs, there was a reason.

*

It won't have gone unnoticed that I haven't talked much about school. No prizes for guessing why. I was by no means the worst student in Dorrigo, but nor was I straighty-one-eighty. At some point, I think I was kicked out of just about every class for being a smart-arsed little turd. It wasn't anything serious in those late primary, early high school years. In science I'd fill kids' pencil cases with gas and light them, or get as many Bunsen burners going as possible. We had frogs to dissect, and as the teacher was old and didn't know how to handle us, we ran around the classroom with frogs in our mouths. It was more skylarking than serious misbehaviour, in the early days at least.

It wasn't that I hated being at school or was hyperactive. I did have periods when I was quite settled and studious. Ever since I'd been little, I'd enjoyed reading books and making models. I could sit for hours building with Lego or model aeroplanes, and if I got into a book I'd read it in a day or two: Roald Dahl's *Matilda*, *Fantastic Mr Fox*, that sort of thing. The old man also used to read to us before bedtime, *The Hobbit* and then *The Lord of the Rings*, a couple of pages a night. I don't know if he got through the whole cycle. But it was hard for me to carry that interest through to school, because the main excitement there was how much you could get past the teacher.

I was pretty cheeky, and around the age of twelve or thirteen I started getting into more serious trouble. One of our teachers was the rugby coach, and everyone knew another teacher was having an affair with his wife. One day when this other man walked past our room, one of the kids said, 'That guy's a wanker.' The rugby coach said, 'Oi, don't say that, he's a good bloke.' I quickly and, I thought, wittily snapped back, 'If he's such a good bloke, why'd he steal your wife?'

I got sent to the headmaster, not for the first or last time. I was going through a transitional period when Mum and Dad must have felt they were just hanging on to me. I'd play soccer on Saturdays and then go fishing with Dad, or hang around the house where he had jobs for me. He got me to help build our home septic tank, which was really tough work, but I would eventually get in trouble, such as when I drove the ride-on mower over our driveway of blue-metal rocks just after Dad had spent all morning sharpening the blades. He came charging at me with a shovel before I knew what I'd done wrong. What made it worse was that he'd been yelling at me to get off but I was wearing my Walkman, listening to my favourite heavy-metal music, and hadn't heard him. In his eyes I was turning into your typical deadbeat teenager. He came after me and caught me across the bum with a full-blooded swing. I didn't cry because I didn't want him to see how much it had hurt, but I still moved far enough away so he couldn't reach me with his second swing.

I was changing, and not always for the better, in Dad's eyes at least. Once, when I was in trouble and he was coming at me, I put my hands up to him. He paused. His face was like, *You've got to be kidding, right?* I said, 'Come on, let's go!' That was a bad move. He was a strong, wiry bloke, with powerful wrists and arms, and he just slapped me to the ground dismissively. He gave me a look that said, *The day you knock me down will be a cold day in hell.* It was a moment that put me back in my place. It's not that I ever thought he was a cruel bastard. It was more me waking up to myself. I never raised my fists to him again.

When I was about thirteen, my misdemeanours began to escalate. Brent had turned into a well-behaved high achiever, and I guess in my typical contrary way I was carving out my own identity. None of what I did sounds like very much individually, but it begins to accumulate, especially in a small town when people want to put you in a pigeonhole, and before long it was my persona to be one of the kids who got into trouble. When you're thirteen years old and you understand that's the way people look at you, you sort of drive yourself to live up to it, or down to it. *If you're going to take that opinion, I'll show you and make it much, much worse than you thought.* I was an extreme character. It didn't matter what direction, I always wanted to see how far I could go, and teenage rebellion was one more opportunity to push the boundaries. When people see who I've become, they wonder what caused the turnaround. Certainly in Dorrigo there are a few people with long memories who can't match up the Victoria Cross recipient with the feral nuisance kid who used to live there! But to me, there's no incompatibility: I've always been drawn to adventure.

I drifted into a different group in Dorrigo, known for more serious mischief. We rode our pushies to the railway museum, a glorified name for the shed and storage yard where an enthusiast kept some of the old steam trains. We opened the doors and started smashing some stuff up. Then we found these big silver canisters and threw one out the door. *Boom!* What were they? We didn't care – there was a whole bunch of them. *Awesome! Whatever they are, they explode when you throw them!* They had a little red disc with two wire straps. We set a few off and egged each other on. I was up for how far could we push it – it didn't matter what, that's what I was all about – so I said, 'Let's take one into town and let it off and see what people do.'

When we got into town, a bunch of kids were hanging out at the park. We told them we were going to set off one of these massive exploding things at the brick toilet. They said, 'Nah, yous won't do that.' Feeling the peer pressure, not wanting to be seen to back away from a promise, I stepped up and said I'd do it.

I tied some string around the wires and hurled it at the wall. It went off like kingdom come, and the kids bolted in all directions. I took off on my bike too, tearing down the laneways between the shops. I was scared but thrilled – I guess from that minute I knew that I loved exploding things.

But taking risks came with a cost. A couple of days later at soccer training, I was putting my boots on. I saw the old man before he saw me. Someone said, 'Your old man's looking for you,' but I already knew. He came over, unnaturally calm on the outside.

'Get your stuff and get in the car.'

'I've got training on.'

'I've told you, get your stuff and get in the car now.'

He drove in silence, but didn't take the turn-off towards home. I thought, *This is a bit different.*

Then he said, 'Righto, where are they?'

'Where are what?'

'Your little mate's told us you did everything, we know, so where are they?'

There was no point fighting it. If I'd been dobbed in, I would only look silly by lying. I basically spilled the beans, took him to pick the canisters up where we'd cached them, and he took me to the police station. The constable read the riot act and told me I'd go to jail. My punishment in the end was to show up at certain times to help clean public areas, like a form of community service without the actual criminal process. At home, Dad grounded me for six months. I could only leave the house to go to school on weekdays and for sport on weekends, and after school I had to come straight home. If I went out, I had to stay with Brent and watch him playing guitar with his mates.

That incident was a catalyst for Dad to ask, *What's going on with my son?* He and Mum began to worry that I was seriously going off the rails. At school I was beginning to be seen as one of the bad kids who'd wreak havoc and smoke cigarettes. I wasn't one of the good kids whose parents were the pillars of the community – Mum and Dad hadn't been there long enough for that. Everyone knew Dad worked at the abattoir and Mum was the secretary at the doctor's and dentist's. The locals would take great glee in telling her what I was up to, which was never good.

The biggest tragedy in my grounding was that I'd been having a little love affair, and all of a sudden I couldn't see her any more. You grow up pretty quickly in a town like that, and even at thirteen, as well as vandalism and experimentation with alcohol, cigarettes and everything else, I was trying to hook up with chicks. There was a lot of pine forest around the school, dropping down towards the river, and we'd skip classes and go down there to muck around. I never had a very serious girlfriend, though I felt strongly about all of them at the time! It was almost a rotational system, everyone hooking up with someone different from one week to the next.

By the time I was fourteen, music had come into the centre of my life. Even when we were little, we painted our faces as Gene Simmonds from Kiss and poked out our tongues. Then we were into rap – outfits like NWA and 2 Live Crew, which had shocking words about shooting coppers and having sex. We immersed ourselves in basket-ball and American culture. We didn't go all out and try to dress like gangsta rappers, but when we saw videos with rappers wearing Chicago Bulls gear, the same stuff we'd been given, we felt a kinship. In Dorrigo, there was no limit to your imagination!

Brent wasn't a big fan of me showing up at parties where he was playing, but once I was over my grounding I was hell-bent on having a good time. We were all getting right into death metal – the faster, the louder, the better. I was into Metallica and bands like Napalm Death, Cannibal Corpse, Gorguts and Pungent Stench. I had no idea what they were singing, I just liked the noise and the music. It excited me, ramped me up. My interest then rolled into the thrash-punk-metal bands like Rancid, Pennywise and Slayer. I didn't know anything about the people who made the music but soon I would be growing my hair long, dye-ing it black, and wearing a lot of the accoutrements of that world.

Mum and Dad were watching all this with growing alarm. The evil-sounding music, the hair, the trouble I was getting into and the people I was hanging out with were all spell-ing bad news. They had what looked like a troubled kid on their hands, and when I was fifteen they had to handle me without Brent's levelling influence.

Brent wanted to study to be a physical education teacher, but didn't get the HSC marks for the uni course. Dad was blowing up about it. He was big on us having what he didn't have, and didn't want us going down his road of getting an apprenticeship and being stuck with that forever. He was adamant that we had to do well in school. But on the other hand, he wouldn't (or couldn't) help us with homework. Anyway, Brent got into a computing course at Newcastle University, and planned to do a year of that before hopping across to teaching. I helped Dad move Brent to Newcastle, but when we returned home, his absence threw the household out of balance. Dad and I butted heads more than ever. I'd always been set on proving myself to him and Brent, but now that Brent had left, I felt that whatever I did, Dad would never be satisfied. I began to retreat into my own world, centred on music, friends and parties.

Before school every morning, I developed a ritual. Mum and Dad both left for work early, and I had some time to kill while I waited for the bus. I went to the drinks cabinet, and stupidly thought that they wouldn't notice if the tide went down a little. I cranked up the music and had a couple of shots of vodka and a couple of rolled cigarettes. That was my morning thing: listen to music, drink and smoke. I thought I was killing it! Everyone would live like this if they could!

It nearly came unstuck one day. I was sitting out the back smoking. The old man had left at 5.30 am, but I heard a car coming up the driveway. It was 300 metres long, so I had plenty of warning. His blue jeep was tearing up the gravel. I thought, *Shit, I'm fucked here.* I stamped my rollie out and stayed outside and kept my distance from him. I poked my head around the corner of the house to say g'day. My heart was racing. He only had to pick something up, and didn't stay long enough to come near me. The relief I felt was not a million miles from when you're hiding in an ambush position and the other side walks right past you without noticing you're there. Living with Mum and Dad was becoming an exercise in concealment.

THREE

Dad was what you'd call a stresser. His own father having died in his forties might have thrown up a red flag, but as Dad reached that age he was putting on weight and getting more highly strung. He blew up at me over every school report I brought home, and also lost his shit when Brent's first uni results weren't as good as he'd hoped. He was on medication for high blood pressure, and I guess our academic performance, or non-performance, wasn't helping.

At night, the dinner routine had become more silent and rigid since Brent had left. We had to shut up while Dad watched the six o'clock news, and he'd whinge at Mum about the size of the servings she gave him. 'I can't eat that, I'm not a teenager any more.' The surprising thing was, when he was younger, he was thin and wiry and strong and always cleaned up his plate. Now, he was eating less but getting heavier.

Maybe I was sensing that he was in some kind of trouble, because after that full-on rebellious period when Brent left, I came good again for a while, working hard at school and getting on better with Dad. I began to hang out with people he liked more. I think he understood that even if I wasn't going to be dux of my year, I was never going to get stuck in the small-town mentality. Probably because Dad was a bit of an outsider, I shared his scepticism about small towns. I sensed that the guys with cars and hot girls, the awesome footy players, the local legends, were stuck. Maybe they didn't want to get out, and that was fine for them, but I knew I was going to. I wanted to see the city, do something different. I was never going to accept the status quo and work for one of the local businesses that soaked up the young school leavers. There had to be something else out there. Dad saw that I was headed somewhere – still a bit of a mystery where, but somewhere better. For all our clashes, I hold on to the idea that he understood this about me before it was too late.

In the early 1990s, after so many years of turning his back on the military, he began to get together with some of the vets from the local RSL. After twenty-five years, he was coming to terms with the bitter memories Vietnam had left him.

The head of the Dorrigo RSL, Bob Denner, and a crew with Vietnam experience decided to meet up for a workshop over a few days in the Lookout Motor Inn in the spring of 1995. I guess a lot of the vets were like Dad, suffering from unacknowledged post-traumatic stress disorder for years, unable to talk about it at home, affected by memories they didn't feel they could share with their families. The night he came home from the workshop, we hadn't seen each other for a couple of days. Just before I went to bed, he came in and told me he loved me. It stuck in my mind because he'd never done that before, off his own bat. We'd tell him we loved him all the time when we were kids and he'd reciprocate, but for him to initiate it was odd. I can't adequately explain how I felt. It was really nice, but because it was out of character it was also a bit confusing. I'm sure it was something let loose by that workshop.

The next morning, he went back for another day of it. We had a school swimming carnival at the public pool, and I was walking from the high school to the pool with my best mate, Murray Steele, smoking cigarettes as usual. A big 4WD came belting along the road and pulled up alongside us. I put my cigarette out against the wall and put chewing gum in my mouth and thought, *Here we go, I'm in trouble again.* Dr Van Dyke, whose reception Mum worked at, opened the passenger window and said, 'Get in.'

I looked at Murray, thinking, *What's this about?*

The doctor said, 'Just get in the car now.'

I told Murray I'd see him later. I got in and said to the doctor, 'What's going on?'

'Just sit here, be quiet and you'll find out in a minute.'

I was thinking, *Shit, I've been busted, but what for?* I was racking my brain. All I'd done was smoking. I couldn't think of anything else. I'd been getting on better with the old man and had cleaned up my act in the past couple of months. Maybe they'd just found out about something I'd done a while ago. I started coming up with plausible excuses for things I wasn't even sure I'd done!

We went to Dr Van Dyke's house. Mum was sitting on the couch, in tears. I sat down beside her and didn't say anything.

'Mark, I wanted to find you before anyone told you,' she said. 'That's why Peter came and grabbed you. Your dad's just died.'

I sat there like a statue. I felt distant from the scene, like I was watching it rather than being part of it. Mum was sobbing and shaking, and Dr Van Dyke was standing to the side.

Every now and then Mum wiped her nose and took a few calming breaths and said to me, 'Are you all right?'

I wasn't crying or doing anything. I asked some questions about where Dad was now. They explained that he was still up at the hospital. Then it struck me that I had to do something. I couldn't sit there waiting for the emotions to hit me.

'I have to go and tell my mates I won't be seeing them tonight.' We'd had something planned, I can't remember what.

Mum said, 'Don't worry about that.'

But I had this overpowering urge to go and let them know. I walked from Dr Van Dyke's house towards the school, which wasn't far. It was surreal, walking down the same familiar path that just a few hours before had been completely different. I felt like I was walking in a void in space, a bubble. The world had changed, but I was the only person who knew about it.

I couldn't find the guys I was looking for, so I found a teacher and asked him to let Murray know I wouldn't make it that night.

I walked back to the doctor's house. Mum was still in tears. When she saw me, she broke down again. I think she was finding it hard, and lonely, that I didn't react at all. I was like an animal under attack, numb until I could understand what was happening and what would happen next.

We got in the car and she drove us back home. I asked if she'd let Brent know, and she said she was going to call him. We got into the house, and I went to my bedroom. I sat on the bed staring at the V8 posters and photos of Kurt Cobain on the wall, but nothing was going in.

*

Dad had been at the workshop with the RSL guys when he'd had some sharp chest pains. He'd got into his car and driven to the doctor's surgery, where Mum was working. His heart attack started there. They put him down on the dentist's chair to chill him out, and Dr Van Dyke gave him some medication to thin his blood and relax his heart rate. He said he felt a lot better; the pain had gone away. Then all of a sudden he crashed, and died there on the dentist's chair, in front of Mum. He'd been hit by a massive heart attack, and one of his lungs had collapsed. Mum and the doc had performed CPR for as long as they could.

For the next three days, our house was filled with people. That first afternoon, I was sitting on the couch as all Mum's friends and the wives of Dad's friends came over with food and to console her. I was watching a TV show, kind of putting on a brave face but wanting to be somewhere else.

The next afternoon Murray came over and took me to the old quarry behind the property where Dad and I had gone to trap rabbits and foxes. Murray and I smoked a packet of cigarettes and talked all afternoon. It was a nice spring day in Dorrigo, clear blue skies, starting to get warm. Without realising it, Dad and I had been getting closer. Brent's leaving had been a rupture, but after we'd got over that we'd begun to relate more as two blokes than as father and son. I felt cheated by losing him – I still feel cheated – because our relationship was beginning to change into something different and better. I often think that if he'd stuck around till I was in my early twenties, we would have got on really well.

When I got back to the house it was still full of people, which kept Mum's mind occupied. Brent eventually showed up from Newcastle, and he was rocked hard. The gutted look on his face hit me too. He was much more open about it than me. I was closed off. It wasn't that I didn't care, obviously, but my way of coping was to keep it all at arm's length. I was trying to think, *What's next?* I needed to focus on practicalities, anything other than letting the enormity of what had happened sink in.

The funeral was a couple of days later. Everyone in the church was crying except me. Feeling everyone's eyes on me, I tried to be tough. Always my way of winning Dad's approval, now suppressing the tears was my way of honouring him. Then an unexpected thing happened. I was soon laughing at the great stories his mates were telling about him. He'd been president of the fishing club, and the kids liked him because he'd give them free soft drinks. The next president wanted to charge them, and the kids had started a protest about how he was nowhere near as good as Dad. One awards night, the other blokes played a trick on Dad by telling him it was suit and tie. He'd got done up, and when he showed up they were all in T-shirts and shorts. I was laughing at these stories, but everyone else was crying. It must have looked strange. But emotions are unpredictable in the way they come out of you. I was bursting inside, but when Dad's mates told these stories, it unstoppered all that tension, which flooded out in laughter instead of tears. I've seen it in combat situations in myself and in others; in some extreme situations the human body can only laugh or cry, and when you're not allowed to cry, all you can do is laugh.

We put him in the ground. Brent was a pallbearer and found it pretty difficult to keep himself from tears. Mum, as well as being overwhelmed by her grief, was stressed out because her stepmother Joan was there, with our grandfather, and getting in the way. Because Mum was small and easygoing, some people thought they could walk all over her. I'm sure Joan was trying to help, but for Mum it was the final straw. At some point during that day she snapped and told Joan to back off. Because Mum losing her temper was so out of character, Joan took it personally and got all huffy.

The wake was back at the house. Brent went back to Newcastle and I took a couple of weeks off school to help Mum. The adjustment to losing Dad was bigger than either of us could have imagined and a catalyst for more change. Suddenly it felt like there was nothing there. He wasn't there to take me fishing or do the other things we did. I thought a lot about how our relationship had been improving, and couldn't control my bitterness. Mum tried her best to control me, but she was so busy, having to work incredibly hard to keep things going, and was dealing with the change from being a family to being a single mum of two teenage boys, one away from home and the other a bit of a handful.

I found myself at home a lot on my own. I got a taste for independence and moved down to the cellar, which had a separate entrance, so I could come and go as I pleased. It was a pretty dingy place, more like a cold, damp dungeon, but it suited me. I got a puppy, a kelpie-ridgeback-labrador cross I named Lister after the character on *Red Dwarf*. Lister went everywhere with me. Tan with a white blaze and socks, he looked like a well-groomed dingo. A boy and his dog are thick as thieves, and I saw Lister as my wingman and confidant. Through Angie and now Lister, I was building a bond with canines that would turn into a wartime partnership that would save my life. In his way, Lister played his role in saving my life back then.

In recent years, I've seen military families when kids have lost their dads. They just want to be with their friends. I think I know what they're trying to do – being with their friends lets them pretend life is going on as normal. If I sat with Mum at nights and on weekends, it would just remind me of what we'd lost. I couldn't face it. I know this was a selfish attitude, and have great regrets about not looking after Mum more, but I was fifteen going on sixteen and focused on my own survival. She wanted to do things together, but I fobbed her off. My mates were now my substitute family, and I saw them as much as I could.

After school, I locked myself in my bedroom with Lister, put on some music, smoked, and then went out to trap rabbits or have a run. I came back and had dinner with Mum, but instead of sitting with her and watching TV at night, I went off to do my own thing. I hitchhiked around the area to wherever friends were having a party. By the time Friday afternoon came, I'd bolt home from school, get changed, and go out and buy some bottles of rum. The parties would go on until Sunday, ranging from Dorrigo down to Bellingen and Coffs Harbour. I had mates in towns down the line and in Coffs, so there were always places to stay and people to meet, girls to hook up with, fights to get into.

It was mateship and loyalty as much as escape that I was looking for. My friends probably saw me as a reliable mate. If they were getting some bourbon for the weekend, I was always up for it. We pushed all kinds of limits, but if anyone got into trouble, they could rely on me. We had a kind of pact: if anything goes wrong, I'm there for you. My closest mates were Murray and another schoolfriend, Vaughan, who was going to do a carpentry apprenticeship. I was probably the biggest risk-taker in the group, getting really drunk and vandalising things, but I was by no means alone.

We couldn't get into pubs or clubs, so we had to make our own pointless fun. We'd walk down the street kicking car mirrors, smashing windows and doors or throwing bins around. We had slingshots and set up ambushes for people who were just walking along: we'd smash the streetlights while they were under them. Or we'd throw rocks up at a balcony where people were trying to have a good night. We'd bump into another bunch of kids and get into a fight, then wash our wounds off with rum. There were some massive street brawls in Bellingen and Coffs. You wouldn't go looking for fights, but it was going to happen with groups of kids wandering around drunk. Our version of a great night was doing that, sleeping it off and then going again the next night. Or we'd find girls to hang out with. We'd make up dares about breaking into places, to see if it could be done. There were other groups of guys who broke into cars and houses to steal, but for me it was for the fun of it, to meet the challenge of getting into difficult places without getting caught. We were quite resourceful, getting a Bunsen burner and hacksaw and breaking locks. The most we ever pinched was a souvenir or two – useless crap, just to show we'd got in. It certainly wasn't the law-abiding life you would hope goes into a soldier's make-up, but to me, the way I rationalised it, we were a unit: setting ourselves dangerous tasks, executing them and getting out undetected, taking huge risks and doing everything for our mates.

That took us through the summer, but when the school year started again there was no let-up in the weekend partying. The amazing thing was, we'd still go and play soccer or rugby on the weekend. We were too young to be getting bad hangovers, so we didn't know we were hurting ourselves.

Mum wasn't blind to what was going on but she didn't know what to do about it, and we fought a lot. I had an undercut, trying my best to look like Kurt Cobain, and lived in this grimy cellar. I remember one weekend she had gone away to Newcastle to visit Brent and I said I was staying at home. I had a rugby game on down the coast. After that I invited a few friends back to my place for some drinks. We got a bit wild and fairly drunk. Stupidly, I took my mate's parents' car for a spin in the paddock. It was then decided that a good idea would be to do a 10-k loop near home. My mate took over the wheel. There were four of us in the car and we ended up rolling it on a dirt road. It was really stupid but luckily no one was injured; the car was totalled but still running. We limped it home to my place, the roof all flattened and one of the tyres popped so there were sparks shooting from the rim. It was a write-off. Dumb idea, that's for sure. We stupidly thought we could fix it overnight, but there was no hope. It is madness doing that sort of thing, and we learnt the hard way.

To create some kind of structure, Mum got me into karate classes at Bellingen a few years earlier and drove me down there two nights a week. My karate teacher, Kathy Sweeney, taught traditional-style martial arts, emphasising respect. I took that very seriously, never seeing karate as a channel for taking out my aggression. Though my life might have looked chaotic from the outside, from the inside I was committed to my causes. There was loyalty to my mates, there was karate, and I was also lifting weights. One thing I wasn't doing was lying around waiting for bad thoughts to get in. In fact, I was frenetically moving, doing anything to create an outlet for that burning feeling inside, the causes of which were transparent to everyone except me.

Unfortunately, I couldn't bring that commitment to my studies. I was sporadically trying to focus on my HSC, but was just getting through the year. A few months before the end, I was pulled out of art class with a few others. The teacher said, 'Here's a test. Give it a go. If you do any good, they'll accept you on a scholarship.' It was a college of fine arts in Sydney. I thought, *Yeah, I'll give it a crack.* I was into graffiti and reading graphic novels. I could never draw that well – better than average, but not great – but it was the best thing going for me at the time, and when I got accepted for the scholarship, I took it as a lifeline. By the start of the next year, 1997, I would be getting out of Dorrigo and off for a new adventure in the big city. My wish to escape now had a physical destination.

Brent was coming home for occasional weekends and his university holidays, and took it upon himself to pull me into line. There was a lot of bickering. One day he asked me to cut his hair in the kitchen with a set of clippers. They were blunt and pulling his hair, but he thought I was doing it deliberately. He got into me, and I said, 'Shove it up your arse and do it yourself then, you princess.'

He burred up at that, and we were going toe to toe. I swung with a closed fist and hit him in the face. We'd always fought, like any pair of brothers, but it had never got to a punch in the face. He took it full-on and grabbed a couple of knives from the kitchen drawer. Mum, who was in the garden, heard the shouting and came in to see us facing off.

'I'm gunna stab you!' Brent shouted.

'Okay, come on, do it!'

It eventually de-escalated, and I pissed off to see what my mates were doing. I didn't come back home until he'd left.

That wasn't the last of our fights during what was the worst period of our relationship – but not the worst period of our lives, which was still to come. On another visit, Brent was going on at me about everything I was doing wrong. I was flunking at school, I was drinking and smoking, I shouldn't be allowed to have a dog, and I wasn't looking after Mum.

'You're not here any more, you don't run this place,' I said. I was going to add, *And you're not the old man.* The thought of that sent me into a rage, and I screamed, 'I'm gunna bash you till you're bleeding.' I charged after him, but he got away and kept his distance. We laugh about it now, but it was a real low point.

Speaking of low points, I completed the HSC with predictable results. The day they were getting posted out, I was sitting in front of the Dorrigo post office. There was a boy there who'd gone to a private school. We sat and opened our envelopes. He asked me what I'd got and I told him.

'What are you going to do?' he said. 'Join the army?'

I sprang up and told him to get fucked. I shoved my finger in his face and said, 'Why would I join the army? I've got a fucken scholarship to a college in Sydney, I'm moving out of this shithole. Have fun working for your dad for the rest of your life.'

The poor guy didn't know how to take it. There was a bunch of other private-school kids, the children of the well-to-do townspeople, hanging around, and I turned to them and said, 'Guess what? Now I don't have to know you any more, yous can go and get fucked!'

They probably thought I was a wanker, and fair enough. It was ironic, too, when you consider where I did end up.

Meanwhile, I was pulling back from all the drinking and fighting and partying all weekend. Maybe I'd had my schoolies a year early. Or maybe it was just that I had to be different from the crowd. Like Dad, I'm a non-conformist, and that went for hedonism as much as schoolwork. When all the other kids let loose and went out partying, I went the opposite way. Now that I knew I'd be moving to Sydney, I wanted to save some money. I went to an extreme in that direction, too. Mum knew a businessman through the surgery who got me a job planting trees. I worked whole weeks, starting at five o'clock in the morning and going until sundown putting trees in the ground. I wasn't afraid of working if I was getting paid for it. It got me out of home and gave me an excuse when people were asking me to go down to Coffs. Some weekends I still got involved, but

I always needed some new kind of stimulation, and I was bored with constant partying. Breaking through the weariness and boredom, getting fit and healthy, sticking with a job – this was the new challenge I was setting myself, and as always I wanted to see how far I could go.

Most Fridays, I was so tired from a week's work I'd crash out and think about Sydney.

FOUR

Despite all the hell I'd been giving her, Mum was tire-less in trying to smooth the way for me. She must have been anxious about me going down to Sydney on my own – Ross and Val were my only relatives there – but, just as she'd organised that job for me planting trees, now she set me up with a place to live.

She knew a clerical worker at the Bellingen credit union. I'd met Chris Watt a few times and had found him weird. He was a bland-looking man, what I'd call a pencil-neck, quite tall and skinny with brown hair and glasses. He was a widower – his wife had hanged herself, apparently – and he had three grown-up children, two daughters and a son. Chris and Mum were friends, but it was pretty obvious to me that he wanted something more. He was ingratiating towards me, trying much too hard to be my pal, and came over to offer to do jobs around the house for Mum when she hadn't asked him. I might have been full of bravado at that time, but I was a pretty good judge of character, and I told Mum not to trust him: he was a weasel. Mum assured me that she had no intention of forming a serious relationship with him. She'd been making a friendship with another guy in town, and when someone said to her, 'I hear you're in a relationship,' she got very indignant and said it was too soon after losing Dad. Chris had acted quite jealous of this other man, which also alerted me to his agenda. But in any case, I was leaving and had to trust that Mum knew what she was doing. Besides, it was only normal that a teenage boy would be protective of his mum when he's moving away, and so maybe I was overreacting to the gut feeling I had.

Chris's younger daughter, Sally, was living in a flat in Artarmon, on the north shore of Sydney. Mum organised for me to move into their spare room for a few months. It was a good location, as the art college was in North Sydney, and I went down and began to focus on my graphic design studies. Well, for a few weeks, anyway. I was soon thinking, *How good is this place?* I was still seventeen years old, nowhere near as mature as I thought I was, and felt like I was in Disneyland. I suddenly found new barriers to try to crash my way through.

Wednesday night was $5-jug night at a pub near the college, and that was the trigger for a five-day party lasting till Sunday. I'd go to live bands and meet a lot of people with similar interests: girls and parties. It wasn't the same as in Dorrigo, where friendship was based on loyalty – it was more that I got on with people who liked the same music and bars and, inevitably, the same partying ways. The friendships were fun but fleeting, based on interests more than deeper affinities.

I lived at Artarmon for a couple of months. Sally was the only one of Chris Watt's children I got to know, and she was nice. Her elder sister, Christine, lived on the Gold

Coast and was somewhat estranged from her father. The son, Jon, had a car accident during this time and became a quadriplegic. I had no idea how that was affecting Chris.

A girl from Dorrigo I knew, Melissa, now lived in a four-bedroom terrace in Camperdown, then a run-down industrial and student housing area in inner Sydney. Five years older than me, Melissa used to work at a shop in Dorrigo and let us smoke cigarettes out the back. She was very pretty, and was now in a lesbian relationship. A room came free, and she asked me if I wanted to move in. It was twenty bucks cheaper and a lot more interesting than Artarmon, and proximity to college was less and less of a priority for me.

Through Melissa I met a new group of people, all older than me. The girls in Artarmon were country girls living in the city, whereas Melissa moved with an exotic crowd. Nelly, one of the flatmates, had done a journalism course and was writing for the Triple J magazine. She was hanging out with indie bands, and crowds of people came over to party. I was the baby of the house, seventeen years old and the only boy. The girls never condescended to me, always including me in their activities, and it was pretty much the dream lifestyle, for a while anyway.

I was starting to realise that college wasn't what I'd hoped for. As much as I liked drawing and other skills, there were a lot of wankers there. It was an industry college and they brought in graphic designers who told us what it was like in the workforce, and it sounded like shit. You had to suck up to clients and tell them how great they were and put up with their rubbish ideas. A lot of it was geared towards the advertising industry, and I was more interested in coming up with artistic ideas and letting designers design. North Sydney had a very businessy crowd, while I was absorbed in that new punkish movement at Camperdown. Life was very different north of the harbour, and I couldn't see a spot for myself in that world of executives in grey suits, with zany ties and socks to show how artistic they were.

Financially, college was a grind too. There was an art supplies shop downstairs from the college, and I stole everything I needed for class. I didn't want to ask Mum for 500 bucks for paper and paint, or for a computer so I could do design. She was already putting Brent through university, and I rationalised stealing as an economic risk I had to take. The girl who worked in the shop knew full well what I was doing but didn't say anything. She knew I couldn't afford to pay. In fact, we became friends and she ended up moving into our house.

There was also a food court downstairs from the college. All the other kids bought their lunch, but I waited until the end of each day, when I'd go to the Chinese restaurants and ask, 'What are you throwing out?' They'd give me a big bag of containers full of leftover food, and that was what I lived on.

I don't want to overstress the poverty, because I did have enough money for food. It was just that I preferred to save it for other things. Alcohol, for a start – there were a lot of parties going on – and my interest was sparking up. I'd go on benders, staying awake for five days to see how far I could push it. I thought it was fun – I just wanted to see what would happen. I wasn't getting into fights like at home, and hanging out with those girls was great. As a house we'd go to the Bank, the Oxford, the Town Hall, all the Newtown pubs. At the Oxford we knew the bouncers, the carpet was sticky, and there was the same bunch every Friday night. No one cared how drunk you got as long as you didn't cause any trouble. It was my kind of crowd.

There was still some of the old north-coast lair in me. Vaughan, my mate from Dorrigo who was doing a carpentry apprenticeship in Sydney, came out with me one night to hear a band at a pub near the airport. Afterwards, we were pushing each other in supermarket trolleys. We came to a showroom in Alexandria, and tried to smash as many windows as we could with our trolleys and then with our elbows. After that it was a street run smashing windows, doors, anything down the street. People came out of the houses. We threw whatever we could at them and continued on. We got away with it, though when we got home we were digging massive pieces of glass out of our elbows.

We revived our old 'can you do it' challenges one night for a concert at the Enmore Theatre; I think Marilyn Manson was in it. We didn't have enough money for tickets, so we started egging each other on about climbing on the roof and getting in from the top. We got on top of the theatre and could hear the place pumping. We found an open air vent and looked down through it – straight onto the stage of this concert! We climbed down into the railings and sat there having a good old time, passing a bottle of rum back and forth. Some rigging ropes were hanging near us, so we scaled down them. If you were in the crowd, you'd have been able to see this pair of feral-looking kids hanging above the stage. Security were watching the crowd, not us. We climbed down onto a little platform, sat there and enjoyed the music for a while. My mate eventually yelled out to one of the dudes on stage.

That was it. Security saw us and went bananas. They couldn't get to us initially. We were heckling them, these big solid bouncers trying to climb the ropes. They put up a ladder, which we pushed away. I said to my mate, 'You reckon we can climb back up the ropes?' He said, 'Don't worry about it.' I followed his eyes. The bouncers were on the platform.

They put us in arm locks, took us backstage and started throwing us around. We were saying, 'Slow down, we're harmless, we're not doing anything.' But they wanted to take it to the next level. The struggle started to escalate into a full-blown brawl. My mate carried a knife with him and didn't want to get caught with it. He started thrashing around and fighting the bouncers, and threw his knife away to hide it. Some kind of supervisor came down and told us to stay there. He was going to call the cops.

We said, 'What are you gunna charge us with?'

'Breaking and entering.'

'The place was open, we just came in.'

While this discussion was going on, the bouncers made the mistake of taking their eye off us. They expected we'd do as we were told and wait passively for the cops, but we noticed that the exit door was right next to us. Suddenly we popped it open and got out onto Enmore Road. There was no way they were going to catch us. We ticked it off as another successful mission.

*

One night during that first year in Sydney, I had a dream that I saw Mum with a soft blue neon light behind her, sort of hovering in the sky. I could see her mouthing words but I couldn't hear her. I was saying, *What are you trying to tell me?* And finally I could hear. She was saying, *Wake up, Mark. Wake up, Mark.* Over and over again. I said, in the dream, *I am awake – what do you want to tell me?* She insisted, *Wake UP, Mark.*

I woke up. It was 5.30 am. It was a vivid enough dream for me to write it down in a notebook. I thought about it, and took the meaning to be that I should wake up to myself and stop trying to be someone other than who I was. I was struggling with college. Was this really me? Did I really want to go down this line? And I was hanging out with a crew of people who were a bit fucked in the head. Maybe on some level she was trying to tell me that. Anyway, I didn't think much more about the dream until the next year.

In the Christmas holidays at the end of 1997, I went back home via Auntie Margaret's place in Newcastle. I might have looked in my element in Camperdown, but visiting the family created a stir. I had a long Mohawk dyed black with streaks of green, tied back, and my head shaved down the sides. I had some piercings, including one in my nose. When I was at Margaret's, one of her grandchildren, my nephew Liam, kept staring at the ring and asking me if it hurt and asking, 'Can you blow your nose?' With my ripped jeans and tattered singlets and hair, I looked like the creature from the black lagoon.

From my appearance and behaviour, it was obvious to Mum what kind of stuff I was up to. I was bored in Dorrigo and hung out with Lister in the cellar. Mum must have been concerned that I was losing my way. I saw Chris Watt again on that visit, and he was still persistent, still weird. Auntie Margaret said she'd only met him once, at his mother's place, and he acted disconcertingly: he was sitting off to the side, outside the circle, and she offered to make a space to let him in. He said no, he preferred being outside, as if he wanted to observe everybody and not be a part of the conversation. Given that he was more or less hosting the visitors, Margaret found that unnerving, but she didn't say anything to Mum.

As for getting myself back on track, I was too full of bravado to be told by anyone else. I had to reach my outer limits for myself. When I went back to Sydney, there was a night I went out in North Sydney and got so drunk that I went to get on the train to go south and ended up two stations north. When I got off, I fell between the train and the platform and took all the skin off my shins, legs and chin. I had one arm on the train and one on the platform and was stuck between them, and the train was about to move. This is the type of thing you read about in the paper: a young drunken idiot getting himself killed by a train. Luckily for me, a guard saw me and stopped the train. I climbed up onto the platform and fell back vomiting, bleeding, blind drunk. The train took off and I was still lying there.

In a haze, and giggling to myself, I got on a train heading south and got off at Wynyard, in the middle of the CBD. I was tipping over garbage bins and couldn't find my way out of the business area. I passed out somewhere, and while I was unconscious I shat and pissed myself. When I came to, I was abusing people. I was just a wreck. I guess I'd achieved what I wanted, which was to find out how far I could push it.

I made it to Town Hall to get a NightRide bus, but the driver wouldn't let me on. I had to stumble the couple of kilometres to Camperdown, and got there as the sun was coming up. I crashed out in my bed, and woke up at five in the afternoon with blood all over me, smelling of piss and shit, clothes all torn, skin off my face and legs. I thought, *I can't keep doing this. I can't keep this up.* When I thought of the night before, I knew how close I'd been to ending up squished on those train tracks. And I'd been on my own, no one looking after me, I'd lost the people I'd started the night with and probably didn't really know them anyway. It was all pretty dire.

The house in Camperdown started breaking up. The girls had a huge argument and we all went our separate ways. Melissa, who was the only one I'd stayed on good terms with, moved back up to the north coast, and I moved into a share house in nearby Chippendale.

That night when I'd nearly killed myself and woken up in my own shit was a wake-up call for me. Years later in Afghanistan, making a split-second decision in that ambush, I didn't realise I'd reached a crossroad that was going to change my life. But in Sydney, sore, aching and embarrassed, it didn't take a genius to work out that I was standing at some sort of junction. Keep going the way I way I was headed and it was going to end badly for me. I made the conscious decision to follow a different road. I stopped boozing hard and partying, and began to get healthy, swimming at the Victoria Park pool on Broadway every morning. Just like in my last year of school, one extreme was followed by an equally extreme counter-reaction. I got a job as a kitchen hand at the Bathers' Pavilion in Balmoral, where one of my new flatmates was an apprentice chef. The other flatmates were a musician and a Dutch exchange student. It was quite a different house from Camperdown, where everyone had done every-thing together. Here it was four guys each doing their own thing, no communal cooking or cleaning. You just looked after yourself. I went for weeks sometimes without seeing them beyond a 'Hey' in the hallway. It sounds like a cold place, but it was just what I needed at that time.

I began cutting out of college early to work double shifts at the restaurant. Because I was cleaning myself up, I was enjoying my new spartan lifestyle. To economise on food, I took the big bags of bread rolls they threw out after each night at the restaurant, and some milk from the fridge. I was making my life simple and healthy.

Mum teased me that I only called if I needed money, and I took it a bit personally, so I wasn't calling her as often as I should have. One morning in April, just after my nineteenth birthday, I woke up with a funny feeling in my gut that I should call her, just to see how she was going.

'Hello?'

It wasn't Mum's voice on the phone, which took me aback. 'Who's that?' I said.

'Is that you, Mark? It's Jo here.' Jo Beaumont was our neighbour and Mum's closest friend.

'What's going on?' I said. 'Why are you answering the phone?'

'Your mum's not here,' Jo said. 'You don't know where she is, do you?'

'I thought she was at home.'

'Well, we're not sure where she is. We think she's missing.'

'What?'

Jo explained that the police were at the house, and a few things warranted them taking a look. She started explaining it quite calmly, but soon got extremely upset and began crying. 'Mark, they think something's happened to your mum. She's missing and nobody knows where she is.'

I don't remember how the conversation ended. My heart was thumping in my throat. I said, 'I'll ring back later.'

I went to work at the Bathers', just trying to normalise things. *When I get home*, I thought, *Mum will have turned up and everything will be okay.*

When I got home, there was a stack of messages waiting for me, none of them good. One was from Auntie Margaret. I rang her, and she said she and Uncle Ken were planning to drive up to Dorrigo. I asked her to wait for me. I'd be on the next train to Newcastle.

On the train, I felt crisp and rational. I could remove myself from my anxiety and analyse the situation. It was uncharacteristic of Mum to do this without telling anyone, but maybe she'd gone camping. She often went away for weekends. In fact, that same weekend, I'd heard, she'd been planning to fly up to Queensland to visit a friend.

The alarm had first been raised when Mum didn't arrive on her flight, and her friend called Dorrigo. A family friend, a young guy named Paul, my godparents' son, who'd stayed at the house a couple of nights a week because he was working as a builder at the pub, had arrived there to drop off his stuff. Mum's car and Lister were there and the house was open, but Mum was nowhere to be seen. Paul had rung Jo and she'd called the police.

When I got to Margaret's place, she was in tears, which confronted me with a truth my cold rationalising could no longer ward off. Something bad was going on. Margaret poured out the facts. There wasn't much chance Mum had left the house to go on holidays. She would have left Lister in kennels or with friends. Bits of information were coming from here and there, but we tried not to make too much of it before we found out more facts. We left for Dorrigo, a four- to five-hour drive, and went straight to the police station. Brent was already in Dorrigo. The policeman, who'd stayed out at the property all night, sat us down and told us they'd found blood in the house, on the staircase and in the garage. He didn't tell us this at the time, but he'd found a bone fragment in the driveway as well. Due to the blood at the scene, the house being unlocked, and the dog and the car being left there, along with signs of a struggle in the house, the police suspected Mum had been murdered. I just sat there, feeling numb but ready to explode at the same time. Margaret was sobbing and holding tightly to my arm.

We went up to the Beaumonts' place, and this was where Chris Watt's name came up. He hadn't even crossed my mind. But the police had told Brent and Jo they suspected Chris was involved, because of what had happened five days before Mum disappeared – Anzac Day.

In honour of Dad, Mum had marched on Anzac Day and laid some flowers at the memorial. After the ceremony, Mum went back to the Beaumonts' and unloaded about recent developments between her and Chris. She got quite upset as she spoke to Jo. Mum had told Chris she didn't want to see him or have anything to do with him any more. She told Jo she felt stupid about giving him the wrong idea, but she'd only wanted to be friends with him, and it hadn't dawned on her until recently that he'd thought the relationship was a lot more than it was. She'd finally told him it wasn't going any further.

He'd started pestering her then, ringing her up and saying, 'I've invested so much in this relationship, you can't end it.' She said, 'It's not about how much money you've invested, is it?' He'd been mowing her lawns and doing other odd jobs, and even though she'd asked him not to, he'd done them anyway. He'd lent her a lot of household bits and pieces, and she told Jo she was leaving the stuff on her back step with a note to him saying he could take it back if he wanted. Mum hadn't wanted to go home, in case he turned up to get his things. She didn't want to be there for any confrontation. She just wanted a clean break. Five days after Anzac Day, Jo saw Chris's distinctive bright-yellow car at our house. Nobody had seen Mum from that day on.

Brent and I stayed at the Beaumonts' for a night. The police let us know that Chris had gone to the Gold Coast. He had been visiting friends near Armidale, at Uralla. He'd told them he was going to the Gold Coast, but they couldn't contact him. His house in Bellingen had been left in a hurry. His neighbours had seen him show up early on the morning of 30 April, dishevelled, and he'd ignored them when they'd said hello. He was going to visit his son Jon, who was in hospital on the Gold Coast. Chris's parents lived in Grafton and it was likely that he took the back road to there from Coffs Harbour and onward to the Gold Coast, where his daughter Christine lived.

Brent and I said we were going to go up there and flog him and find out what he had to do with it. Margaret and Jo were saying, 'We don't know if it's him. Let the police do their thing.'

Frustrated, I stomped around the place. A lot of people were coming around to the Beaumonts' and I started having similar feelings to when we'd lost Dad. I wanted to find some mates and have a drink and get away from all this overwhelming interest. It was suffocating, everyone being in the one place moping around and talking about it. I wanted to *do* something. Lister came with me everywhere. We went down to the pub for a few beers. The publican was nice and let me have Lister in to lie by the fire.

People were going in search parties into the bush down the back roads between Dorrigo and Bellingen and to the Bellinger River. Then we got the news. Chris had been found in the car park of an RSL club in south-east Queensland. He'd taken some pills and left two suicide notes, neither of which said anything about Mum. To say he took the coward's way out is to get across barely a fraction of the anger I felt, and still feel.

Brent was the same. We were saying we should have gone to the Gold Coast and got him while he was still alive, and were mad at ourselves for not doing so. He might have already committed suicide by then anyway, but at least we'd have done something. 'If he hadn't done that,' I said to Brent, 'he'd have ended up dead anyway if I'd got my hands on him.' Brent agreed. That was how enraged we were.

I still feel that fury to this day and would still do that to him. It's quite violent, but I would make him suffer. What did she ever do? She did nothing, nothing at all. I have no words to describe him. There's no lower human act than to take an innocent person's life and then be such a coward as to take your own.

We stayed in Dorrigo for three weeks, driving around looking for her. People were walking the banks of the rivers. Notices went out in the papers asking for information, and there was a bit on the TV news.

The police ended up digging up Chris's wife's body, suspecting there might have been some foul play. In a cruel irony, Mum had only befriended Chris in the first place because his wife had died, and someone had told Mum that it might be good therapy to share experiences. Chris's wife had hanged herself, but there were parts of the story that hadn't sounded right. She'd bought material for sewing and done her ironing that day. It was uncharacteristic of people committing suicide to do those sorts of things. But nothing could ever be proven, and either way it wasn't going to help Mum.

It can be hard to believe genuinely nice people exist, but Mum was truly one of those types. One of my friends said, 'This sort of thing doesn't happen to people like Bernadette. She was supposed to grow old and sit on a rocking chair on the front porch watching her grandchildren run around.' That's right. She was an authentically good person and deserved the best. One of the things that really gutted me was that she always trusted people, and it was that trusting personality that brought about her end. I think it changed my perception of how to treat people, and whether I wanted to or not, I would be wary of others because of what happened to her.

It is kind of sad that we took her for granted. You tend to just assume that your parents will always be there. The older I got the more she would have to put up with. Especially after Dad died and I was going through those couple of wayward years.

She was happy for me when I moved into the room under the house. I was smoking cigarettes down there, stupidly thinking she would not be able to smell it. She caught me off guard one morning before school. I came upstairs to have breakfast and just out of the blue and in complete calmness she said to me, 'if you're going to smoke that's fine, but at least go outside so it doesn't make the whole house stink.' Silence. I must have had a bit of a stunned look on my face, then just said something like, 'Uhhh, okay . . . thanks!' She was good like that. I know she didn't like the fact that I did it but knew I would do it anyway, so she compromised and that relaxed the feeling of tension in the house, for me anyway.

I can say that I had no concept of how I was making her feel by taking off on a Friday down the coast to go partying and not showing up till Sunday night, having not talked to her all weekend and her not knowing where I was or what I was up to. It is hard because I snapped out of that selfishness and became aware of how much I had troubled her only shortly before her tragic death. In being patient and not aggressive, it helped me and I owe her my life for that. I think if she had been any other way – if she had intervened or forced me – then I believe it would have pushed me further away. It would have been difficult for her too because Dad had been a hard taskmaster and had anger problems. There were probably times when she needed to use his approach in dealing with us.

My memories of her are centred around a feeling that she made everything okay and safe. Her positive attitude, no matter what was happening, really rubbed off on us. She would encourage us to try our best and remind us that we could achieve whatever we wanted. Mum had a special way of making us kids feel as if there was nothing we couldn't do. Even though Dad was great to have fun with, if it wasn't done his way it was wrong. You had to perform with Dad or he would explode. Mum had a better way of letting us figure it out for ourselves without making us feel useless if we didn't. A unique talent.

Before she disappeared, Mum had been planning Brent's twenty-first birthday party. We decided to go ahead with it. Jo cleaned the house, and Brent and I moved back in. I was still separating myself from it all emotionally. It was only on the first night we moved back in that I shed a tear. To this day I haven't done it again. There's no mistaking how emotional it is for me, but I've never let it overwhelm me. Maybe I don't know where I'd end up if I did.

We made the best we could of Brent's twenty-first at the Beaumonts' place. Brent's mates from uni were all there, trying to keep it from being an understandably sombre occasion. While we were at the house together he and I had a lot of talking to do, and one night we had a big argument. He was lecturing me about how I had to get myself back on the rails, and I snapped, 'This is just like when Dad died. You're trying to tell me what to do again. It's not like that any more. Where were you when I was in Sydney doing all this stuff and getting in trouble and going down this slippery slope? Where were you then? If you're such a good brother who looks after his little brother, where were you then?'

The look on his face showed that he hadn't realised I felt that way. It upset him and he took it pretty hard. I didn't understand how badly I was hurting him – then again, when you're arguing with your brother, you *want* to hurt him.

There were signs that we were cracking up again the way we had when Dad died, but this time it was different. After we simmered down, we agreed that there was only the two of us now. We had to look after each other.

That was the closest I came to getting really emotional

about it. It wasn't quite a pact, just an understanding that we'd stay in touch and be good to each other and not grow apart. Years later, Brent and I can go for long periods without talking to each other, but when we're together we don't argue any more. He's my best friend. And for fifteen years we've been all that's left of our family, only the two of us to look after each other.

FIVE

We had a service a couple of weeks later, to put a plaque on a rock in the park in Dorrigo. A lot of townspeople were there, to show their horror at what had happened and their respect for Mum. There were a few seats for family down the front, but I didn't want to go there with people looking at me, so I stayed off to the side with Lister.

Joan came over and said, 'Come and sit with the family.'

'I want to be here,' I said. 'This is where I want to stand.'

She took the hint and went back to her seat. The spooky thing was, as she went to sit down she fell off the back of her chair. Margaret to this day says Mum was there and tipped Joan off as a last message.

The service was upsetting, but in a different way from Dad's. This time there was nothing we could hang on to. Dad had died and we put him into the ground. With Mum, one day she was there and the next she was gone. I never had a doubt what had happened; Chris had no other reason to commit suicide. There would be two coronial inquests, eventually finding that he'd probably murdered her, but we didn't need that for confirmation. Years later, after the second coronial inquest and thanks to advances in DNA technology, it was deemed that the blood found in the back of his car was Mum's. To this day she's never been found – no remains, no personal effects, nothing. An empty absolute nothingness. It was not only a brutal and cruel thing to do, but unthinkably self-centred. We were at the park trying to think about Mum and bring back all our good memories, but that was hard to do when I was so stirred up by anger and disgust for that person.

I hung around for another week, in no hurry to go back to college. Mrs Hogan, my high school art teacher, had been at the service. She came up and made the mistake of asking, 'How's school?'

Grunting, I said I'd decided I didn't need that shit now. This was the second parent I'd lost. I'd thought about it on my way up with Margaret and Ken. The last thing I wanted was to continue with a degree I didn't like. I told Mrs Hogan I was going to travel and see things. In those days, there was a bit of a battle going on, with plenty of friends and family encouraging me to stick with my education. No way in hell. I had a kind of unbreakable determination now. It didn't yet have any positive direction, but I knew with certainty what I *didn't* want to do.

I went down to Sydney and saw the management of the college. They said, 'You've only got three months to go, why don't you stick with it? We can work something out.' I said, politely but firmly, 'It's not going to happen. I don't want to do this any more.'

After a week in Sydney, I found I couldn't cope and headed straight back to Dorrigo, moving into the house. Brent went back to Newcastle, where soon after he met

Kate; they would go on to marry and have a beautiful family. We all deal with these things in our own way, and my way, as it had been after Dad's death, was to seek out my loyal old mates.

A lot of them were in Dorrigo, and once again they became my surrogate family. To escape, I dived into the drinking and partying with them. But as they say, you can never step into the same river twice. The guys were still living the same way, doing the same thing. For me, it was fun at first but had a shorter lifespan. Things could get out of hand too easily, and the thrill wasn't the same as when we were sixteen.

One night down in Coffs Harbour, we were drinking a slab of VBs on a roof over the pedestrian mall in the centre of town, chucking bottles down to smash on the pavers and scare the people walking past. The next minute, we saw coppers in leather jackets climbing up towards us. We sprinted across the tarmac and climbed down the side of the wall, but they caught us and gave us 'move on' notices.

Later that night, we were back in the mall. A drunk man with his arm in a cast came up to my mate, who was a 100-kilogram tuna fisherman, also pretty drunk, and started asking him for a cigarette. My mate said no, and the bloke took a swing. My mate took a haymaker back at him, but missed and fell over. We were standing there laughing at him. It was pretty funny that he'd been so pissed he couldn't even lay a hand on a pissed bloke with a broken arm.

But then the man with the cast kicked him in the face. We just ramped up. The bloke took off. After my fitness kick in Sydney, I ran him down pretty easily. I was just wrestling him, and he clipped me in the face with his cast. I lost it. I grabbed his hair and drove my knee into his face. Other people showed up, and I had lost all feeling of making this a fair fight. The guy was getting rag-dollish, but I kept going. I landed a few uppercuts in him, picked him up and drove him into the pavers.

'How do you like it?' I screamed and kicked him in the face. Some girls were screaming at me to stop and charging at me to pull me back.

Someone yelled, 'Cops!'

It was the same ones as earlier in the night. A paddy wagon materialised behind me. I ran down the back alleys with the coppers chasing me in the paddy wagon. I remember looking back behind me at full sprint and clearly seeing their faces as they tried to chase me down. I jumped a fence and got away. I was too quick and knew it too well. I ended up at a beachside block of flats and jumped into a garbage bin. I was slowing my breathing while I heard the cops just outside, talking about me: 'He went this way.' They went away, and I waited till it was really quiet. I got out and looked around.

We had a rendezvous point we'd agreed on, to meet at four o'clock in the morning if we split up and got into a fight. True to our sort-of-military spirit, pre-arranging an RV was how we used to do it when we were kids. I was walking along towards that point, thinking about the fight. I'd been motivated by taking care of my mate, who was lying on the ground getting his face kicked, but I'd been in those situations before and not lost control. This time, the way I'd laid into that bloke with the cast was frightening. In all those years of karate, I'd known how to control myself in a fight and not do anyone serious damage. It was like the day with Brent when I forgot the rules and swung at him with a closed fist – but much worse. I could have killed the bloke. Losing control of myself didn't make me feel good. Suddenly a Falcon pulled up beside me. I thought it was some more guys looking for a fight, but it was plain-clothes coppers. I tried to escape, but they ran me down.

They took me to the police cells, and there were my mates.

'Hey!' We had a laugh.

I said, 'I guess we're not going to make the RV tonight.'

The police put us in separate cells, and I was trading stories about the night with the bloke I was put with. The coppers were bringing plenty of drunk people in. Meanwhile my mate, the tuna fisherman, had worked out how to undo the latch of his cell. He didn't plan to escape, just to make them look silly. When the cops came past the next time, he was casually leaning against the outside of his cell.

'What are you doing, mate?'

'Just wondering if I could get a glass of water and take a piss.'

We were given court dates, but I was the only one who showed up to the hearing. I pleaded against the charge, which was vagrancy, and the magistrate said words to the effect of, 'You're a piece of shit. You're going down the wrong track.' He fined me a few hundred dollars. I didn't care. I was beyond caring. I should have cared about what came out of me when I let loose at that man with the cast. From this distance, it's pretty obvious, and I'm sorry for the bloke who happened to get in the way of so much pent-up rage. I can see, from here, where my loss of control came from. He couldn't help it if he wasn't the person I really wanted to kick the crap out of.

SIX

Whether or not I admitted it to myself, I was in a churned-up state. You can go through the loss of both of your parents without breaking down into a blubbering mess, but that doesn't mean you won't be affected in other ways. If you hold down one part of your nature, the trauma's going to pop up somewhere else.

While I was in Dorrigo, I caught up with my ex-flatmate Melissa, who'd moved back north after the break-up of the Camperdown house. We were sitting in the back seat of a car chatting and waiting for people to come out, and all of a sudden we were kissing and carrying on. It was weird because we'd known each other for so long and lived with each other, and because she'd just got out of a relationship. But we'd always got along well, never mind the age difference.

I was vulnerable and it had something to do with that, but it developed into something more. A summertime love almost. When all the fuss died down, she and I had an idyllic few weeks, swimming in waterholes, going to the beach, living one day at a time. She was kind and soft, and if there was something maternal in how she cared for me, I'm not going to deny it. In a strange way it was just what I needed.

One day I was going through my notebooks and found that the day Mum went missing was a year exactly since I'd had that dream about Mum saying, *Wake up, Mark.* I hadn't mentioned it to Mum, or anybody. Melissa was a spiritual person and she sensed a message. I'm not sure. I've only told a handful of people about it, and even my close mates have looked at me strangely. I guess if Mum hadn't gone missing, the dream wouldn't have meant anything and it wouldn't have stuck with me. But she did, and it has.

*

I still wanted to go back to Sydney, though I didn't have any specific direction. Vaughan was doing his carpentry still, and we moved into a place in Croydon in the inner western suburbs. Melissa drove me down and helped me move in. I wanted to save money, for travel and whatever eventuated. Vaughan was still heavily into partying, which I'd gone beyond. Instead, I threw myself into working in a city restaurant as a kitchen hand, working out in a gym, and doing boxing sessions in the backyard with Vaughan. I got back into karate, working towards my black belt, and laboured on building sites. In my free time I took Lister for walks. Melissa was underpinning everything in my life, and I was enjoying the time with her more and more.

Deep down, I was in limbo. I was very active but the pieces weren't coming together. Was I going to keep working as a kitchen hand forever? A labourer? I didn't quite know why I was in Sydney any more. Vaughan was off on his own trip, which ultimately took a bad turn: he had an undiagnosed schizophrenic condition that was just coming out, with a bit of a hand from too much weed. I was starting to feel adrift.

Towards the end of the year, I decided to move back up to Dorrigo. Margaret and another auntie came down and helped pack the car and move me up. I was lucky to have that support; they'd do anything for us at the drop of a hat. The house was still there, untouched apart from a bit of maintenance Jo and Gary Beaumont had done to keep it tidy. I got my old job back with the tree-planting company, doing reforestation. Melissa moved in and we stayed until the end of 1998.

A hellish year ended in a hellish way. On New Year's Eve, Melissa's dad, a dairy farmer, was in a car accident and had a stroke. She was really upset. He didn't fully recover. Melissa moved up to Lismore to be closer to her family, which made things tricky for us. I hitchhiked ridiculous distances, spending up to a couple of hours waiting for lifts, all to see Melissa. My work moved up to Grafton, which was a bit closer, but her life had taken a pretty dramatic turn and I think her focus had moved from being with me to caring for her dad, which was fair enough. We eventually called it quits, with no hard feelings either way. She'd been an essential person in my healing process, and now she was being even more important for her dad.

While I was living in Dorrigo, I linked up with an old surfer named Kelvin, who lived at Wooli. He and his wife had been friends of Mum's, and Brent and I knew their kids. Kelvin was stumpy and brown, and we called him 'Bilbo Baggins'. He definitely had his own way of doing things. Kelvin taught me how to surf, something I'd always wanted to do but hadn't spent long enough at the beach to put in the commitment. It was such an amazing feeling getting a wave, a total escape, with the sea water performing its own magic, delivering its own hypnosis. Kelvin became a personal mentor too. I was obsessed with surfing and wanted to do it every day. I loved the sense of adventure in finding a wave. I'd put my board under my arm and hitchhike to Sawtell and stay at the beach all day. When you were hunting a wave, there was nothing else you needed to think about. Kelvin showed me I could heal myself by switching from unhealthy to healthy addictions.

I'd like to think some wisdom or self-awareness came with it. I could definitely feel the anger and aggression draining out of me, and saw the pointlessness in a lot of what I'd been doing. It was like a detox. Surfing taught me not to give up: when you're getting smashed and your arms are noodles, you just have to drive yourself on. Sometimes I crammed three long sessions into a day. No half-measures! I'd hitchhike for three hours and find the surf was absolute crap; it didn't matter, I'd still go out alone. I loved how surfing was simply me against me. The only person I was proving a point to was myself. Nobody cared whether I made a wave or not, or survived a heavy wipe-out.

I think I've taken some of that philosophy into my approach to soldiering. When you set a successful ambush and complete the mission, it's a great feeling. But too much emphasis can be placed on winning. It's important to strive to win every gunfight you get into, but it's when you're on the back foot that you need to find your resolve. You can be successful even when you're getting pounded. Combat situations are not always under your control. When you're under fire, when it all changes and goes the other way, a lot of guys get panicky and lose their clarity, because they're all geared up for winning. But I love adversity – it's where I see a chance to prove myself to myself. I think I got it through Dad, and Mum, and had it reinforced when I got into surfing and copped some frightening beatings from the ocean. They were qualities I think came to serve me well in Afghanistan and might have saved my life more than once.

For the first time, I developed a bit of hero-worship for someone doing something in public. This was the year Mark Occhilupo came back from a pretty hopeless state and won his world surfing championship. I thought, *Shit, this guy's gone through all this stuff, similar to me in a sense, and then dealt with it and come through.* It was unusual for me to read that much into a sportsman's life, but I was ready to take inspiration wherever I found it. I've always loved team sports, learning how to manoeuvre towards a common goal, but the individualistic side of surfing really appealed to me. Your own mind is your toughest competitor. Playing against another team or opponent can be hard, but fighting your own self-doubt can be even harder.

I remember reading or hearing something a surfer once said: 'If you're a surfer and you're not surfing good waves, you are denying yourself an opportunity.' For whatever reason it really struck a chord with me. Why settle for mediocrity when you could be enjoying the best parts of life?

I realised that I'd risked missing out on my chance to enjoy this stage of my life. I had to look at the positives in suddenly having no parents. If there were any, it was that losing them gave me an opportunity for freedom. I could do what I wanted with my life. Nobody was telling me to live a certain way. It was all up to me. What an incredible gift.

Brent had been motivating himself in a similar way. He'd become a PE teacher, as he'd always wanted, and had a beautiful girlfriend he was in love with. Life was working out for him, but he was concerned about me and was still into me for quitting college.

'Where are you going to be in five years?' he asked.

'I'll show you, just wait and see.'

Gary Beaumont took me down to the Dorrigo pub to meet the manager of a company laying optical fibre. 'It's not a nine-to-five job,' he said. 'It's two to three weeks on, you travel and stay with the crew, and then have one to two weeks off.'

'How much?' I said.

'Twenty-four hundred a fortnight clear.'

I tried not to jump out of my seat. In the tree-planting job, you were paid per tray. There were twenty-five trees per tray. You had to plant fifty to sixty trays a day – 1250 to 1500 trees – to get a half-decent wage of $100 to $150. The terrain varied and you might only get ten trees in a row before you had to walk somewhere else to plant more. They were long and difficult days.

'When do I start?' I said.

The cable-laying wasn't difficult: 8 am starts, helping guys on huge Unimogs – multi-purpose, off-road, medium-sized trucks – by digging holes and guiding the cables that spooled out of their machines. I worked for them for a year and a half, up the north coast, out west to Tamworth, Dubbo, down from Sydney to Melbourne in one contract. I loved working with the older men, a lot of whom were good-natured Kiwis. They always had plenty of jokes and funny stories. There were only twenty people in the company and six machines, so I was given more responsibility the longer I was there.

Without realising it, from that job I got some of the basic elements of working life that I would enjoy and develop later in the SAS. One was that we had plenty of autonomy to solve problems as a team out in the bush, and were free to take the unconventional approach. The Unimog was a 15-tonne 4WD truck with a winch that we hooked up to a big plough-like wedge that moved along the ground behind it. The cable connecting the truck with the wedge would go out up to 100 metres, but if the wedge got stopped by a rock, the winch would start lifting the Unimog off the ground, nose first. At the wheel, slowly winding the winch, going back and over and almost upside down, you could manipulate the weight of the truck to lever up the rock. I'm sure it wasn't the way they were designed, but there wasn't as much OH&S in those days!

The physical danger in the job also appealed to me. Once, a younger guy had to chain the Unimog to a bulldozer to keep it weighted down. The tension in the cable was enormous, and it wasn't long before it snapped with a loud *crack!* The Mog, with operator inside, went flying backwards before slamming upside down into the earth. The driver, shaken up but extremely lucky, escaped with a minor injury. Another day, a branch had fallen over the cable and an executive came up in his car to move the branch. The operator in the Mog didn't see him and winched the wire taut. It came up and clipped the executive in the head and spun him 360 degrees. He flew over, hit the bonnet of his car, and tumbled onto the ground. He hadn't been wearing a helmet, and part of his scalp was missing. He tried to stand up, but was staggering about. We ran over and told him to sit down. He went to hospital and ended up with brain damage. They were dangerous machines – nothing like being in a war, but the presence of life-threatening hazards kept me sharp.

Another aspect of that kind of work that carried over into the SAS was the sense of humour you develop when you're in a team out alone in the bush. Outside Goulburn, we were digging a trench trying to find an existing Telstra cable. The company's representative was overseeing our work, and I couldn't resist a prank. We got a couple of broken offcuts of optical fibre and buried them in the trench. When the Telstra man came around again, we told him we were pretty certain we'd nearly found it. Then, as he stood there, we drove the shovel into the dirt through the pre-cut cable and cried, 'Ohh, shit!'

He saw the cut cable and, thinking we'd just severed the main line between Sydney and Melbourne, turned white as a ghost and started stammering and gibbering. He ran to his car and got straight onto his mobile phone to his boss. Pissing ourselves, we grabbed the broken cable out of the trench and threw both pieces onto his bonnet. He had to take a few looks before he believed us. It was a priceless moment. He was a good sport about it and had a laugh at himself. Since then, I've always thought that a well-constructed practical joke can be one of the best team-building exercises.

In the winter of 2000, we were working near Canberra and I had two weeks off. My cousin Christine, Margaret's youngest daughter, was living at Jindabyne. Her boyfriend Adam worked with the snowmaking machines at Thredbo. She said I should come down for my weeks off and see if I liked the snow.

Did I what! Snowboarding was a revelation, like surfing. I was hooked, first day out. *Yep*, I thought, *I want to do this properly*. I had visions of travelling to surf and snowboard and see the world.

While working for the cable-laying company, I'd saved up ten grand through living frugally and working hard. I'd bought a V8 Sandman panel van, and when I had my weeks off I threw in the surfboards, took my trusty Lister and went where I wanted. It had been a good job, but again, it wasn't what I wanted to do forever. Now, just when I discovered snowboarding and thought about travel, fate stepped in and gave me a push. The company was under strain. One day they told me I could take a week off, so I went snowboarding. By the time my week was up, the company had gone under.

While I hadn't planned on losing my job, having a bridge burn behind me was good. There was only one way forward. I spent a few months working as a labourer and farmhand on the mid-north coast of New South Wales and surfing some great waves on days off. I was having a good time, until one weekend in Sydney my beloved V8 was stolen. Van, clothes, two surfboards – all gone. I was pissed off, and of course I had no insurance, having prioritised replacing the gearbox, the diff and the clutch after all the burnouts I'd done. It was a hard way to learn that maybe insurance is just as important as upgrading the parts. Oh well, at least they could never steal the great memories.

I decided to travel to Canada to go snowboarding. Why Canada? My aim was simple: minimum cost, maximum snow. Hoping to test myself in extreme conditions, I wanted to go deep into the country, off the beaten track, rather than to a big resort full of Australians such as Whistler Blackcomb. My research pointed to the town of Fernie, far into British Columbia, with a population of only about 4000. It got as much as 10 metres of snow every season – that's a lot of snow. So in December 2000, I just bought a ticket, packed a small rucksack and a snowboard bag, and asked Brent to drive me to Sydney Airport.

He and Kate were getting married after Christmas, and I think he had his doubts about whether I'd come home for it. In fact he was a bit puzzled about what I was doing in general. Here I was with massive dreadlocks hanging down the middle of my back, off on some unspecified 'adventure'. It reinforced all of Brent's worries about me.

'But what are you going to do over there?' he kept asking.

Telling him I wanted to snowboard and make my couple of grand last as long as possible didn't seem to satisfy him. Eventually I shrugged and said, 'Something'll happen.' And when I jumped out of the car, I grinned at him: 'See you at the wedding.'

He looked at me as if to say, 'Yeah, right.'

I think he was probably a little worried.

SEVEN

How did I ever end up in the Australian Army, let alone its most elite unit? My family and friends still shake their heads. When they think of what I was doing in those years after Dad and Mum died, nothing could have seemed further from my future. How could this deadbeat kid end up having a personal audience with the Queen? I was anti-authority, anti-commitment, looked like something out of *Mad Max*, and prized, above everything else, my personal freedom. I refused to answer to anybody. What could have been further from the military? I was on track for a professional career as a dirtbag. They saw me as the image of my father, which in many ways I was, and I was living the young man's life he couldn't live at that age because he spent those years in Vietnam. Anyone who knew me would have seen a total rebel, the opposite of a uniformed soldier. For them, the truest statement I'd ever made about my future was when I burred up at that kid outside the Dorrigo post office when he'd said, 'What are you going to do, join the army?'

'Get fucked!'

When I did eventually join up, it looked like a massive U-turn. 'What's he doing?' my family asked. Some of them predicted I'd last one week. At best, two months. But to me, it wasn't a change in direction at all. In my mind, I was always heading on this path – if not to the SAS, then something like it. I may not have taken the direct route, but in the five years between Mum's death and my joining up, even if it looked like an extended party, I did have a sense of purpose. If nobody else understood what it was, that was okay; it took me some time to understand it myself.

*

By the time I flew into Vancouver twenty hours after saying goodbye to my brother, I was jumping out of my skin. The city was blanketed in snow, with as many snow ploughs as planes at the airport. I was tingling. *How awesome is this going to be? Where's it going to take me?*

The only negative about the next few weeks was that they passed too quickly. In Fernie I stayed in a big dorm-style house with about eighteen people sharing four or five rooms, with a hot tub out the back below an elevated deck, and made lots of great friends with the snowboarders. Whether it was improvising runs using a handrail and a ramp off the back deck of the house, or going into the back country, I was feeding my lust for adventure. Often I thought, *If only Dad and Mum were here.* Probably they'd have been worrying and telling me what I should and shouldn't be doing.

Brent's wedding, on 13 January, was coming up fast. On New Year's Eve, a few of us decided to catch an eighteen-hour bus ride down to Vancouver for a party. I was trying to pack a lot in, and knew I was running the risk of missing the wedding if things went off the rails, but that was the spirit of the adventure.

The snow was really dumping, and getting to Cranbrook, the nearest airport to Fernie, to catch my flight was no sure thing, but I made all my connections and got back to Newcastle the day before the wedding. The surreal part was, the surf at Newcastle Beach was cranking, so here I was, on a pristine afternoon, getting sunburnt as hell, the day after I'd been snowboarding in a tiny inland town in Canada. The more extreme the transition, the more challenging the adventure, the more it suited me.

Brent and Kate's wedding was happy and very emotional. There were tears everywhere when they made their speeches, talking about Dad and Mum. I was best man, and thought I had to lighten the mood – they were killing their own wedding! – so I made some jokes about how Kate had a life of punishment ahead of her if she realised that soon he'd be dragging her into the backyard to bowl cricket balls all day and get flogged in one-on-one footy. Jokes aside, I was really proud and ecstatic to see them so happy. I was on a bit of a high myself, and these were good days to remember Mum and Dad.

Two days later I was back snowboarding in Fernie.

I stayed in Canada until May 2001, living from one day to the next, loving my snowboarding and ice hockey and making new friends. I left the big share house I was living in after breaking the caretaker's rule of no hot tubs after midnight. One night I brought about ten people back from the pub, guys and girls, and we all piled in nude. We started a competition to see who could get the furthest away and make snow angels. The caretaker stuck his head out the window and told us to shut up. One of the people I'd brought back, an Australian named Mikey, made a snowball.

The next time he poked his head out, *wham*, Mikey nailed him.

To keep myself going, I got some work helping Mikey clean the spas in the resort on the mountain. It wasn't the worst job: we were paid cash to do the cleaning up after the guests, and were allowed to take whatever food and beer they'd left behind. If we were in the mood, which was most nights, we'd have a bit of a spa party ourselves.

I found the snowboarding as rewarding as surfing. It was amazing to be flying down a mountain at breakneck speed and laying down long, hard, sweeping turns in the lush powdery snow. It had a really relaxing effect on me and I was able to just focus on making the turns, picking the best lines down a cliff or through a forested section. It was the feeling during those moments that attracted me to it so much: just being with myself, executing a difficult but exhilarating task, in the wilderness.

At the end of the ski season, when I was thinking about going back to Australia, Mikey said, 'Who wants to go on a trip through America for three weeks?' I had a simple motto: 'Say yes to everything.' So we formed a group: Mikey, two girls, Misty and Lou, another guy, and a little blond Canadian snowboarder named Drew. He and I established an instant friendship.

My travel mates knew people everywhere, and Americans let us sleep on their couches in Seattle, down through Oregon to California. If we couldn't crash in someone's home, one of us would go to a hotel and book a double room, and then, when none of the staff were looking, the rest would pile out of Mikey's van into the room and sleep on the floor. I celebrated my twenty-second birthday in northern California in a seedy pub with my mates and some of the locals, and couldn't have thought of a better way. We got wetsuits and boards and took Drew surfing for the first time. It was far colder than anywhere I'd been in Australia and conditions weren't great, but he absolutely loved it. He got hooked as instantly as I had and a few years later I would meet him on his own surfing odyssey.

Living on a shoestring, we all had the same lack of a plan. Each day we'd just go where we'd go. We went to San Francisco, Big Sur to see the redwoods, the Grand Canyon and Las Vegas. It was snowing when we were in the red desert of Arizona and Utah, which looked bizarre, but that countryside struck a chord with me for some reason. I fell in love with Monument Valley, which became my favourite place, climbing around the rocks in the Valley of the Gods nearby. After all that had happened, I felt like I was leading a different life, that it was many years ago that Mum had disappeared.

But it had only been two years. On the anniversary of her disappearance, we were on the Californian coast, and I took some time out and dropped a flower in the ocean for her. Not a day went by when I didn't think about what had happened. Every year, on her anniversary, if I can be by the ocean, I drop a flower in for her. What I was think-ing about most, I guess as a way of suppressing my feeling of being cheated, was how much I'd love to tell her what I was doing and where I was. That's the thing I'd lost: being able to share this with her, even if it was only in a letter or a phone call.

I missed her and Dad especially when we were in Lake Tahoe. There was a bridge where Mikey had seen some massive steelhead trout swimming by. You weren't meant to fish there, but he wouldn't be stopped. We went on a mis-sion at night and chucked a lot of bait in but didn't get one hit. It looked easy, but they were probably so used to being fed they weren't going to be tempted by something on a hook. But the act of finding this fishing place, and doing it on the dodgy, made me literally ache to get on the phone and call Dad. It was the type of thing he'd do. And the next day we walked out onto a jetty on the lake, and Drew and I were daring each other to jump in. When we jumped, it was fucking icy – everything froze up. We had to swim 25 metres back to the ladder to climb out. I'll never forget it. That 'will I or won't I' anticipation, and finally having the eggs to jump, felt like being on holidays with Dad and Mum and Brent.

We headed back north, through Salt Lake City, Utah, then Wyoming and Yellowstone National Park. There were a few more weeks' worth of snow in Fernie in May, and we took another trip up into the north-west of Canada, mainly to fish and spot wildlife. The end was coming, though: I was close to running out of money. To evade a per-passenger fare on the car ferry from Prince George to Vancouver Island, Lou and I hid under the blankets in the van and Mikey and Misty drove on. Once aboard, we scrambled out. The sun didn't go down till ten at night, and we sat on deckchairs enjoying the incredible scenery, the fjords and the whales bobbing up, while finishing off a bottle of rum. I had just one ratty dreadie sticking out the back of my head. In every new place, I'd cut one off and left it there. On the deck of this ferry, I stood at the rail and cut off the last one, marking the end of the trip in a ceremonial way by dropping it into the ocean. Only, the wind caught it and it landed on this bloke's shoulder on the deck below. He hadn't seen it. It was tickling his neck and he was scratching at it, then he grabbed it and absolutely freaked out. He jumped like it was a rat or something. He looked up, but we were rolling around laughing, out of view.

We finished the trip with some more fishing and camping on Vancouver Island, where a local lent us a lot of gear. The people were so spontaneously generous, for me it was like a cleansing of the spirit. After seeing the worst a person could do, I felt I was now seeing the best. I wanted to say to Mum, *Here, see, there's goodness in the world too*. I was beginning to really value the world I lived in, and wanted to protect it. Every small gesture could help in that way. Just before I left, I offered Mikey the rest of my Canadian dollars. He wouldn't take them, so I snuck out and stashed them under the visor in his van. It was just a couple of hundred bucks, but I wanted to say thanks somehow. Years later, we met up again in Sydney, and he said, 'That was you that left that money?'

Vancouver Island was a beautiful place to finish. One day near the end, we were by the water when a bald eagle landed next to us. For my future, I felt as free as that eagle. Until this trip, had I ever lived completely in the moment? I might have thought I had, but this was really my first experience of it. I finally understood the gift my parents had left me: the present moment is all there is and it is precious. Because the past had been broken away from under me, I didn't sweat about the future.

EIGHT

While I came home refreshed, with a new perspective on life, the family were worried sick about me. Brent and Margaret were convinced I'd gone off the rails. I thought the opposite – I was finally making sense of things – but it was impossible to convince them.

An important event when I got back was the sale of the house in Dorrigo. To have the soft option of sinking back into the old house closed off was a good thing for me, but on the other hand, I didn't quite know where home was.

I moved into the timber house my cousin Christine and Adam were renting at Dalgety, outside Jindabyne, and started work at Thredbo as a snowmaker. My shifts were at night, either 4 pm to 1 am or 1 am to sunrise. The life was pretty carefree. I saw a skidoo as an invitation to hoon around the empty mountain. Between shifts, we could grab our boards and go out on the snow all afternoon, free lift passes being one of the perks. When I had a few days off, I cut for Bermagui or Ulladulla with my surfboard, just searching for waves up and down the south coast. At the end of the day I would go to a local pub for a feed and a few beers, then just find a car park near the beach and crash out in the car and do it all again the next day.

It came to a sudden end, however, when one day, after a shift and some snowboarding, I headed down towards Dalgety to get the house warm before the others arrived home. Tony, Christine's brother, was with me, and when we came past Jindabyne we saw a grey cloud rising. 'Someone must be burning off,' Tony said. Then, as we got closer: 'Oh no, that's the house!'

By the time we got there, the house was gone. I felt terrible for the owner, and for Christine, who'd lost everything she owned as well as some guinea pigs and other pets. I'd lost nothing of real consequence, just some gear and a couple of souvenirs from America: a lump of salt from Death Valley, a bit of wood a beaver had chewed. The investigation found that it was an electrical fire. I felt really guilty. It might have been an electric blanket I'd left on so my bed would be toasty when I got home.

We moved into a caravan park in Jindabyne, but the fire turned out to be a catalyst for change. Adam and Christine had been drifting apart, and decided to separate. For myself, I'd put in an application to work at Deer Valley in Utah, on an exchange deal between the snowmaking companies, so that I could work in both the United States and Canada.

It had been three years since I'd quit college and begun this string of jobs, and even though I was enjoying the snowmaking, a little seed was growing in me and gnawing at my insides. I needed to push the adventure further, not settle into a groove of repeating what I'd already done.

At the snowmaking company in Thredbo, I met a man who said he'd been in the SBS.

'What's the SBS?' I said, thinking of the TV station, but he was definitely not a TV kind of guy.

He told me all about the Special Boat Service, the elite Special Forces unit of the Royal Navy, and I got interested in his descriptions of the ship assaults, the canoeing, the diving exercises. It sounded like an adventure lifestyle where you got paid, which didn't sound at all bad. This was the direction I was beginning to move in: to try to convert my love of the outdoors and pushing for a new challenge into a job, instead of what I was doing, which was working to fund the adventure lifestyle.

I made some enquiries about joining the fire and ambulance services. Neither was taking on new staff. I thought about the police, but given my background it didn't feel right. At the end of the season, I was mulling these things over, really thinking about what I'd do after I came back from my next trip to America. So much for letting the future look after itself! But I was entering a more complicated phase of life, and, as it turned out, so was the wider world.

*

I sometimes doubt there's such a thing as coincidence. In September 2001, I headed up to Newcastle to stay with Brent and Kate. I did some work pulling cables through pits for Kate's brother Danny, and met a guy called Dominic Freestone, from Woolgoolga, near Dorrigo. He was a great bloke, roughly the same age as me, a bodyboarder, and we liked the same music. We'd surf every afternoon after work at Newcastle Beach, and if we went out at night, we'd catch rides home on the empty coal trains. Dominic was half-Papuan, and we got so filthy after sitting in coal cars, we joked that he'd got so dirty, even the palms of his hands were black.

One night, I got home to Brent and Kate's unit in Lambton. I flicked on the TV and saw this building with a big gash in it, which they said had been made by a plane. *What's all this?* I couldn't drag my eyes off it. It took me a while to realise it wasn't just a movie. Then I saw the second plane. I started thinking about friends, wondering if they were in New York. From the commentary, you thought planes were going to start raining down everywhere, even in Australia. *Holy shit*, I thought, *this is a big thing.* Brent came home late from work and I said, 'Check this out, two planes have flown into the World Trade Center.' I stayed up for hours watching it all unfold. How could somebody do that?

The next day I rang my travel agent and asked if my plane the next month was still going to leave. People were saying I was crazy to fly over there, but things calmed down, and my plans wouldn't be disrupted.

I can't say that September 11 was the trigger, but it was an important piece in the puzzle that was falling into place. I was gripped by the horror of what had happened, and cut out and kept newspaper clippings about it. Lots of things seemed to be coming together around me, as if they had a mind of their own. I had started running and going to the gym. Brent had a friend in Newcastle who'd been at school with us in Dorrigo. He was in the RAAF now and he made it sound pretty good. Then one day I picked up the newspaper and there was this double-page spread advertising the anniversary of the Special Air Service Regiment. They were described as the 'most secretive unit in Australia' and were being deployed to Afghanistan already. There was one picture of a soldier free-falling, and another of a soldier standing with a gun. I found out later this was from a painting by Ian Coate titled *The Sentinel*. I thought, *What is this? It looks like something I'd really enjoy.*

I cut *The Sentinel* out and put it in my wallet, in the transparent slip for ID. Every time I opened my wallet, there was this SAS trooper. It inspired me. These guys obviously did something special. I asked my RAAF mate, who said he had a friend who'd been really fit and trained hard, but didn't pass the SAS selection course. He said, 'It's not a job you really want to do – you're away six or seven months a year.' To me, that sounded perfect – *just* what I wanted to do.

Before I went to America, I went home for Murray Steele's mother's funeral. Kirby Steele had been, along with Jo Beaumont, a kind of second mum to me after Mum's death. I could walk into their houses and eat food out of the fridge, and they wouldn't care. I could be myself in their houses. Going to that funeral service and putting Kirby in the ground was very emotional for me. Murray had come to my parents' services and got tearful. He'd got on very well with Dad. They talked about Vietnam, Dad showing him scars on his legs and telling him what to watch out for if he ever joined the army. I'd think, *Why are you telling him, not Brent and me?* I asked Mum, and she said he'd find it easier to talk to boys who weren't his own children. He liked Murray showing an interest in it, and liked Murray generally.

There's something about being one step removed from the centre of attention that can unleash your feelings. At Mum's and Dad's services, when I'd been in the middle and everyone was looking at me, I put a defensive cordon around my emotions. At Kirby's funeral, when I was on the sidelines, I broke down. When you're part of the crowd, you're free to be yourself. I understood now why Murray had gone to pieces at my parents' services.

He and I hit it really hard after the funeral. Smashed, I drove my blue Ford Laser all the way to Coffs Harbour just to go to Macca's. On the way back, Murray was asleep,

I was drunk, and I drove onto the wrong side of the road. I hit the mountain and pulled the drive shaft out. We were lucky to survive. If I had gone right instead of left we would have plummeted over a cliff and probably been seriously injured or killed. Murray woke up to see me kicking the dented guardrail and throwing rocks at the car. It was four or five in the morning, and he couldn't help laughing at the tantrum I was throwing. Eventually a bloke came past in his ute and gave us a lift up to Dorrigo, where Murray's stepdad blasted us. Murray's cousin had died in a car accident a few weeks before, and we'd just put his mum in the ground. Fair enough.

I got the car fixed and for some reason was wondering if Sally Watt was still working at the bank in Bellingen, where she'd moved back after her stint in Sydney. I'd heard she was getting married. I thought I should stop in, just to say hey and tell her there was no bad blood.

When I got to the bank, the lady behind the counter said, 'How can I help you?'

'I'd like to see Sally Watt.'

'Who are you?' I could tell by the way she looked at me that she already knew, but I told her. It was the same bank Chris had worked at.

'Oh. Okay, can you just wait out the back and I'll see if Sally can come out.'

She did come. We said hello and had a chat. I explained that I didn't blame her, her sister or their brother for what had happened. 'I'll never forgive your dad for doing that to us and taking her away,' I said, 'but I've got no bad feelings towards any of you.'

Sally became quite tearful, and I was trying to hold back my own emotions. She was apologetic. She told me how they'd dug her mum up and she wasn't too sure what was going on. We had a bit of a hug and she said she was thankful that I'd come and spoken to her. She'd been wondering for years what Brent and I thought. She might have been scared of us.

As I drove back towards Newcastle, I felt an amazing lightness. It was like I'd been doing squats for a long time and now could put the weights back on the shelf. I'd never felt like that up to then. Obviously I'd been carrying something around in there. I just felt so happy that I had closed that chapter.

Another piece in the puzzle was my opportunity to go through the files from Mum's case, a lot of which I hadn't seen: family history material, Chris Watt's suicide notes, all the evidence that had been laid out for the coronial inquiry. It stirred up a lot of memories, and pressed home that what had happened had marked me out in a special way. Maybe I had to do something of the same magnitude as what had happened to Mum, to put the universe back in balance. Brent and I both felt guilty, at some level, that we hadn't been able to protect her. Maybe I could atone by taking on the role of protecting others, helping them out, doing what I hadn't been able to do as a kid. That's a little deeper into my subconscious than I was thinking at the time, but as time has gone by and I understand myself better, I can see that the urge to protect and to fight was my way of saying sorry.

NINE

Little by little, that picture of *The Sentinel* was burning a hole in my wallet. I remembered that man from the SBS talking about ship attacks and Brent's RAAF mate talking about how hard the SAS selection course was. When I got to Park City, Utah, to work as a snowmaker at the Deer Valley resort, I spent my nights on the internet looking up stuff about the SAS Regiment. The book and movie *Black Hawk Down*, about the incident in Mogadishu in 1993 when the Americans got hammered, came out, and put the hook in me deeper still. I was fascinated by its portrayal of Delta Force, which I imagined was the US equivalent of the SAS. The Delta operators, it suggested, were in but not *of* the armed services: that is, they did the most dangerous, out-there tasks but were given a freedom to make their own decisions. They were like military mavericks, able to decide how to wear their uniform and cut their hair and pretty much run their own race. To me, it sounded like the best of both worlds.

As I worked, I went for long runs in the snow in shorts and a jumper, pushing myself, visualising myself as doing pre-selection training. There was a winding road I'd get my flatmate, Chris, to drop me at the bottom of in the middle of the night, and I'd run up the hill to work. He was asking, 'What the fuck are you doing?' I wasn't ready to tell him or anyone else, but I'd made the commitment in my own mind, for myself alone. I couldn't afford to make a promise; promises are too easy to break. I was swimming laps at the local pool, doing push-ups. I was still having a good time when a party was on, but there was a fire I was feeding.

When I had time to snowboard, I'd go by myself out through the ropes onto the off-piste areas, which were quite dangerous if they'd had a big snowfall. I felt safe, doing big cliff drops – it was all about that addictive adrenaline rush, and also the risks that came with going out alone and being self-reliant. Any trouble I got into, I'd have to get myself out of.

Sitting on top of those mountains and taking in those amazing sights was something I will never forget. The beauty of the mountains is almost hypnotic, especially when all is still and quiet up there. A bit like when you're the only one out at a surf break: you get a moment to focus on the only task at hand. You live in that one moment and get a chance to find yourself.

This private, obsessive regime culminated on New Year's Eve when I left a party to get to where I was living, about 15 kilometres away. I treated it like an SAS selection task. I stopped at a 7-Eleven and got a couple of boiled eggs and a chicken hero. I could see the glow of where we lived, and headed across country, drunk, with two boiled eggs and a chicken hero in me, across people's backyards through thigh-deep snow. Next thing I knew, the snow was up to my chest and there was only loose scrub underneath. Every step, I slipped and sank. I was in jeans, a T-shirt and jacket, freezing, dehydrated, falling over, fighting through this snow. I started to dry-retch. Then I told myself, *If I'm going to join the SAS, I've got to be able to do this.*

Eventually I popped out, and was lying on the highway trying to get my breath back. Welcome to 2002. It was nearly daylight when I walked into a servo, my jeans, frozen solid to my legs, crunching like cardboard. The guy said, 'You all right?'

'Yeah mate, I'm right.'

It could have turned really bad, but my mental state was all about training and pushing myself beyond my limits. Any chance for a challenge, no matter how insignificant it seemed, I'd give it a go. Setting myself and completing those small challenges delivered little rewards that drove me further.

My time in the States was excellent. I have so many fond memories. The job was great and hooning around the backcountry on snowmobiles in the middle of the night was one of the best parts of snowmaking. We would often get all the guns set for a few hours of quality snowmaking and then go through to the next valley to visit mates doing the same job for a different resort. Other nights we would take our snowboards and skis out with us while doing checks on the snow guns. We'd take it in turns to shuttle each other up the runs to have some stealthy night runs. It is not so easy boarding down a hill at night, trying to use the hue of the white snow to keep from ploughing off the tracks. Management would have had a pink fit if they'd ever caught us.

During our limited time off, we once made a trip out to Nevada because fireworks were more readily available there. We got up before dawn; five blokes, skis, snowboards and gear all crammed into and onto a VW Golf. A few hours later we had managed to load up with trolleys full of fireworks. On the way back to Snowbird Mountain, which we were riding that day, we almost set the car on fire no fewer than five times. We learnt that fireworks are extra loud in a confined space like a VW and that attaching them to the rear bumper and having multiple 20-foot sparks flying out really does make the car go faster – as evidenced by the surprised faces of the drivers of the cars we were overtaking. Looking back, we were very lucky not to have been caught by the police. I'm sure they would not have found it as exciting as we did.

By the time I went home, I was really fired up, but still wanted to keep my plan to myself. My family thought I was drifting. Uncle Ken had asked what I was going to do, and I'd said vaguely, 'Leisure management at uni maybe, I dunno.' I knew they were going to be shocked when I applied to join the army, but there was no contradiction in it for me. Adventure and helping people – that's what I wanted, in a nutshell. There would always be the question of how I could handle authority, of course. The army was not some kind of holiday camp where you did cool things whenever you felt like it. And I'd been living by my own timetable for a while now. But I didn't see authority as a problem any more. Getting told what to do was just another hurdle, as much as getting tired or hungry. I wanted to know if I could handle it. Could I prove it to myself? I'd proved a few other things to myself – what about this?

TEN

Secretly, I started putting in my application forms to the army. I moved back in with Brent and Kate, got my old cabling job with Dom, and bought a motorbike. I designed a proper training regime. Monday: a five- to eight-kilometre run after work. Tuesday: weights training, sneaking into the university gym on Brent's membership card. Wednesday: hill sprints near the uni. Thursday: more weights. Friday: interval training. And a lot of swimming and surfing in between. I stuck with it religiously, always trying to improve my performance, telling myself, *If you want to survive a gunfight, you've got to survive this. The more you prepare yourself now, the more ready you'll be when the time comes.*

I have fond memories of those training days. Brent knew I was applying for the military and as a PE teacher was trying to help me out, but I was doing it on my own, hurting, faltering, telling myself to push on harder. I knew that in the army I'd get yelled at and tormented, but physical fitness was something I could control. At work, I treated the cable-pulling as a form of incidental exercise. We competed to be the quickest at ripping the Parramatta ropes through the pits. I thought if the military wouldn't take me then I'd go to the US Marines, and if they wouldn't take me I'd go to the French Foreign Legion. There were no limits to how far I'd go.

An appointment was made for me to front up to the army office in Sydney, and I went down to stay with Ross and Val for a week. The army letter had said to show up with your gear in anticipation of not going home. When the day came, I had a bag packed and said to Ross and Val, 'See you later.' If I got through the tests, I'd be on my way to Kapooka, the basic training camp near Wagga Wagga, by nightfall.

The office was on Oxford Street. I was sat down and given some straightforward tests. The interviewer said, 'Your application says you want to go into the infantry. Tell me what it's about.'

I regurgitated what I'd read on the army website. I would learn shooting, bush and infantry skills, be in a team environment, learn how to dig in, perform section activities. I expected to get yelled at and do physical training. He said, 'Okay, no worries.' If applicants hadn't done any research, they got sent back to find out more. The army didn't want them going in blind. Then, as an afterthought, he added, 'And you're going to do drill as well.'

I didn't really know what drill was, apart from what I'd seen in movies. I didn't like the look of it, and have never liked it since. I guess it's worthwhile, in a punishing kind of way. But perfecting open-order marching wasn't why I joined up.

They sent me down to HMAS *Kuttabul* at Garden Island, and put me through a basic physical: push-ups, sit-ups, swim, beep test. As soon as you'd reached their standard – thirty push-ups, or 7.5 on the beep test – they stopped you. From there, I was sworn in on the Queen's oath and put on a bus. We sat and waited for a few more recruits, and when they'd filled two buses we were off. I was in the army.

*

The bus drove through the night, about seven hours from Sydney to Wagga. I knew that everyone on the bus was nervous, but it was interesting to see how differently people expressed it. Some were boisterous, high-fiving and cracking jokes. Others were subdued. There were guys with headphones, going inside themselves. There's a basic human nature to how people behave in a group, which I've seen repeated all the way through from Kapooka to Afghanistan, and most of us are the same all the way through. For myself, I was apprehensive but excited. I wanted to get it done, get started on this adventure I'd been thinking about for so long. This was step number one. Outwardly, I was what's known as a 'grey man', the one who gets on with it, stays under the radar, doesn't speak much. Big ears, big eyes, small mouth. 'Going grey' wasn't a deliberate pose: it's my nature.

When we pulled into the barracks at Kapooka, military police (MPs) stepped onto the bus and started yelling and screaming at us. They lined us up and told us to put our belongings into bags, which they took away. I was at the rear of the line, and they assigned us numbers: I was in Bravo Company, 11 Platoon, 1 Section. That was it. The MPs shouted, 'Remember that number to tell the corporal at the desk.'

I went to the desk and said, 'Donaldson, Bravo Company, 11 Platoon, 1 Section, *sir*!'

He nearly exploded. 'It's corporal! Everything you say, it's corporal!'

I squeaked, 'Yes, sir.'

'I'M NOT SIR! I'M CORPORAL!'

'Yes, si– yes, corporal.'

I toddled off, nervous but not scared. I wasn't fazed; I didn't feel my temper was challenged by having my head ripped off. I was happy to do what they said, because it was taking me one step closer to what I wanted to be part of.

Usually the basic training at Kapooka took twelve to thirteen weeks, but the army was trialling a new method of recruit training, which saw us in and out in half the time. We were housed in a long barracks of four-bed rooms, with a divider between the two sets of bunks in each room. The system marked you out by what tabs you wore on your epaulettes. For the first week, as a 'jubie', you had no tabs and were treated like a piece of shit. You couldn't even go to the toilet when you wanted, and every morning you had to be lined up outside your room at six o'clock, having been shouted at to get out of bed, with your bedsheet over your shoulder. Everything you did, you had to be like an automaton, accepting authority, marching everywhere as a group.

In the second and third weeks you had red tabs, and then you moved on to blue tabs. Gradually the insulting, pointless part of it was relaxed. Under blue tabs, you didn't have to march to and from the mess, and could walk in pairs. By then you were too close to the end to be overly bothered by it. For the last week you got gold tabs, which meant they took you into the bush for a bivouac, you did a navex, or navigation exercise, and were taught some basic soldiering skills.

Every Sunday we had to go to church, but one of the privileges of being on gold tabs was that you didn't have to. I thought this was two hours I could have to myself. I'd write a letter to Margaret and Ken, Kenny and Julie, or Ross and Val. I rang Brent once. It felt good to be able to tell them I was enjoying it and not copping out. And I really was enjoying it, no doubt to their general astonishment. I didn't make any close friends there, more friendship through necessity, but I think I was convivial generally and don't remember being a prick or ostracising anyone. I was always there to help people out if they were struggling, and wasn't part of a clique. For me it was just a mission to get to the next step.

Kapooka was a training institute, not a place for culling. The instructors weren't dickheads for the sake of being dickheads (that came later, at Singleton). At Kapooka we had a really good one, an ex-infantry soldier called Rollingston, nickname Lurch. We joked about his inability to do PT, or personal training, with us. He popped a magic purple pill every day, Naproxen, because his back was fucked and his legs were fucked. He'd been in Somalia, and I felt like I could learn from him. I asked if Somalia had been anything like *Black Hawk Down*. It makes me cringe to remember, but I was green. When I go to Kapooka now and the recruits ask questions like that about Afghanistan, I wonder, *Was I ever that young? Did I ever come across that way?* They look so impressionable and naïve, like a bunch of scared sheep. Surely I never looked like that? But I'm sure I did.

Overall, I found it less challenging and more friendly than I'd expected. The sense of camaraderie was already there: you could leave your belongings out, because even in this first stage of the army it was understood that thieving from your mates was a bigger crime than murder. I liked the trust and teamwork they were trying to build. The PT, the shooting, the navigation and soldiering exercises were fun. The drill wasn't, but I could get through that. There was a weird exercise one night, when they darkened the hallway and locked us in our rooms. A corporal came and grabbed us, one at a time.

'Righto.' The corporal came to our door and looked at me. 'You ready for this?'

'Yeah. What's going on?' I could hear muffled shouting from somewhere down the hall.

'You'll see.'

He took me to a door, pushed me through and slammed it shut behind me. Inside it was pitch-black with a bunch of strobes going off, flashing all around me. There was a rifle on the floor and voices were shouting, 'Go! Pick up that weapon! Load! Action! Instant! Unload! Get on your guts! Get on your knees!'

To be honest, I think they'd just found a couple of free hours they wanted to fill in. But I thought, *This is how I thought it would be the whole time.* Instead, that was an exception.

Although the army couldn't afford to discourage new recruits too much, a few weeks at Kapooka caused some attrition. One guy in my room flaked out when he was driven nuts by the basic petty stuff. With making our beds, they required the army standard of having one bayonet-length folded back every single morning. They'd make you rip your bed apart and remake it in three minutes. Or they'd make you take something out of your locker and iron it pronto. These were all games to annoy you and test you, but also to teach you how to work quickly under pressure. This one bloke decided he couldn't do it any more. But unfortunately for flake-outs, it takes time to get their paperwork done and withdraw them from the system. They can't stay in the platoon, because they'll be infectious and bring everyone down, so those who flaked out were segregated into a kind of limbo. At mess times they were sat down on the other side of a partition. This guy was still in there when we left, waiting for his papers.

Flake-outs were put into the Digger James Platoon, named after the highly regarded officer who lost his left leg and his right foot in a mine strike while serving as an infantry platoon commander in Korea, where he was also awarded the Military Cross (MC). He subsequently resigned, studied medicine at Sydney University and rejoined the army medical corps, rising to the rank of major general as the head of Army Health Services. My view is that the naming of 'Digger James Platoon' at Kapooka sends the message that people can overcome injuries and continue on to achieve great things.

I never saw anyone who flaked out get taken back in. Sometimes people had a more acceptable excuse than just being unable to meet the standards. In our shooting phase, there was an Indonesian-Australian with a soft manner, who the instructors had been riding a bit. He wanted to be a medic and help people. When we got to the shooting, he said, 'I'm not here to kill people.' They said, 'Mate, understood, but you need to do this.' He said because of his religion he couldn't do it, and dropped out.

We had three girls in our platoon, and luckily none of them dropped out for the wrong reasons. It could be tricky in the mornings, when everyone had to line up in the hall in their identical blue pyjamas, trying to drape their sheets in such a way as to cover their morning hard-ons. But there wasn't much you could do about it with the corporal yelling at you and someone over his shoulder pulling a face. I copped that once from a British guy who'd been in the army before and was coming back in. He was always taking the piss, doing everything they asked but also giving plenty of good-humoured advice. One day they picked me to be the one they yelled at. I was there in the hall, trying to say, 'Yes, corporal', while my so-called mate was behind the corporal, swaying from side to side to make me laugh. Keeping a straight face under pressure is another essential military skill.

Between dinner and lights out, which was ten o'clock, we'd have whatever free time we could fit in after doing homework, navigation theory or ironing. Teamwork became important. I've never been any good at ironing my clothes or shining my boots or having the brass the right way. I tried but didn't have a knack for it. Some of the trainees could belt out an ironed shirt in seconds. I'd say, 'Can you do mine, and I'll do something for you?' He might need help doing a navigation theory test, or improving his push-ups, so we could barter our skills with each other.

During that free time, we'd talk to each other about why we were there. About 80 per cent were there for a job, and the other 20 per cent knew exactly where they were headed. One guy wanted to drive tanks and blow shit up. Another, who'd moved from America, wanted to be an engineer: he wanted to be up front to find and defuse bombs. I chatted with people who, like me, were headed for infantry, but I didn't put it about that I wanted to be in the SAS; that would have been presumptuous. But it sort of seeped out. A couple of times Rollingston pulled me aside, out bush or at the range, and said, 'Hey, are you thinking of going into the Regiment?' I said, 'Corporal, all I want to do is make the infantry first and then think about that.' He said, 'Mate, you won't have a problem.' The worst thing for me would have been to believe him, so I deflected the compliment as best I could.

There were a couple of encounters with SAS visitors at Kapooka, and my antennae were on high alert. One of them came along to a PT session and said to us, 'Let's see how many push-ups you recruits can do in two minutes.'

I thought, *This is what I've been training for.* I think I got to eighty and was the only one still going after two minutes. He said, 'Not too bad. We'll have to keep an eye on you.' I didn't say anything and just hid my blushes, thinking, *That's pretty good if an SAS guy said that to me. I'd better not fuck up now.* Inspired, I did the beep test and almost beat the company commander. I was nowhere near as good as the instructors, but I was doing well enough to be able to apply myself to the things I wasn't good at.

The SAS aura went beyond push-ups and beep tests. On an overnight exercise, where we'd hump – walk with a heavy pack – and navigate during the day, get put into an imaginary contact with the enemy, do some shooting and go on to a bivouac, we were walking along and I heard people whispering, 'There's the SAS bloke.' He came up from nowhere in his cams, all rigged up to go hunting with a bow and arrow. He had a chat, bagged us out and ran off into the bush. We were blinking back our amazement at how fit this guy was, like we'd just met Superman. The reality was probably that he'd got out of a car 100 metres behind – but he sure made an impression!

On the last day, I was sitting at the mess with the American, and an unusual-looking older bloke sat next to us. He didn't have slides or a name tag, and his gear wasn't ironed. He had scuffed-up black boots, not the standard brown ones. He slapped down the sand-coloured beret with the winged dagger on it. We might as well have been getting a visit from God.

'How you going, fellas?'

'Yeah, pretty good.'

He looked at me. 'I hear you've done not too bad on this course?'

'Yeah, good.'

'Where are you going?'

'Infantry.'

'You ever thought of coming to the Regiment?'

I said 'Yeah' and tried to change the subject. I was in awe of this bloke and didn't want to make a goose of myself. Things got silent as he ate his breakfast. Finally I said, 'So what are you doing here, sir?'

He just gave me this look. I thought, *Okay, maybe I shouldn't have asked that question.* I've got to know him since I joined the Regiment, and I've asked him about it. While he can't remember the episode, he says he was probably just shooting us a look to show how hard he was.

At our March Out Parade, he was sitting in the crowd in his beret, his polys (the ceremonial dress), and the red sash showing he was a warrant officer. I kept thinking, *Why is this guy here?* I stopped myself short of thinking, *He must be here for me.* Maybe I did, just a little. It was hard not to be deluded that they had someone from the Regiment to check us out for possibles. But even if it wasn't real, I was getting encouragement at Kapooka. They weren't out to cut you down or belittle you. Every instructor I came across was willing to give me tips or suggest someone else who could help. Towards the end of the course, they said, 'We've got a special treat for you today,' and sat us in an amphitheatre to watch *Black Hawk Down*. I sat next to Rollingston. He was talking to me about Somalia. My chest puffed a bit; I felt I'd earnt a little of his respect.

Brent offered to come down for the March Out, but I didn't want to make a big deal of it. It was only six weeks, only the first step. 'Maybe if I get through the next part,' I said.

The next part was a whole different world: infantry training at Singleton. By the end of that, I would appreciate seeing some familiar faces.

ELEVEN

The Kapooka graduates were sent out to all corners: Sydney, Melbourne, Puckapunyal, Townsville. I was put on a huge coach to Singleton with four others. There was plenty of room to spread ourselves out.

Immediately on our arrival, it felt more like the real army than Kapooka. NCOs were yelling and carrying on, trying to organise us and several dozen other new recruits. The barracks were named after battles in Australian history: mine was named after Samichon River in the Korean War. I was getting a bit nervous, but still excited and positive. I was in IET or initial employment training, learning to be an infantry soldier. We did our paperwork, went over some weapons drills and were shown the camp layout, taking instruction from an old corporal whose voice was so hoarse and crusty he would eventually need a throat operation.

'You guys think you're good enough to get in the infantry?' he rasped. 'Right, we're going to do some push-ups.' Then he'd get right in your face and shout, 'Down!'

I thought, *No way is he going to beat me.* He dropped into a push-up position and held it just off the ground. 'You reckon you can hold it longer than me?' the Corporal croaked.

I did my best, glaring at him while my face was breaking out in a sweat and my arms and legs were turning to mush. I was trying to feed off him. It was tough, and soon people were dropping out of the infantry left right and centre. I revved myself up by saying to myself, *This is what I came here for.* In a funny way, being a rebellious person by temperament was something I could turn to my advantage, getting through by sheer bloody-minded defiance.

Our biggest tormentor was our platoon sergeant, who I had for twelve weeks. He had no reason to be a dickhead. He just wanted to be, or so it seemed. He came right out of the classic military-style negative-reinforcement textbook. The regulations gave us free time from Friday night until Sunday night, but the platoon sergeant could take it away from us on his own say-so. Early in week one, he said, 'That's your Friday night gone straight away. The corporals told me you weren't here in time.' No one had done anything wrong. We hadn't been late. We were really fucked off. But this was only the beginning of it.

Our weeks had hardly begun before he was taking away our Friday nights. One of the more pointless set tasks was to pull up the hems of our trousers for inspection, to show if we'd rolled our socks over our boots in the correct manner. He exploded at someone: 'Right, that's Friday night gone for the lot of you!'

The aim was to bring us together, make us accountable to each other, so we could say to any miscreant, 'Mate, get your shit straight because you're fucking the rest of us over.' But this sergeant was so over the top, there was no incentive to improve. Some weeks, by the time we'd got to Monday afternoon, he'd already stripped us of Friday night, Saturday, Saturday night and Sunday. One week, we really busted our guts and made it to Thursday without having lost our weekend. We were doing an exercise out in the field, and the sergeant lost his shit over some rubbish he'd found uncollected. He got the three garbage bags we'd filled up, ripped them up and chucked the trash everywhere, going off his head, screaming and carrying on. 'You leave rubbish at a camp, you kill your mates, you kill your platoon!'

We just stood there thinking, *Please don't take our Friday night, not when we've made it this far.*

After he cooled down, he said, 'Right, you've got thirty seconds to pick up all this rubbish, and if you don't, that's your Friday night gone!'

We were desperate. Everyone was scrambling around, trying to pick up the rubbish he'd strewn about.

'Thirty seconds, that's it!'

We formed up and were looking around, thinking, *Okay, we've done it.*

Then this one little plastic wrapper blew out of a guy's hand. In slow motion, flipping and rocking back and forth like a feather, it twirled in the air, taking forever, right in front of us, before it landed on the dirt.

'Right, don't you dare fucken touch that! That's Friday night done! Dump all the rubbish on the ground!' He went bananas, kicking it at us, through us, picking it up and chucking it at us. I was right at my limit. *If this prick throws it at me, I'm going to go him.* Everyone was the same.

'Right,' he said. 'Now you've got *twenty* seconds to pick it all up!'

It was spread around everywhere. We did it, thinking we might win back our Friday night, but he didn't care.

'That's it,' he said. 'Saturday and Sunday – gone.'

Each Friday we'd sit there grimly watching other platoons tear off into Newcastle for the weekend. We learnt to hate that bloke. I just wanted to go to my brother's place and hang out with him and Kate, or my mate Dom. After six weeks at Kapooka and four weeks at Singleton, I was craving a weekend off.

On the weekends, the corporals and sergeant were home with their families and left a duty corporal who'd tell us what to do. We had to sit in our rooms for hours. On the hour, every hour, all through the weekend, we'd have to lump our gear to the duty room, take it apart and repack it as per standard operating procedure. First hour, we had to be in field order. That meant our combat webbing and packs plus 35 kilos of gear standing in perfect rank and file waiting for an inspection. By the start of the next hour we had to be back there with our plastic army storage trunk, our field order laid out on the ground with our pack and webbing, all to be unclipped. Every pouch, belt, clip and buckle laid out on the grass. If anyone had anything missing, they'd put it on a list for the sergeant on Monday. The next hour you'd have to be there standing in field order, all put together again, for the same procedure. This would continue from eight o'clock in the morning to ten o'clock at night. We'd just do that all weekend, pulling our stuff apart and putting it back together.

What a fucken waste of time, I was thinking. This was the first test of my resolve. I was starting to question what this was all about. Brent had told me the surf was pumping at Newcastle. It was hell. There was a rec room to watch TV, but the rest of the time there was nothing. We weren't allowed to go to the gym by ourselves, so we'd go and do push-ups and chin-ups out the back of our lines. We'd make our own circuits. We had no internet. I didn't have a mobile phone. All there was, was army.

When, in about the fifth or sixth week, we finally got to go out on the weekend, everyone went nuts, overcompensating. At least I had somewhere to stay and family to hang out with. Some of the trainees were seventeen years old with nowhere to stay, had saved up some money and were full of pent-up frustration. Friday nights were massive bitch sessions about the platoon sergeant, and the next thing some of the guys were back at Singleton, having taken their money and blown it all in a few hours of drinking and gambling.

Being out after all that time in Kapooka and Singleton, I had the strangest sensation. We had to wear jeans and a collared shirt in public because we were still representing the army. Wearing civilian clothes felt as bizarre to me now as wearing cams for the first time. Even though there were women at Singleton, we rarely saw them. Our days were heavily structured and the women were not doing the infantry training we were. I said to Brent, 'I feel really weird. I'm in unfamiliar clothes, I'm seeing females walking in the street. My idea of normal has been changed.'

He said, 'Isn't that what they're supposed to do to you?'

'I guess so. I'd feel much more normal if I was in a pair of cams.'

For the three months we were there, the barracks at Singleton started to feel more normal than Newcastle. I enjoyed going out in the bush and doing section attacks. There was one crucial week when, if you were going to fail, you would. It was the section contact phase. If you weren't looking through your sights when you were shoot- ing, if you weren't in the right position to fire, you received a warning called a safety breach. The second warning was a standards breach. If one of the instructors walking behind you saw you doing an improper drill, he'd write it down and say, 'You've fucked that.' The punishment was to go back to repeat it with a platoon that might be two or three weeks behind you in the training. My view was, *I'm not doing this twice*, so I made sure I got it right.

Singleton was a big step up from Kapooka in their attitude to culling people. They weren't going out of their way to get rid of you, but to their credit, they still had a standard you had to reach. The instructors prided themselves on being hard. The two main ones, corporals Meehan and Barrett, held a lot of the PT record performances and used us, their sections, to compete against each other, whether it was on the obstacle course, the bayonet assault course or overall.

I had my first experience of the mindset of violence we'd need. Ultimately, your ability to kill someone might be the difference between your own life and death, and is one of the tests of whether you can be a combat soldier. Back in Kapooka, we'd had bayonet training – the routine of 'Left parry, right parry, butt stroke, smash, slash, in, out, on guard'. We did it with bayonets fixed to Steyr rifles, using them on a rubber car tyre attached to a metal rod. The rod was on a spring system that would bounce back up, like those clowns you can punch down but come at you again. A corporal at Kapooka did it so vigorously that on his first slash he snapped the blade out of his Steyr. It was quite eye-opening when you saw how aggressively he attacked something that was a stand-in for a human being.

At Singleton, as we lined up with our bayonets, the instructors paced up and down in front of us.

'What are you gunna do?' they shouted.

We had to scream: 'Kill! Kill! Kill!'

That's what they were teaching us. There's a technique to using bayonets, but ultimately it's an act of violence. They didn't overdo it, but it was my first glimpse of what would be a long indoctrination. I wasn't sure how I felt about it, but I wasn't scared by the idea. My attitude was, *Let's cross that bridge when we come to it.* Even now, when I certainly have crossed that bridge, I think it's one of those experiences that no matter how much training you've done, you never know how you'll handle it until you're confronted by the real thing. Although I also feel that being real with yourself – accepting what you may have to do in this job and being at peace with it – will set you up for dealing with those feelings when it happens.

Meanwhile, in section attacks we had to throw grenades and assault a pit. We put two shots into the enemy and yelled out, 'One dead enemy!' or 'One enemy KIA!'

Given what I'd been through, I suppose I have to wonder whether I had a different view of life, not only because of what had happened to Mum, but through Dad being a Vietnam vet, loving his hunting so much, and his work killing live animals. Was it somehow programmed into me that I found it easier than the next person to take a life?

I don't think so. I could equally argue that what happened to Mum left me valuing life more, not less. When I was doing that first training in how to kill, I didn't find that it unleashed pent-up reserves of violence from inside me. I didn't go into an uncontrolled frenzy when I charged with a bayonet or put shots into an enemy. In fact, they were looking for that kind of crazy-eyed behaviour, and weeded those people out. I was quite calm and controlled. The whole exercise was about unpeeling our natures. Some of the trainees really didn't want to be a part of that. Some took it too far. Those of us who could handle it, and went through the course, were in the middle ground.

As the end of the IET approached, I got excited about marching out. One day towards the end, we were all pulled into the platoon sergeant's area. He passed around a newspaper that reported a bombing in a Bali nightclub that had killed at least eighty Australians and injured many more.

Holy hell. It cemented in me the purpose of being there. It had happened in the United States and now it was at our doorstep, affecting our country and the people who live in it. More than ever, my personal drive to excel in the army was being woven together with a bigger cause.

The final phase involved ten days of living and digging in fighting pits to establish a defensive position, climaxing with shooting, a pack march, a stretcher carry, an overnight exercise where we were up all night doing defensive work, then a big stores carry, and finally a bayonet assault course with the instructors shooting blank ammunition and throwing smoke at us. A few made it right up to that last day but were told to do the last couple of weeks again.

After a pretty difficult three months, I was ecstatic to be an infantryman at last. On the last night they said, 'Righto, this is your turn, you can take the piss out of us.'

I knew what I was going to do. *Here's my chance.* I put a big stack of beer cans in the middle of the circle and started going off my head like the platoon sergeant had that day in the bush, kicking them everywhere. I kicked one straight at him and the beer went all over him. I stopped. He took it well, I'll give him that, but I thought at that moment, maybe I'd pushed it too far.

Although he was a prick, he had a job to do and I have to give him credit for being pretty effective and maintaining standards. And there was probably a decent bloke underneath it all. One day at Singleton, another trainee and I had been staying back to help him prepare for a live fire exercise with Claymore mines. He was ex-Reconnaissance, and was doing them up in a Recon way rather than the standard infantry procedure. As we worked together, he was handing out tips and passing on information about guys in the SAS Regiment he knew. We hadn't seen this side of him. It was good to break down that barrier. When he wasn't playing his role of hard-arse platoon sergeant, he was actually a decent fellow. Three years later, when I was in the Regiment, I ran into him, just by coincidence, in a mess hall in a camp in Iraq. I sat next to him and said, 'How're you going?'

He kept eating his food. After a while he said, 'So you made it, eh?'

His demeanour had changed a bit. At Singleton he'd been on a pedestal. But there in Iraq, among everyone else, he just seemed normal. I'd changed too. I thought he looked almost happy to see me with the Regiment. A little bit proud, perhaps.

I invited Auntie Margaret and Uncle Ken to the Marching Out ceremony. Photos were taken, and I had short hair, a number-one buzz cut, a far cry from when I'd dropped in to their place in earlier years. It made me happy to win some awards in front of them: best shot, best PT, most outstanding soldier. It was nice for them to see that I'd earnt some respect in that environment, and was going to stick at it.

When we were standing around, it was announced which Royal Australian Regiment we'd be going to. 3RAR was parachutes, and initially I'd wanted to go there. Paras had high standards and worked hard and went everywhere. The parachute culture prided itself on its ability to take hard knocks. They had the mentality that comes with being skilled soldiers who are trained to drop in behind enemy lines and fight their way out.

There was appeal in other regiments too. 4RAR was Commandos. 5RAR had amalgamated with 7RAR to become 5/7RAR, the mechanised battalion, working with the armoured personnel carriers, or APCs. Their culture was known among the other regiments as 'Ramps down, pants down', because they got fucked on (so to speak) while moving alongside the APCs. 1RAR and

2RAR were air mobile, which meant they went in and out by helicopter, in theory anyway. In practice, there was a helicopter shortage.

But the overriding rule is that whichever regiment you're in, you think it's the best. The corporals at Singleton and my section commander at Kapooka had all been in 1RAR, and they'd convinced me to put that down as my choice. They told us that 1RAR was always the battalion that would go somewhere first. That gives it prestige, builds a spirit in the corps and gives the guys something to hang on to. I thought they sounded like the most professional soldiers.

So when we were told we were going to 1RAR, a couple of us were cheering away and jumping up and down, saying, 'We're going to Iraq!' As it was happening, with Margaret and Ken being there, I had this flash from the past. In 1991, when the first Gulf War had started, we'd been on holiday at Tanilba Bay. On TV we saw the tanks and helicopters and Scuds, and the old man was fixated. Whenever it was on screen, he'd shut everyone up. Margaret and Ken were taking the piss, saying 'It's not Vietnam any more.' He said, 'Shh, it's on, the world's at war. They're gunna start conscripting you, Brent, we'll have to hide you up in the roof.' Brent said, 'Dad, I'm only fourteen!' Dad said, 'This'll still be going on when you're eighteen.' When everyone else had gone to bed he'd stay up at night watching it.

Well, he was wrong, but he was also right. Australia was about to send troops back into Iraq, twelve years on. And it looked like I'd be going, not as a conscript, but voluntarily, just like him. I could see him there, in front of the TV set at Tanilba, as clearly as if it was yesterday.

Happy first birthday, 1980. On the Sandy Hollow property with the old man. He was a hard worker and set in his ways. His hair must have been fashionable at the time.

The Donaldsons – me, Mum, Brent and Dad – in 1980.

Playing with the black snake under the house in Sandy Hollow in 1981. Apparently I wasn't supposed to. Lucky Dad had already killed it.

Swimming on the Hunter River, 1981, with Mum keeping a close watch in the background.

Two young, proud brothers, 1985. Brent with his under 9s Best and Fairest trophy and me with our Major Premiers trophy for the Denman Devils. We were undefeated that year. Maybe if I'd had some talent I might have had a different career...

Mother and son. This was when I was giving my mum so much grief, in 1996 or thereabouts. I like this photo, but I think her eyes give away the heartache she was going through. My hair is a giveaway of bad choices.

Me, aged 17, sleeping off another all weekender of partying, vagrancy and trouble. At least my dog Lister was there to help me sleep it off.

Somewhere near Goulburn, New South Wales, 1999. It's me behind the wheel of this Unimog, trying to drag a machine behind it to lay optic fibre cable from Sydney to Melbourne. These were loose OH&S times. If you were not on the trigger or if you lost control of the winch it could obviously end badly.

Checking out the sites in Banff, Canada, 2001. The mountains were like nothing I had ever seen. I instantly fell in love with the remoteness of the place and the amazing snow they get. Check out those dreadlocks!

Domestic Counter-Terrorism training, 2005. All about the Black. Many men have spent long days and hours in this get-up. If it wasn't for them, we would not be where we are today.

In the back of a Hercules aircraft, on personal security detail with Prime Minister John Howard, Islamabad, 2005. This was his first trip into Afghanistan. We had a rough start to the trip, but managed to crack on and get it done.

Getting some respite in the shade of the Long Range Patrol Vehicle near Chora, Afghanistan, 2006. One patrol we did was just over three weeks of living and working out of them.

Resting after an early morning physical training session. The memorial behind me is dedicated to a killed US Soldier. 2007, somewhere in southern Afghanistan.

The aeromedical evacuation helicopter that came extremely close to crashing on top of us east of Uruzgan in 2008. Apparently this is classed as a 'hard landing'. Those ripped up blades were only metres from us.

The Chinook that brought in the recovery team after the incident east of Uruzgan in 2008. We only had to wait five hours. I was lucky enough to get a lift back to main base with them while the rest of the recovery team pulled apart the downed helicopter. The Bushmaster cannot be shown due to operational security reasons.

Our patrol in 2008, minus Bruce who was sick. Me on the right with the flaming beard. Taylor is next to me. It was his second mission in Afghanistan. The view from up there was quite spectacular.

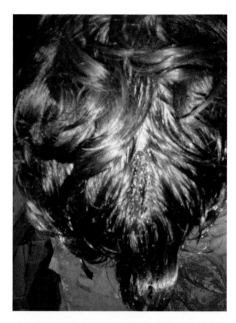

The injury that nearly took Taylor's life: he is one lucky bugger. Only his third time outside the wire in Afghanistan and it does not get much closer. This photo was taken moments before we washed out the wound and stapled it shut. 2008.

Carl's rifle. You can see where the enemy bullet has struck the ejection port and split the receiver. He was extremely fortunate not to be hit as he was shooting the rifle at the time the bullet struck. Some of his blood is still on the weapon, just above the trigger. 2008.

Helping out the others with some first aid with dried blood and gore still on my face. Not long after we returned through the gates of Forward Operating Base Anaconda, 2 September 2008.

The day after the ambush. This is what was left of the joint AUS/US patrol. We had begun with 36 personnel, not including the Afghanistan attachments or interpreters.

Me on one of the last jobs of 2008. At least we were getting a lift in a Chinook this time.

Returning from another night mission. Standing on the helipad not far from the gates of Camp Russell, Multi-National Base Tarin Kowt, late 2008.

Trying to sap some shade from under a Bushmaster to sleep. The heat can be relentless. It was a rough way to do things but kept the enemy on the back foot as he never knew if we would come by foot, vehicle or helicopter. It was times like these you needed a good crew to share some laughs with. In the desert between Tarin Kowt Bowl and the Mirabad Valley 2008.

Marrying my sweetheart in 2008. We were so happy and she was so beautiful.

AP/AAP

The moment when Quentin Bryce the Governor-General pinned the Victoria Cross medal to my chest. It was an amazing experience and one that I will never forget. Government House, Canberra, 16 January 2009.

KYM SMITH/NEWSPIX

Emma, Kaylee and me in the gardens of Government House moments after having the Commonwealth's highest award given to me by Governor-General Quentin Bryce.

In 2009 I handed over my Victoria Cross to the Australian War Memorial. I felt the first Victoria Cross for Australia should be on display so all Australians could see it. It was the right thing to do.

Sharing stories with Ted Kenna, the Victoria Cross recipient from WWII, in 2009. A unique experience I will never forget. Lasting advice of 'Don't let it go to your head'. Good advice.

Enjoying the view at Yarralumla, January 2009.

TWELVE

I had a week off before travelling to Townsville, where 1RAR was based. While waiting to leave, we had to stay on barracks. Upon graduation, we'd exchanged our crossed-rifles badge, for School of Infantry, for the Skippy badge, a kangaroo with a wreath, which denotes that you're a full-fledged infantryman. Although I was only a private, the badge brought some privileges: we could go out every night if we wanted, as long as we were back by curfew, and we could go to the mess at any time.

That feeling of being at the top of a tree only lasted until I got to Townsville. I'd never been that far north, and as I looked down at the brown expanse of Stuart Hill, I thought, *What the fuck is this place?*

At the base, it was a whole new atmosphere. A jaded duty corporal sent us to our lines without any welcome. As soon as we started walking through the dusty ground between the barracks a nasty yell came from somewhere: 'Swing your fucken arms when you walk in this place!'

It was like a reset, first day at a new school. The next day they were marching us around, showing us the lines, which were multistorey barracks blocks, and told us which block belonged to each company. In a weary drone, the NCO announced each one: 'Heavy weapons, direct fire support, recon, snipers, mortars, signallers, pioneers, extra support.' There were soldiers who'd been there six, seven or eight years, and they had a hard-bitten, salt-of-the-earth look.

1RAR has a green puggaree, the band around the slouch hat. The green puggaree was first worn by 1RAR during the Malayan Emergency in 1959–60. The Australian Army was unable to supply 1RAR with new puggarees so a local tailor was commissioned by the unit to supply them made from the same soft green material as the British Forces green shirts. As a tradition they are still worn to this day. We still had plain khaki ones, so everyone knew who we were. Suddenly there was a shout of, 'You fucken lids!' and a volley of half-eaten apples and oranges were thrown at us. I was thinking, *Jeez, this is different from the training establishments!* It was free rein up there. I was excited, and it really did feel like a step up. *You don't want to fuck up here,* I thought. *This is where it's all gunna happen.*

The barracks were dingy and filled with asbestos. The rooms were dormitory-style, four beds in each, and our platoon of thirty occupied its own level in the block. Downstairs was an office area where the support companies hung out. Every morning we'd rock up to work in running shorts and a blue 1RAR T-shirt. We had to form up, march to company headquarters, and then do PT. It was pretty full-on in the summer heat. There was a run called Tank Hill, up to a water tower. Our secco, or section commander, was a huge, chunky fellow known as Rhino, from DFSW – Direct Fire Support Weapons – where they pride themselves on being big. I was surprised by how fit he was for his size.

This hard run soon sorted us out. In Singleton, an older soldier had said, 'Whoever the first guy is who wants to come and talk to you, he's usually the worst soldier and the biggest fuckwit.' Soon after I arrived in Townsville, this one bloke was making a beeline for everyone to tell us how everything worked. He was the authority. Others were the first to gob off or try to be smart-arses. Within minutes, the senior men had them pinned. They'd pass it around to each other: 'That guy's a knob, he's been here all of two minutes and he's mouthing off already.' And then, on the Tank Hill run, it was just as I'd been warned, the know-alls were the first to peter out.

When this started happening, it was a struggle for those of us who were doing it easier to know what to do. At training it had been all about helping each other out, and your team's only as fast as your slowest member. So another of the fitter ones, Monty, and I decided to go back to pick the stragglers up. One of them said, 'Fuck off, leave me alone!'

'Come on mate, you'll be right.'

A PT instructor (PTI) came back and told him to hurry up. To us he said, 'Fuck off back to the front of the group.'

This set the tone. You were there to strive ahead for yourself, and be at the head of the pack. Good, fit soldiers earnt respect within the wider group. Those who struggled at PT or soldiering were denied that respect. I wanted to be as good as I could be, but there was also a catch. You didn't want to stand out as being too good, with the attitude to match. I reasserted my 'grey man' approach: just get on with any task without any carry-on, do my best but keep my head down and my mouth shut.

*

We started at Townsville at the end of 2002, and the regulars were soon going on holidays. As newcomers, we only had a week's compulsory stand-down, so I rang Brent and said I'd stay in Townsville over the break. You got one free trip a year to your next of kin, and I said I'd save it up for when I'd accrued more leave.

I loved trying to surprise Brent, however, by turning up when he was least expecting it. Sometimes it backfired on me. A couple of years earlier, I'd gone to his place at Bar Beach and he hadn't been there. Thinking he'd be home soon, I bought some sushi and longnecks and sat on his step. It got dark, started to rain, and I'd been trying to break in when an old bloke, a neighbour, challenged me with an umbrella. This was when I had the dreadies and half a beard, so I must have looked pretty suss. I ended up out in the rain all night when Brent didn't come home. I didn't even have a mobile, because I didn't like people being able to contact me. I was free. And then I joined the army.

Anyway, after getting some Christmas leave, I rocked up at Brent and Kate's house by surprise and again they weren't there. But I tracked them down at a party, and had a bit of fun seeing Brent's face. We were even closer as brothers since I'd joined the army. Outside that world, he could seem like my only constant.

But his world was changing – he and Kate were about to start a family – and so was mine. I let battalion life envelop me. As we got more senior we could move into better rooms, little efficiency apartments where communities of blokes formed. You had a bit more freedom and more of a social life once you moved there. Every weekend we went into Townsville, where each battalion had its own pub. It's a garrison town, but weirdly I never came across anyone from 2RAR there.

We weren't getting paid much, about $500 a week, much less than I'd been getting before I joined the army, but there was nothing to spend it on, so you saved what you earnt. As in Singleton, the younger lads blew their cash. At midnight on Wednesday night, your pay appeared in your bank account. So these guys would go out, wait till twelve o'clock ticked over, withdraw the maximum and hit the casino. Come Friday morning, they'd be hitting you up for a loan.

Our early hopes that we'd be off to Iraq didn't materialise. We heard that three of the four companies would be sent to East Timor, and I got excited about that. But my company, Bravo, had just been to Malaysia for some training before I joined, so we were the ones to miss out. That was disappointing enough, but the hierarchy was selective in who it actually left behind. Our best section commanders and 2ICs were cut away to go to East Timor, and we were left with the weaker soldiers from other companies and us rookies. It felt pretty shithouse, to be honest. The war in Iraq had started and we were stuck in Townsville, at the bottom of the 1RAR barrel.

I turned every setback into fuel for my ultimate goal, which I never lost sight of. I was reading lots of books about Special Forces. I did a field medic's course so I could be the first responder to look after someone in the 'golden hour' before they get a proper medic. Those courses didn't come around very often and were hard to get into. I also tried out for a PTI course, anything to expand my skills.

I didn't mention my plan to others. I didn't want to be laughed at. People might want to tear you down if you say you're going to the Regiment. So I sat back and watched and waited. Discreetly, I kept asking questions about the Regiment. Nearly everyone told me that you had to wait four years before they would even look at you, or do a support company course like Recon or DFSW first. The multitude of theories added to the mystique. I looked at that information and the people telling me and thought, *Well, these guys are not in SASR, never have been and never tried out, so how would they know?* I decided to do the exact opposite of what they said, and go for the most direct route possible.

*

As compensation for not going to East Timor, we got a trip to Hawaii to train with the US Marines. Having read about them, I was amped up. And going to Hawaii, as a surfer, was a buzz.

The departure was routine army frustration. The army has this notorious fudge with time. The commanding officer (CO) tells the officer commanding (OC), 'You've got to be ready at 8 am.' The OC then tells the 2IC, 'We need to be there at 7.45 am.' The 2IC tells the platoon commanders to be there at 7.30. And so on down the line, every person in the chain of command taking his fifteen minutes, and before you know it you, the soldiers, are there at 5.30 am with all your gear on the parade ground. No one else is there. The platoon commander rocks up half an hour later, and it's hours before the OC turns up, all ready to go, wondering why everyone looks pissed off.

Anyway, we got onto the Hercs and flew to the Marshall Islands. I was excited, watching the white rings around each island, wondering where the surf was. I still do that now. Even going into Pakistan on the way to Afghanistan, there's a part of the shoreline we always fly over, and I see this perfect point break. You could have it to yourself, guaranteed.

After a one-night stopover, we went up to Kaneohe Bay, on the eastern side of Oahu. It being summer, the famous beaches on the North Shore, like Pipeline and Waimea, were a lake. I didn't care. I was excited to train with the Marines, so I ended up being surprised by how unfit they were. Their patriotism, however, is unparalleled. We did some fast rope training and flogged them in a run. They did things very differently, to say the least. They ran as a platoon while chanting and singing together. We just ran.

We did the obstacle course, and unknowingly were doing it back-to-front. This Marine captain showed up, had a bit of a chuckle at what idiots we were, and said to our platoon commander, 'You want a competition? Get your best five against our best five through the obstacle course.'

Our captain was pretty cocky and chose five blokes. I wasn't one of them. He said, 'How about we do it with webbing on?'

The American said, 'Webbing? No, we don't do that.'

'Okay, mate, we'll do it with webbing and you do it cleanskin.'

We all cheered madly on the sidelines, and our five had finished in the time only three of theirs had. Our commander was chuffed, and as we wandered off we could hear the Yanks getting screamed at. 'These goddamn Aussies have beaten you on your own fucken obstacle course!'

When we had some time off, I hired a huge mal as the waves were fat and paddled out to one of the breaks at Waikiki. There was this one blond guy chasing everything. I could hear him talking in a Canadian twang. I said, 'G'day mate.'

He was giving me a funny kind of look.

'Where are you from?' I said.

'Canada. Are you from Australia?'

I said yeah, and we were sitting there looking at each other.

'Mark?'

'Drew!'

It was my snowboarding mate, who we'd introduced to surfing in northern California. We leapt off our boards and grabbed each other in a headlock. The chances of running into each other were infinitesimal. I'd hired that board for an hour, and chosen that break out of six or seven different places to paddle to. I was blown away.

Drew was on a surfing odyssey, leaving behind his snowboarding, at which he'd been on track to becoming a professional. But ever since that day we'd taken him into the ocean, he'd been hooked, and here he was.

We caught up later and got drunk together. He was amazed that I was in the army, but he wasn't one to question or judge. He just said, 'Hope you're having fun.' He was going to university to study philosophy. I still wonder at the chances of our bumping into each other like that, and think of what different directions our lives have taken.

*

The longer I was at the battalion, the more my determination firmed up to go for the SAS. I was continuing my obsessive reading about Special Forces, and moved with one of my best mates at the battalion, Nate Hall, into a house in Townsville. He was dead keen on being a sniper, and was a better soldier than me overall. It helped me lift my standards to spend time with a bloke who wasn't going to sink into mediocrity. Recently, after years of me pestering and hounding him to come across to the SAS, Nate finally gave it a shot and got accepted. I was happy for him because I knew he was always keen on doing it.

I was getting desperate to move on from the battalion. Life was filled with pointless exercises. As a digger, of course, you don't understand the massive moving parts of the machine you're in, but to fill in your time, they'd devise mindless tasks such as digging in rocks on a hill for three days. Guys got pissed off, and rightly so, as they weren't advancing their skills.

The final straw for me was Operation Croc, a big multi-unit exercise. We were to load up onto HMAS *Kanimbla*, sail down to Rockhampton and fight some make-believe enemy. It at least had some potential for real war-fighting stuff, which made the ultimate let-down all the harder.

Our trip down on the *Kanimbla* took twelve days, and my old rebellious spirit started to rise up again. I had some run-ins with officers. Navy are a different breed; they take things very seriously as far as rank goes. We were calling them 'mate', and they'd burr up. If you call an army officer 'mate', at worst he might say quietly, 'That's "sir" to you.' But in the navy it was a screaming fit. 'YOU'LL COME HERE, STAND AT ATTENTION, CALL ME SIR, SHOW THE PROPER RESPECT!' That's how they treated each other all the time. It was back to being a recruit.

They had a letter code – ship state Zulu, Yankee, or whatever – meaning what doors and hatches had to be shut. They were very strict on it, but nobody had explained any of this to us. A door had Z on it, but we didn't know we were meant to shut it, and when I got pulled up by a naval officer I said, 'Mate, nobody told us.'

'Don't you "mate" me, I'm an officer of the Royal Australian Navy!'

And so on. I'd keep saying, 'Okay, mate, don't worry.' Eventually a senior officer had to come in and calm him down. We weren't being mongrels on purpose. It was just a clash of cultures.

But I was getting restless to the point of desperation. According to the scenario, our ship got 'sunk', but that meant we had to do an enormous loop of 150 nautical miles, taking three or four days, before returning to the same spot. There's always someone at the bottom level being fucked around in the army, and on Operation Croc that was turning out to be us. We got outside the heads and the ship was getting bashed around by the seas. I've always had a bit of a problem with motion sickness, and was green and throwing up, hating it, thinking, *Fuck this, this is bullshit!*

Once we got onto land, we were moved around on a map by some CO in his little tent – just like all military history! We ended up tromping all night to an ambush position. After we were fucked around a bit more, I said to the secco, or section commander, 'Why are we here? What are we ambushing?'

'Dunno, mate. This is a fucken joke.'

The higher-ups' theory was that we didn't need the overall picture of the campaign, we only needed to know our objective for the moment. My secco said, 'Welcome to these exercises. This is our part.' We had no sense of purpose, no ownership of the plan. The boys were generally very professional in their soldiering, but had lost all interest in Operation Croc.

The final straw was when we were told we'd be assaulting a target by helicopter. We thought, *Finally we're going to do something.* But at the last moment the decision was changed. Instead of sending the assault forces in, they were sending the headquarters: the OC, the 2IC, all their staff. We were in uproar. It didn't make sense! Why did *they* have to be on the ground first? Wasn't the idea for us to secure the ground, and then they'd come in to expand the operations?

It turned out that the HQ people got their helicopter ride, but were rendered 'battle-ineffective'. We could all see through it. We were never going to go. We were stuck for another three days on the airfield, digging pits to defend it. Even our secco was muttering, 'Get fucked, yous can fuck off.'

I got back to Townsville feeling disillusioned. I still had a high expectation of what the battalion could do, but they were getting let down by the hierarchy. I'd joined up to jump out of helicopters and go bush and attack targets, but the scenarios were just a matter of ticking boxes that someone had come up with, and Operation Croc was the biggest crock of them all.

Personally I needed more, and Croc gave me that last push. During Croc, we'd crossed paths with some army commandos, who showed us the weapons and technology they had. It was so much more advanced than the gear we used in the infantry, and their being there was almost like a recruitment drive. They had an SAS Regiment man with his sandy beret, and I had a chat to him. He gave us a spiel about Special Forces: 'I'll put it to you like this. If you want to do some Special Forces shit, join the Commandos. If you want to do Special Forces shit *properly*, come to the SAS.' It was quite funny, because all the commandos were calling him a wanker, but I was impressed and used it as more fuel. The farce that Operation Croc was turning into wasn't pushing me to get out of the army; it was pushing me to get out of the infantry and into the SAS.

I'd seen a few blokes training for the Regiment. They'd gone off to Perth for the selection course but had missed out. There were all sorts of legends about how tough selection was, but I set about gathering real information. I was asked if I wanted to do a sniper course but said no.

The commander said, 'What do you mean, no?' I'd only been in the battalion for less than two years, and it was quite a compliment, at that time, to be noticed that early and invited to do the sniper course.

I told him I'd got the SAS paperwork off the computer. 'I want to do this,' I said, placing the forms in front of him on his desk.

To his credit, he said yes and signed off on it right away.

I was very determined not to do another of those pointless exercises. To this day, I can happily say that Croc was my last one.

THIRTEEN

I'd made a resolution not to eat any fast food for a year, and felt much healthier not to have that in my system. I got into the recommended training program and was panelled for the three-day Special Forces barrier test in Singleton. You had to do a certain amount of testing for them to decide if you were up to trying out for Commandos or SAS, or neither. The old way had been that the guys who were culled out of SAS selection were moved down to Commandos, but the skills required for each were quite different, so now they were trying to stream from the outset.

A couple of blokes I knew came to do the barrier test with me. Julian, a good soldier who I didn't yet know very well, was a sniper from the battalion. There was another sniper nicknamed 'Head', because he had this massive head and ears, who had tried out a couple of times before but got injured. He was telling us everything about how it was going to be. It was another case of beware the loud one.

I was thinking, *Do what you should do. Don't fall into the trap of doing what the others are doing.*

The tests were challenging but not overwhelming. There were push-ups, sit-ups, swimming in cams, treading water for five minutes, a 3.2-kilometre run in boots and cams and carrying a rifle that you had to complete within sixteen minutes. They put you in a series of tight tunnels, pitch-black, full of mud and shit, and you had to crawl for a couple of hundred metres. We did some rappelling off towers to test how we were with heights. They showed us an action-instant-unload drill on a weapon we'd never seen. We had to watch it once, mimic it and get shown again, and the next day they tested us again to see how well we'd remembered it. We did a 15-kilometre pack march that we had to complete in two hours fifteen minutes, fully loaded with marching order, and then a navigation theory exercise.

Just before the practical navigation test, or navex, there was an interesting exchange that gave me an insight into the SAS way of doing things. We were all sitting down listening to an SAS man giving us the grids and our first checkpoints. One of the guys said, 'Can I wear my MP3 player while I'm doing this exercise?'

'What?! Are you for fucken real? Where are you from?'

He said he was a signaller, a 'chook', from 152 Squadron in Perth.

'You're from fucken Perth and you're asking me if you can wear an MP3 player on a navigation exercise? You've got to be one of the dumbest cunts I've ever come across.'

This chook did get through. He turned out to be someone who genuinely liked listening to his music, but also liked to get a reaction out of people.

The navex was exciting, and more tense than the other tests, which were more physical than mental. This navex was one of the first times I had to navigate for myself in the bush when it really mattered. You did navexes in the infantry, but you were always near someone or you'd only do a leg, and the stakes weren't high. This time, if you made a mistake, you had to quickly figure out where you'd gone wrong and fix it, or else you were out. Luckily for me, it had only been a year and a bit since I'd been on this same Singleton layout for infantry training, so I had the advantage of knowing where I was and could pace myself. What made it harder than usual was we weren't told how long the course would be. At each checkpoint, there were people barking questions. 'Where did you come from?' 'When did you leave?' Then they gave you the next checkpoint. It was a lesson in keeping your thinking clear while you were under pressure. Each student went somewhere different, so you couldn't just follow people. I made a few mistakes but ended up second and got all ten checkpoints.

Next was an interview with a hard-looking RSM (regimental sergeant major).

'What do you do?' he said. 'What are you?'

'I'm just the scout in my section in the battalion, a rifleman.'

'What do you mean, you're *just* a scout, *just* a rifleman? You're the lifeblood of the infantry.'

'I didn't mean that,' I said. 'I meant I haven't done all the support company courses the other guys here have done.'

He cooled down a little. 'Righto, but remember, you're never *just* anything.'

It was good, actually. He was telling me I was on a level playing field, no matter how inexperienced I was. Whatever we'd done or hadn't done, we were all starting from the same point.

There were other interviews. When they asked me why I wanted to join the Regiment, I said, 'I want something more for my soldiering, I've read a lot about the SAS. I want to go there to improve myself and my soldiering.'

'Okay. What if we took you in, and one of the blokes you're working with is gay?'

'I don't have a problem with that. If that's the way it is that's the way it is. I might not snuggle up with him at night, but I don't care as long as he does his job.'

'What do you think about women in the infantry?'

'I don't know if women have a place in the infantry, but if that's the way it's going, that's the way it's going. I can't do much about it.'

'What do you think about women in Special Forces?'

'I'm not in Special Forces so I don't know. I can see there might be a benefit somewhere down the line.'

The questions seemed odd, but they didn't care about my opinions. The point was to make sure I wasn't a nut job who got emotional about certain issues.

After the barrier test, they sat us in a room where we waited anxiously for the result.

I was called in to see an officer. 'Private Donaldson, we think you're suited to go and try SAS selection. Is that what you're happy doing?'

'Yes, sir.'

'All right, sign here. Here's your joining instruction. Go back to your unit. Get in touch with our orderly staff. We'll see you when it starts.'

I turned to leave.

'Private Donaldson?'

'Yes, sir?'

'How old are you?'

'Twenty-four, sir.'

'You're a bit older than other guys who come through here.'

I didn't say anything. Nor did he.

My legs were torn up with chafing from the march and the navex, and I had a lot of gauze bandaging on my thighs.

He said, 'Make sure you look after those legs. It'll hurt when you rip that stuff off.'

'Yes, sir.'

*

When I got back to Townsville, I had three months to train for the SAS selection course. Since 1968 when it started, selection has knocked out two out of every three candidates, often more. I dedicated myself to sticking to the program down to the last detail. It helped that my platoon commander, Lieutenant Cocksedge, was supportive. I'd say, 'I have a pack march to do for selection,' and I'd get up at two o'clock in the morning to do it. He counted that as my PT for that morning and ticked my name off the roll. Not every platoon commander let you do that, so I was lucky.

The Croc experience kept motivating me. I didn't join up and put in all this effort to go back to doing that year after year, and didn't want to do this training three or four times. I wanted to do it once and get it right and get in. I still had doubts about whether the SAS would consider me after the short time I'd been in the army, but I knuckled down anyway. I saw myself as average at PT and an average soldier, so I would have to perform to my absolute limit to even get a look-in.

Weeks two to five of my program overlapped with the Christmas break. I owned a Toyota HiLux, and asked Brent if I could drive down and stay with him and Kate for my holiday. They lived at Corlette, near Anna Bay in Port Stephens, and were fine with me coming down.

On the way, I stopped at the Gold Coast to stay with a girl I'd known a couple of years earlier. I'd driven down from Townsville in one go and got up early, went for a surf and did some training. I explained what I was doing, and she said I was nuts. When everyone else was winding down for summer, I put my army pack and cams in the HiLux, drove out to the Gold Coast hinterland, and found a mountain to hump up and down. The requirement was that you carry a 28-kilogram pack, eight kilos of webbing, and a 4.1-kilogram Steyr rifle. I made my pack 33 kilos, my webbing 10 kilos, and had a metal bar made up that weighed seven or eight kilos. My theory was, if I can do the march in the required time carrying extra in training, I shouldn't have any dramas on the day. I don't know if that makes sense scientifically, but it did in my head.

When I got to Brent's place, I found sand dunes to train in at Stockton and a firebreak trail alongside a powerline. I marched in the sand dunes in all my gear. In the firebreak I measured out a one-kilometre interval by parking the HiLux at one end, and did my interval sprints.

I did it on my own the whole time. Once Brent said he might come with me, and I said, 'Okay, I'm getting up at 4 am to do this walk.' He reconsidered. Kate was a swimmer and water polo player, and she said she'd come do some laps with me at the local pool. When we got there, I got into my cams and boots, jumped into the pool, and swam fully kitted up. People were staring, wondering what this bloke was doing, and I thrived on that too.

That training was pretty hard, especially in the summer heat, and it took a lot of mental work to push myself through it alone. Much as I loved my music, I didn't let myself train with headphones. I remembered the SAS man's contempt when that chook had asked if he could wear his MP3 player. I wouldn't be allowed to listen to music on selection, so why would I do it in training? There was also a pleasure in hearing the real world around me. While snowboarding, I never liked having music on. The sound of clipping your boots into your board, the crunch of the snow, the smooth sound of your board sliding through the snow: my heart rate goes up even thinking about it. In the United States I'd go into the back country on my own and shut my eyes. It was so quiet it was beautiful. It was similar here, just me and nature, though the cicadas meant it was never silent.

Brent and I had had some conversations about Mum and Dad. I'd asked him to tell me stories about Mum and Dad that he might have known and I didn't. All of this stirred up a lot of thoughts and memories while I was out training.

I remembered always trying to prove myself to Dad, whether it was taking on a bigger kid on the football field or in a muck-around fight or karate. I remember going to a karate competition as a fifteen-year-old and coming second in the state under-18s, fighting black belts, just on determination. I never feared a bigger guy bashing me. Even when I had a white belt I was like that. It was stuff I did because of my own personal stubbornness, but also a little to win Dad's approval. It must also have been a quality I'd inherited from him. When he was twelve, thirteen, fourteen years old, he had it very tough emotionally. His mum had men friends over, and she'd lock him in his bedroom. He'd yell out, and she'd come in and tell him to shut up. When he had the chance, he took off to the beach for whole days. He told us how, after a huge storm, he'd gone running through a wall of solid foam. We said how great it must have been and he snapped, 'No, it was dangerous!' He just hadn't wanted to be at home. He didn't feel safe. It was a tough way to grow up, and no wonder he left when he was fifteen. It shaped his whole life. And when it came to raising us, no matter how tough we thought he was, all he was doing was what any parent would do, which is give us a better time in our family life than he'd had in his.

For Mum, it wasn't all that different. When her mother had died and her sisters left, and her father remarried, all Mum had for company was a rabbit and a cat. It had to have been lonely, but it built her character. She didn't act tough, she was small and quiet, but she wouldn't take any shit. If she wasn't happy with what someone said, she'd put them in their place. As a mother, she instilled that determination in us. 'Never think you can't achieve something, never feel worthless,' she said. She'd been made to feel worthless at home and thought she'd never become anything, and was adamant that we'd never have any self-doubts about what we wanted to do.

I thought about the two of them a lot while I was out slogging in the heat. They'd just tried to give us a better life than they'd had. They never manipulated us children, which was what had happened to them in their homes. Thinking about that filled me with a lot of steel.

During the training, I got bad chafing on my back from where the pack rubbed. I told myself it was going to get worse than this. Every time I wanted to skip training and have a rest, I'd say to myself, *Nup, your mum'd be disappointed.* I'd think about her last day. I don't know what she went through, but I'd say to myself, *This is nothing compared with what she went through that day.*

Sadness drove me further. One of the last times I saw her, she'd asked me to go on a short car trip with her somewhere out of Dorrigo. I hadn't seen her for a couple of months, but I said no. She thought it might just be a nice time to spend with each other. Instead, I went and got drunk. Hindsight's a beautiful thing, but I regretted a lot of small things like that. What I'd give for a car trip with her now.

*

Brent and Kate went for a holiday up north, and I lent them my HiLux. On my own at the house, I whittled life down to the essentials: training, cooking up big feeds, surfing, reading books and watching surfing movies. Sleep, eat, train, surf. It was gold.

When they got back I headed to Townsville. On my way I stopped at Wooli and had a surf at Wilsons Point with Kelvin. It was fantastic to be back there – I really love that part of the New South Wales coast. Good uncrowded waves. He was still riding his mini-mal, and I was riding a 6"1'. We had a good chat. It was weird going back there, because it brought back that immediate aftermath of Mum's disappearance, when Kelvin had helped me through a period of crisis. Now, though, I was much more self-confident and happy.

We were sitting out the back of his house one afternoon. Kelvin was having a beer. I was drinking water.

'So, you're in the military,' he said.

'Yep.'

'What are you training for?'

'The SAS.'

'I thought you might.'

'What do you mean?'

'When I heard you were joining the army I was pretty certain you were going for the SAS side of it.'

That was funny. Kelvin was about the most out-there, non-military person I'd ever met. I said, 'Of all people, how do you know about the SAS?'

'I don't know about them, but I know they exist.'

I didn't relent on the training while I was there. I got in the car and marked out the kilometre, and ran the intervals in the middle of the night, between Wooli and Minnie Water. It would've been pretty arresting for people to see this maniac in cams with a metal bar running in the night.

Without consciously planning it, I was taking stock of my whole life. I could sense that something big was about to change for me, and driving up the coast I was reliving parts of my experience.

Having touched base with Kelvin, I stopped in Toowoomba to see Vaughan and his parents, Dee and Phil. The parents of my friends had been so good to me in my darkest hours, and even now, Dee, a physiotherapist, had time to think about my wellbeing. She told me the runners I was using were wrong for me: I had flat feet, and she said my runners would bugger up my knees. I was spewing: I'd just spent $200 on them. But she was right, and typically willing to sort me out. When I think, nowadays, of 'defending my country', there are a lot of things that come to mind, but one is that great debt I owe to such people who helped look after me in Dorrigo.

Back in Townsville, I maintained my focus. When my mates were getting on the piss, I'd offer to drive them in and out of town. At two o'clock in the morning I'd take off to Paluma or Bluewater and hump for six hours. I got home and slept until the early afternoon, then trained through the night. I wanted to play mental games by making myself tired and sleep-deprived, because I knew they'd exploit that in selection.

In the last two weeks the training program tapered down – which I needed. There was a long pack march in there and I did it with Julian and two sniper mates to see where we were at. We went up this high mountain near

Innisfail, and I remember noticing how much they were struggling. We spent the night. They had hammocks and I slept on the ground. For my smarts, I woke up with leeches all over me, even in my mouth.

We linked up with some others to do a similar thing, including an officer. He had no shirt and was wearing headphones, and he was smashing the start of the walk, more or less bolting away from us. Maybe I hadn't trained as hard as I should have? We stuck with the rough track, picking our way among rocks. Near night-time we caught that officer and he was spewing his guts up.

I said, 'Are you all right, mate?'

'I'm all right, I'm all right, keep going.'

At the end of the descent, when Julian and I got to the car park, we were wondering if we'd have to go back and find him. He eventually turned up, full of excuses. 'I've hurt my ankle . . . I was sick.' We sort of went, 'Righto.' It was good to see where I was at compared with others going for selection, but it was all about competing against myself, not them. When I'd been out in big surf or going down a 40-foot drop on a snowboard, I was on my own and there was no one to brag to later. It took me a while to understand that fully. Even in Afghanistan, I'd never rate myself as the best soldier, nowhere near it. There are numerous things I always do wrong. But it's about doing it better next time. If you're going backwards, there's something wrong.

On the eve of leaving for Perth, I rang Brent. He wished me luck and warned me to watch out for the mind games. He'd spoken to someone who'd done selection, and they'd told him about one huge walk where a truck waited for them at the end. Every time they got near the truck, it would pull away from them, to taunt them when they were totally fingered. 'They fuck with your head,' Brent said. 'Anyway, try your hardest and show them what you're made of.'

It was one of the first times he'd acknowledged that he was proud of me. I'm sure he always was, but he hardly ever said it.

FOURTEEN

So this was it. On the Qantas flight over to Perth Airport, everyone seemed to be an expert on selection. I sat tight, not thinking about my chances, set on just trying my hardest and running my own race. My goal was to get selected, but I didn't let myself dwell on that overall result. Instead, I just focused on getting through the first day. Then I'd deal with the second. If I could get through one day, I thought, I could get through twenty-one.

There were 120 to 140 candidates starting the course. We were met at the airport in the late afternoon by a man whose T-shirt said 'DILLIGAF', as in 'Do I look like I give a fuck?' He barked out instructions and handed us three pieces of paper each. 'Study them on the bus trip, don't talk to anyone. You have to know them all on this course.' One was the first two verses of 'Advance Australia Fair'. The next was the words to 'Lili Marlene', the SAS Regiment's song, about a prostitute out in front of a barracks. The third was a fake language they'd made up – words for mother, father, brother, yes, no, north, south, east, west. It was just a memory exercise, to see if you could pick things up and retain them.

We weren't driven to Campbell Barracks, the SAS headquarters in Perth's seaside western suburbs, but straight out to one of their training facilities at Bindoon, an hour away in the bush. There was a big metal hangar and a sheltered area with an ATCO hut where the kitchen and barbecue were. We had a feed and handed over our papers before being told to line up in the hangar in a big grid, each of us behind the armband with our candidate number. The opening spiel began, with instructions on what we needed. 'If you do not have any of these items one of the DS [directing staff] will come and assist you.'

Someone put his hand up. A DS went over and the next thing we heard was, 'Why the fuck didn't you bring this?'

We were given a short 'cover story' on a piece of paper, and had five minutes to memorise it. We also had to write an essay about ourselves: your life, your military life and why you wanted to go into the SAS. There was also a six-page maths exam. It started easy, and then went into calculus and harder stuff. I was looking around, thinking, *No way can I do this*. One, I was shit at maths at school, and two, I didn't have a calculator and couldn't remember these theories. I was stressing out, thinking, *If I fail this, I'm out*. In the end I just did what I could, which wasn't a lot.

One of the first things they did was tell us to strip naked and put our stuff – phone, watch, all non-military stuff – in our echelon bags. These bags are heavy duty, olive, drab col-oured canvas bags with a zip and two carry handles, similar to a duffle bag. So there we were, more than a hundred of us, standing in the nude.

'Now the RMO is going to inspect you.'

The regimental medical officer came around and looked us up and down and checked us out. With one RMO and 140 candidates, it took quite a while. We weren't allowed to talk. For some, this was already planting doubts in their minds.

The RMO stopped at me and said, 'You've got flat feet?'

'Yes, I use orthotics.'

'Do you think that's going to be a problem?'

I was panicking. *You can't take me off, after everything I've done, just because I've got flat feet.* It had never been questioned before. It wasn't like the old days when flat feet could disqualify you from military service.

I said, 'No, I don't think so.'

'We'll see,' he said, and walked off as if here was one they could already cross off the list. I took a deep breath: at least they weren't going to send me home already. *Push that out of your mind. There's a job to do here.*

We put our cams back on and humped off after a guy with a red lamp on his head. It was now dark and we were sliding on the honky nuts – big brown gumnuts – and pea gravel. They marched us around in the bush for a while, and then lined us up in rows from A to Z in front of rectangular sheets used as camouflage and shelter, known as hootchies. The officers were first, then the rest of us. We had to sort ourselves into pairs.

There were stories about how they woke you up on your first night after half an hour's sleep. But we didn't get to lie down until two o'clock in the morning, and although we were waiting for it, no wake-up call came.

I'll never forget the bullhorn that hit us at 6 am, though. We ate breakfast and they had us standing in marching order. Somebody might not have stacked his breakfast dish the right way – there was always some little thing – and the DS said, 'Drop your packs and webbing, assume the push-up position.' We did about fifty push-ups in slow time, then had to follow the DS as he ran down a road. I was trying to do my best, and noticed some candidates already struggling.

I drew strength from that. You don't feel any compassion. Each one who drops out is one competitor less.

After that pack march was a 3.2-kilometre run with webbing and rifle, around a course with eight or ten stands where you had to stop and do a task. There was how to use a radio and use point of origin, how to tie knots, how to use a rope pulley system, and how to take apart a .50-calibre machine gun. These were all unfamiliar to me, and part of me was thinking a couple more years of experience might have helped. But on the other hand, some of the candidates might have done some of these things under different systems. So at least I had a clear head going into it, learning something new rather than unlearning old habits as well.

At the end, we had to sit down for a test in that language we'd learnt on the bus. It wasn't a big deal, just another box for them to tick or cross. We were still very much in the easy stage.

That night, half an hour after lights out, the bullhorn blew and we were up for a two-and-a-half-hour smash PT session – boxing, kicking, heaving metal bars.

The DS walked around and looked us in the eye and bollocked us. 'Go on mate, there's a truck over there, go on over, go back to your battalion and be a big man in the battalion, off you go.'

They've changed it now. They find candidates feed off that abuse, and it gives them an advantage. It had been that way for me at Singleton, where I strove to defy my sergeant. Nowadays, the unit has changed SAS selection to a principle of silence: no talking. And that freaks guys out, especially in the military, where they're used to getting feedback.

I'd done a lot of work with bars, but this PTI was inhumanly strong. He was doing one-armed raises with a 10-kilogram bar, counting them out to fifty. We were all struggling to keep up.

'Look, that's seventy, can you keep up?' He just wouldn't stop.

Other DS walked around saying, 'It's not hard, just lift your arm up. Why are you having so much difficulty, candidate? Just lift your arm up.'

Some were dropping off. This was in the middle of the night, after half an hour's sleep and a hard day's work. I was counting how many the PTI was doing. He got up to 120, 130 reps. Then he said, 'Rest!' and he was holding his bar out horizontally.

'HOLD IT OUT STRAIGHT! . . . Right! Change arms!'

And he was off with the other arm. It went on forever. I was convinced, and still am, that the bar he was using was hollowed-out and weighed about a kilo. It probably wasn't, but the thought helps me sleep.

After those two and a half hours, we were allowed to stagger off to bed.

Two hours later, they woke us again. We had to run up and down a road, doing lunges, holding a fast rope off the ground, putting it down when they told us, dragging it through the bush, walking on it, doing push-ups on it, holding the squat position with it held above our head. Every minute the DS were mocking us. 'Why are you having so much trouble?'

At the start of the course, they'd given us a slip of paper we had to carry. It said, 'I [name] voluntarily remove myself from this selection course.' If you handed that over, that was it. No second chances, no coming back in a couple of years, you've had your chance, you're done.

Already this night, there were candidates stepping up to hand in their slips. In front of everyone, the DS made a big point of turning around and being incredibly nice to the bloke who was dropping out.

'Okay, have a rest, get a drink of water, take a seat.' The DS started treating them like normal people. 'Sure, mate, go and sit in the truck. There's a stretcher for you. We'll take you up and give you some hot food.' It was obviously a mind game to provoke the rest of us, and some of the guys got pissed off, taking it as an insult that the flakers would be treated like kings while we were getting kicked like dogs.

Attrition was high in the first seven days. Some mornings, you'd wake up and see a bed-roll and pack missing. Just gone, flaked out. The DS came and reorganised us without a comment. We never knew if the absentees had handed in their slip, or been removed, or got sick or injured. They just vanished.

The first phase to see how we worked in isolation came in the way of a solo 36-hour navigation exercise, or 'navex'. At each checkpoint, you were grilled. Out of nowhere, a DS jumped out and got you to do all ten knots from the earlier knot test. I struggled with the .50-calibre weapon when it had a stoppage. A round came out and the DS asked me to see if it was hard struck or soft struck. If it was hard struck, showing the mechanism had worked, there was something wrong with the round and you replaced it. If it was soft struck, there was something wrong with the firing pin and you had to take the whole thing apart. I struggled a bit. The DS was shouting, 'Mate, did you even listen in the lessons? You don't know what you're doing, do you?'

After running a leg of the navex, with the general fatigue piled on top, it was hard to think clearly. At one checkpoint, the PTI told me to hit one punching bag fifty times, hit another one fifty times, run around a tree, and in twenty minutes do as many laps as I could. At another stand there was a video you had to watch and then answer questions on. A really fit bloke from the battalion was there. I was shocked to see him filling out his slip. The DS was working on the video player, and I whispered, 'Oi, Foogsy, what are you doing?'

'Mate, I'm done.'

'Come on, keep going, put it in your pocket, he's not looking.'

'Nah, mate, I can't do it.'

I was in shock as I watched this special police video from South Africa and did the questions. I thought, *Fuck, this is hard but it's not so difficult I want to get that bit of paper out and give up.* I kept telling myself to get through the day and not think ahead. But it's a lot easier said than done. Foogsy used to paddle from Townsville to Magnetic Island and back, for fun, seven kilometres each way. I wouldn't have been able to do that. But here, he'd hit his limit.

That officer I'd tested with in Townsville, I saw him broken. 'My back's fucked,' he said. 'My foot's fucked, I'm not doing very well.' I said, 'Okay, good luck,' and kept moving. He handed in his slip.

We had a full day of patrol skills, where we were tested on our ability to work as a team. At one checkpoint, we had to stand in a grid and answer questions, and if any of us got one wrong the whole section had to do thirty push-ups and start again with a new leader. It demanded a complicated mixture of knowledge and spatial memory, and by the end we'd done a lot of push-ups. I could see the guys who were getting it wrong, but they weren't necessarily marked down as much as those who, knowing the right answers, were saying 'You fucken dickhead' to the one making mistakes.

There were tasks where you had to cooperate and innovate to move a wooden pew with weights and tractor tyres through an area, and negotiate a course down an airstrip with a telegraph pole that could only be moved by flipping it end on end. The DS made a specialty of picking up the slightest mistake and punishing you, and studying how this would reveal character traits. Some candidates would say, 'I've got a blister,' or 'My knee's hurting.' Others would sit down and eat out of their ration pack while the heavy lifting was going on. I felt as if nothing went unnoticed. The stress of keeping up was doubled by this feeling of always being watched and assessed. It was relentless.

The night we'd finished those patrol skills, they got us out of bed to do more PT. Then we went in a Unimog up to Lancelin, a sand-and-saltbush beach hinterland area further out of Perth, for a five-day navex on rations and water. Shut up in the Mog, we weren't shown where we were going. We were let out at this crossroads and shown our first checkpoint on the map, and told to go there. Everyone sort of looked at the DS and thought, *But we don't know where we are.* We had no GPS or anything. How could we get *there* if we didn't know where *here* was?

I stood there, loaded with five days' rations and water, webbing, rifle, a sleeping bag, radio, spare batteries, medical and other equipment, and a checkpoint on a map. Eventually I figured how to do a resection using what features I could discern, which wasn't a lot. It took me a while. I plotted it, and it was 12 kilometres away. And that was just the first leg.

Lancelin was hellish to slog your way through, with deep sand and thick saltbush. We called one area Mordor, from *Lord of the Rings* – it was all black burnt-out banksia that seemed to have a mind of its own, poking you and springing back on you and pushing you away.

The context of the navex was a race – we were up against each other individually – but we didn't know where the end was. I couldn't pace myself, because I didn't know what the endpoint was. I just had to go my hardest, for five days, in a terrain with no landmarks and hard, resistant bush. We couldn't talk to anyone, and if we were caught walking on a marked track, we would be removed from the course, no questions asked. If we got lost, we had to shoot some rounds in the air. We were only allowed to move between 7.30 am and 10.00 pm.

Losing weight fast, I had to stop myself from going hell for leather and burning out. I'd walk for four hours and have a thirty- to fifty-minute break, during which I'd de-kit, chill out, have a feed, rest, and most importantly stop thinking about it all. I don't know if that was tactically sound or not, but I did it in the middle of the scrub where no one would find me.

It was a hard slog, but for the first time in my life I saw the Indian Ocean. My second leg was to a beach hut, and I was excited to see the surf peeling beyond it. I thought, *If I get through, I'll come back and surf here.* I watched the sun set over the ocean, which I hadn't seen since America and which is always a thrill for someone from the east coast. These little glimpses of beauty were what I used to get myself through all the torment.

At the end of the third day, after a long slog through deep sand dunes, I arrived at a checkpoint down the end of the beach. The DS said tersely, 'That's enough for you, go and get some water.'

'What?'

'That's enough walking, have a drink.' His voice had a finality to it that brought me crashing. I was thinking, *Fuck, there must be a cut-off and I haven't done enough k's.* I checked my sheet and added up what I'd done. I'd covered more than 100 kilometres. Surely that wasn't too bad? I knew I'd gone twice as far as some candidates I'd seen battling along the way.

Another bloke was sitting near the checkpoint.

'What have we done wrong?' I said.

He shook his head. 'I think we're done, mate. That's it. We've been sat down to wait for the others to catch up.'

The DS came up and said, 'Rest up, get out of your gear, have a feed. If you want, have a swim.'

It seemed bizarre, to think one moment I was being sent home, and the next I had finished the navex two days early. Half-expecting the DS to pull me up and tell me he'd only been tricking, I stripped off, ran into the ocean, and washed all the nasty red bush ticks and grime off me. It was regenerating, like growing a new skin. I enjoy the feeling the ocean can give you of being alive. I had some blisters as well, but not as bad as some of the guys were sporting when they came in over the next day. We were made to do more PT while we were waiting. Eventually, when about forty had turned up, the DS were yelling at us for losing some gear, and suddenly said, 'Right, get on the trucks.'

Julian had made it, and I said to him, 'What's happening? Aren't they going to wait for everyone else?'

He shook his head. 'This is it.'

Of the original 120 to 140 who'd started selection, about eighty had started the navex. Now we were down to forty. And the biggest challenges were still to come.

*

They took us to the public park in Lancelin, where we could shower up and have a barbecue. It was a very brief respite before we were bussed back to Bindoon for the third and final week.

There was a slight easing of pressure after the navex, before the final onslaught on our minds and bodies. Over the next day we did roping exercises on big suspension ropes strung between towers ten storeys off the ground. The hardest part was a regain, which is flipping over the rope and pushing yourself with your legs and pulling with your arms. It wasn't physically hard so much as a test of your fear ten storeys up.

Fear was a big part of the last week. There was a tunnel system leading into the Embassy, which was a big mocked-up building the Regiment used for practising assaults. I went in and it was black, not a speck of light. I thought I was alone until I heard someone grunt in fright just ahead of me. I came to a ledge with a big drop into a pit. I jumped down into the pit and put my hands up. I could feel a body.

'Fuck, sorry mate!'

I thought it was that guy. There was a horrendous smell in there, and the sound of dripping water.

'Mate, are you right, you need a hand?'

He was still there. I thought, *What is it? You right, mate?* I put my hand up again and touched a paw – *Fucken hell!* I pulled my hand away, then groped around to work out what I'd been touching. It turned out there were a couple of dead kangaroos dripping with blood above us. We had to use them to get up and climb through the next hole. When I got to the top, I turned around to the kangaroo, grabbed his hand and shook it and said, 'Cheers, Skip.'

There were two more exercises. One was a six-kilometre circuit that we had to do fast, carrying a bloke with a weapon over our shoulder in a fireman's carry. That night they followed it with another PT exercise, but our minds were on the big iceberg looming ahead: the notorious Lucky Dip.

Legend speaks of Lucky Dip as pure hell. I might have felt pretty hardened after the first sixteen days, especially that navex at Lancelin, but I'm sorry to say, Lucky Dip fulfilled all expectations.

Split into sections of twelve, we were dropped off a truck in what we were told was an area filled with enemy combatants. We rushed off into the bush, where the DS came and nominated a commander and told each section what we were doing. They asked me to be 2IC, and I went around to make sure everyone had everything squared off ready to go. I didn't really know what I was doing, but followed what we'd do in the battalion.

It started pissing down. A man came and said in a funny accent that he needed help from us Australians to get his gear to the next camp. 'Who's in charge, who's the 2IC, why aren't you ready? I thought you Aussies were supposed to be hard and tough! Look at you, you aren't laid out properly, your gear's a shambles, you're not ready to go, you don't want to work.'

His stores included wooden poles, signals gear and wooden ammunition boxes with rope handles. 'You just follow us,' he said, exasperated, 'and we'll take you there.'

It turned out to be six hours of humping this stuff through the bush. The crates were filled with rocks, but their shapes were different, so the weight was unevenly distributed, and they were awkward as well as heavy, about 40 kilos each. If we stopped for a rest, I was told off for not having a section defence set up. The punishment was having to do push-ups in our webbing, keeping our rifles off the ground, a simple punishment session.

We came to a road we had to cross without touching the ground. The only conveyance we had was some 44-gallon drums and painter's planks. It was a punishing exercise, getting all those stores across, constructing some kind of bridge or mechanism with the drums and planks. We needed two blokes on security on each side, so manpower was limited. The DS were constantly telling us the scenario had changed and we had to do things differently. It started to break down people's minds, the mental exertion and the frustration, being wet and cold, knowing it was getting dark soon, the goalposts always moving.

At night a new DS came in, as fresh as we were tired and hungry. He took us off for an ambush. We had to walk really slowly in single file, as slowly as possible.

'I'm going to stand over here in the bush,' he said, 'and if I hear a single noise, you're gunna keep walking until I can't hear anything.'

At the end, we had to stop still for ten minutes and be perfectly quiet. It's pretty hard to walk through the bush without making a leaf rustle or a twig snap, and it went on until about three in the morning.

We were now disoriented by cold, tiredness and over-whelming hunger. Once we lay down, everyone instantly fell asleep. The fatigue was so heavy, you'd even fall asleep while you were laying an ambush. When you woke up, you didn't know if you'd been asleep five minutes, half an hour or two hours. You didn't even know if everyone was still there. In another section, a guy got left behind and woke up to find himself in the middle of the bush in the dark on his own. Just as he was seriously panicking, he bumped into the back of his patrol. Pure luck.

That night, they told us about the next morning's scenario. We would have some wounded – stretchers with 80-kilo sandbag dummies on them. We had to bash through the bush from checkpoint to checkpoint in six hours, keeping security all around us the whole way. It was relatively straightforward, but the pressure was always on. If one of the team went down, we couldn't just go every man for himself, we had to help him up. As an individual candidate you might gain strength when someone drops out, but when you're in a section exercise you develop a bond with people you don't know, and it's camaraderie through hardship that brings you together. You do have to achieve a mission and work together. The DS were watching and taking notes the whole time. If they noticed something, they'd wander over in a sinister way and say, 'Hey, candidate 23, what's your name? Where are you from?'

'Private Donaldson, 1RAR.'

They had a blue pen and a red pen. They wrote something down. I saw the red pen – or were they just playing with my head? But let that get to you, and you can ruin your chances; you're a nervous as well as physical wreck.

At midday, we got a short break and then had to lug a big plastic container full of outboard motors for Zodiac boats. They were thrown together in an awkward box, which we had to carry with three metal poles of unequal length and ropes to tie them together. Once we'd contrived a carrying apparatus, we had to haul them for another six hours through unforgiving bush, while keeping our bearings and not getting lost on the way to the checkpoint.

We came to a broken-down box trailer, with a separated axle and only one wheel. We had to get the outboard motors on top of it and transport them somewhere else. Another six hours and another task. This time the trailer waiting for us contained a big fuel bladder, full of fuel or water and quite heavy. We had to push the trailer up rutted dirt roads, still with two guys as security to the sides, and another up the front navigating. The one in command had to decide how to rotate resources. The DS were just looking for initiative and nous, who takes leadership, who works in a team. You don't realise it so much when you're one of the candidates, but there was always someone putting their hand up for the easiest jobs. There were those who would shirk altogether. There were also those who'd be happy to volunteer to carry stuff, but never wanted to contribute ideas or leadership towards solving a problem. The DS sat back and noticed everything.

The physical ordeal throughout the day was tough, especially not eating. SAS soldiers are nicknamed 'chicken stranglers' for their ability to live off the land, but often it's a matter of living with starvation. For the whole five days of Lucky Dip, we each had one 24-hour ration pack. I allocated one muesli bar as my food for one day, and three Arnott's biscuits for the next. The packs contained two muesli bars, a pack of M&Ms, a small block of chocolate, a tin of cheese, a three-pack of biscuits, a little tin of two fruits, and some dehydes or dehydrated rations, which were either black bean beef or a disgusting seafood mixture. We couldn't make a fire to cook, so if we wanted them we ate them raw. There was sugar, tea and coffee, but likewise, if you wanted them you just had to eat them. You always had to have two litres of emergency water on your webbing, which you didn't drink from, plus 10 litres in your pack. You were pretty much living on water.

We were being tested on how we worked and thought when we were feeling like absolute shit. The night-time was a respite, but they'd get us up to do one nebulous task after another. In our minds, we questioned what the hell we were doing. During the day, we had a purpose, and could concentrate on putting one foot in front of the other. But at night we had to build a platform out of gum-tree sticks that were lying on the ground, and it had to be three feet high. We had to fit all our packs and all of us on it. 'Once you've achieved that,' they said, 'you can go to sleep.' So everyone worked really hard to get this thing built, rummaging around, one guy maintaining security, everyone dragging big trees back. Then the DS came back and said, 'Actually this is pretty good, but we've had some information from the locals that we're in a creek line and there's some rain coming, so it'll get washed away. We have to move 30 metres over there, but we can't take any of this with us. We have to build another one. And this time it has to have a roof on it.'

I was thinking, *Fuck this shit. By the time we've got this built, the sun will be up and we'll be sent on a new six-hour daytime task.*

There's a lot of psychology behind selection, but I think the quality they were testing, above the physical and mental and teamwork and all the rest of it, was simply our desire. I had the advantage of being totally pig-headed. I wanted to see what happened at the end. Why would I come all this way and not see what happens at the end? If I was going to remove myself from this course, it would have to be through a broken leg. I didn't want to give up just because I started doubting my own ability and confidence. Looking back, it's a really hard thing to push through. I thought, *I'm not gunna let that beat me. I'd rather break down physically than say, 'That's it, I'm done.'* It was always tempting to give up, but I knew I'd hate myself two hours later when I was sitting there thinking, *I let building a stick hut beat me.* I'd only be thinking of that, not the accumulation of things that had led up to it. I thought, *It's not going to last forever. I just have to not give up. If they don't remove me, I'm doing all right. If they take me out at the end or not, that's irrelevant, I have to get there.*

I had another advantage, in a perverse way. I had no warm, cosy family nest to go back to. I wasn't yearning for that, because it wasn't there. No girlfriend or wife, no parents, no family home to lure my mind away. It helped me not to have anyone or anything to go back to. I'm not saying there's nothing else I could have done with my life, but I wasn't wondering what my wife and kids were doing, what my mates were doing at the pub. There wasn't some beautiful world I was missing. I had left myself with only one way to go.

*

On the third day of Lucky Dip, we had to carry a baby goat in a crate. It got weird. The goat was called Bung, after a character in the Vietnam War film *The Odd Angry Shot.* We had to have a shrine and a prayer for Bung, and a teepee to put everyone under in the middle of the night. We were absolutely falling over we were so tired and hungry, and then we'd be told to get down on our knees in front of this goat and chant a prayer. It was almost enjoyable; it was so ridiculous I had to laugh, like I was delirious. And it still wasn't easy to make the teepee. By the end of the night, we'd built three half-made teepees and had fully finished one, and even then, when we were lying under it trying to get one hour's sleep at best, I remember looking up and thinking, *If this thing falls it's going to crush all of us.*

They were seriously messing with our minds now. The next task, carrying a fully inflated Zodiac with all its boards in, was all about frustrating us and seeing who would crack. The boat weighed about 120 kilos, which is not a lot, but we were so tired, and with guys of different heights throwing the boat out of balance so it never sat right on our packs and shoulders, trying to get it fast through bush that snagged and blocked it drove us crazy. We then had to get it across a dry riverbed on a pulley system, but fast, with a lot of random restrictions. I don't remember our patrol achieving any of the nebulous tasks properly, but that wasn't the point. They were watching how we behaved in the patrol group. Guys snapped, threw tantrums, burst into tears. One had a UD, or unlawful discharge, of his weapon. We were walking along and − *Bang!* − a round went off. They were only blanks, but it was a big deal. Everyone stopped. 'Who was that?' The DS all rushed over. It's a massive thing in the army to fire your weapon negligently anywhere, let alone on an SAS selection course. You'd be seen as lacking competence. It should never happen. The DS didn't do anything about it until that night, when they slipped in and quietly removed that candidate.

In the final part, it got more interactive, with scenarios involving conflict. We were in an 'enemy guerrilla camp', and were accused of hitting on the guerrilla chief's wife. In five minutes, we had to write a poem and deliver it to a woman in a veil. Mine went something like, 'Roses are red, violets are blue, if I had a wife like you, I'd be happy too.' My poetic creativity was never very high at the best of times.

They had us on the go all night. We did drill on the road: about turn, left turn, right turn, marching up and down. The bizarreness of it really challenged me. I was wanting to laugh like a madman. Then they'd tell us to build a chicken pen. We scrambled around, got the pen built. Then they told us to remove it and build it again a few metres away. This kind of thing went on all night.

As it went into the last days, the pace accelerated. In the morning, on no sleep, we had to carry some heavy weapons for six hours. Halfway there, we realised we hadn't remembered the yoke, a kind of support part on the tripod for the gun. So we had to carry all this stuff back to the beginning. It's awkward enough carrying the weapons in pieces down these dirt tracks, without having to do it twice. The frustration drove us spare.

Then we had to be inspected by the 'general' of the guerrilla camp. He had cardboard cut-outs on his shoulders and ridiculous tassels, like an Iraqi general under Saddam. We had to do slow marching past him, very slow, kicking our toes forward, eyes to the side, struggling to stay on balance with the heavy weapons on our shoulders.

For the next task, the nine or ten of us remaining in our section had to carry sixteen full water jerries to a dam, trudging through the bush. At the dam there were 44-gallon drums and ropes to make a raft out of, and we had to carry the water jerries and the DS across the dam without anything getting wet. I think our raft sank halfway across.

Throughout all of this was the constant hunger and tiredness, and getting bollocked by the DS. Amid the tasks, there was always something trivial to slow us down. If someone's pouches were open, they made him stand there while everyone else in the section did twenty push-ups. One of the blokes had lost his hat. The DS said, 'Right, that's it! You can't go anywhere until he gets a hat!'

We were saying, 'Nobody's got a spare hat.'

'Figure it out! Come up with something!'

We had little square bright-blue foam mats that we slept on. The hatless guy cut a hole in that and stuck it over his head. He walked along with his head sticking out of this blue square. The staff were pissing themselves, and so were we. Having a laugh was like getting a shot of some magic medicine, briefly.

It was getting dark on what we hoped was the last night, though we didn't trust them. They took us down the road and told the section commander to come over. A lot of hotboxes had been left there.

'Tell everyone to get their cups canteens out, there's some food for yous.'

In one container was half-cooked rice. We were allowed one spoonful each in the bottom of our cups canteens – the metal cup around our water bottle. The other box contained a boiled pig's head. The only meat on it was the cheeks and snout, and the ears. There were a lot of hairs on its head. We didn't care. I took the head out and put it on the lid and started cutting strips of meat off it. We were all tearing it apart. I put the snout aside for myself. It was fatty and rubbery but seemed like one of the best feeds I'd had in my life. I was still picking pig's hairs out of my teeth a while later.

When we'd finished, they lined us up and said, 'We're going to give you two items. Each individual has to eat them one at a time.'

They came along and put two sheep's eyeballs into each person's cups canteen. They stood and watched us eat them. We had to bite it and chew it and swallow it. Sheep's eyeballs explode in your mouth. I was that hungry, I didn't give a toss. I gagged a little bit, but wasn't going to throw up. The explosion in my mouth of all that warm blood was pretty disgusting. One guy couldn't hold it in – all this black blood and bits of eyeball were oozing out of his mouth and the DS were saying, 'Don't you dare throw up or you'll be off this course!'

They left us for an hour, and everyone lay around aching and sick. We'd devoured so much fat in a frenzy after not eating a thing that our bodies shut down, lacking the energy to digest it. We'd thought they were testing our ability to stomach something so disgusting, but maybe they'd been testing our ability to restrain ourselves.

We were sat in a big circle, and this bloke came in and spoke in a boring monotone, dead flat, no breaks between the sentences. He made a big pot of tea. It was hard to tell what he was about. He asked, 'If-you-could-be-anywhere-right-now-where-would-you-rather-be?' Everyone else said they'd like to be in a pub having a counter meal. I said I'd like to have a swim in the ocean – and then have a counter meal.

He droned, 'Righto-now-it's-time-to-get-back-to-work.'

We had to bury some 44-gallon drums as a cache in earth that was so hard-packed it was like rock. The DS said, 'You figure it out. Aren't you supposed to be able to use your initiative?'

Guys were racing around looking for star pickets or anything to dig with, but it basically came down to digging with our knives and cups canteens. All through the night we were lying on our sides, digging and scratching. All I could hear was *Tink! Tink!* At times we got swapped out to sit in the dark and do sentry. It was like a last act of inhumanity, putting us through something like we were old-time prisoners of war.

In the morning, that monotonous man was completely different, all bubbly and full of life, like he had bipolar. 'Come on, let's go for a run! Let's do some push-ups, sit-ups, get us moving in the morning!' Needless to say, it was the last thing we wanted to do. We came to a Land Rover that was weighed down with a load of heavy APC tracks. We had to push it for six or seven kilometres: up and down hills, on dirt tracks. It was another really tough task, and the DS capped it off after several hours by telling us to sit down. He jumped into the Rover and drove it off. That was demoralising.

Some Mogs drove up, and we were told to get on. Everyone just sat there, not trusting them.

'Come on, what are you doing?'

I didn't trust them either. Were they for real, or were the trucks going to drive off just before we got to them?

We got on. There were only eight left in our section of twelve. We were haggard and hollow-eyed, looking at each other thinking, *Is this the end of it?* One guy was saying, 'Nah, they're taking us to the next thing.'

We hit a tarred road. Were we done? I almost couldn't believe the possibility that we were at the finish line. A ration pack was sitting in the Mog. We started ripping it apart, hooking in. The bloke with the foam hat was hoeing into a pack of wet food, squeezing the last drops from above his head into his mouth. A filthy stench filled the cabin, and then he started vomiting out the back. The ration pack had been left in the sun, obviously, and this fish-flavoured feed had had a hole in it. I reckoned it was a set-up.

We got to the hangar at Bindoon, where we'd been standing nude three weeks before, and lined up behind another patrol. The DS started calling candidates out for a two- or three-minute chat.

'Private Donaldson. What's your cover story?'

Shit. I was trying to remember something I'd read for five minutes three weeks ago. I had remembered most of it, luckily. It was another nasty thing to do, make us feel comfortable and relieved about finishing, and then challenge our memory by taking us back to what seemed the least important thing in the whole course.

Of the original 120 to 140 candidates, about forty had made it to Lucky Dip. Now, we were down to twenty-eight. There was no fanfare or even a word of congratulation. The DS just said, matter-of-factly, 'Righto, fellas, stand up, there's a feed on over there, you're at the end of the selection course.'

They didn't tell us if we'd passed or failed. It was simply the end. They told us to shower and get some clean cams on. It wasn't exhilarating; it was weird, awkward. We were wondering if it wasn't just another trick. We loaded up the trucks. No one talked to us or said, 'Good on you.' Just, 'Get on the buses and go back to Swanbourne [Campbell Barracks].' On the way back, most slept. Some were cracking tired jokes. I managed to squeeze a bit of sleep in and mostly wondered if I'd done enough to be selected. At Swanbourne we had to clean up our stuff, go to our rooms, have dinner and be back at the DS office by eight o'clock the next morning. The emotional flatness of it all was unnerving, like they wanted to puncture any sense of achievement.

I phoned Brent and said, 'Yeah, I've finished it, but I don't know if I've been selected or not.' I rang Margaret and Ross and Val. I think they were pretty proud. I told them I'd lost six kilos. Some had lost up to 12 or 15 kilos.

We were walking around like emaciated ghosts. We gorged ourselves in the mess and some of us were sick again that night. Blokes' feet had swollen up and they couldn't walk for a couple of days. My toes were numb for four or five weeks. I had a hell of a lot of chafing on my back, but over-all suffered from soreness rather than injuries.

It's only been recently, when I've worked as DS, that I've seen how scientific it is behind the scenes. Every activity has a thorough briefing on what the Regiment wants to see in terms of initiative, teamwork, aggression, weapon handling and other attributes. The DS make notes on a slip in red or blue pen, with the reasons why, and the slips go into a big bin to be sorted out at the end, when the DS convene to talk about what was good, what was bad, should they keep or lose this candi-date. It's very rigorous, but even then, they don't always get it right.

*

At eight o'clock the next morning, we had to clean some weapons. A few guys were getting called out for extra interviews. There was an officer who'd made it through selection, and after this interview, he came back to us, shattered. He looked like he'd been crying.

'I've come to say goodbye, boys, I'm out of here tonight. I didn't get through.'

We were stunned. After he left, everyone was quiet. Someone said, 'Ah, fucken hell.' Even though we'd been told it might happen, it was a shock that after we'd got through selection, they were still telling candidates they hadn't made it.

A couple of others got pulled out. Then the DS called everyone remaining into an annexe and said, 'Righto, welcome, you've all passed.'

And that was it. No one-on-ones, no being called to the office, just a terse group announcement.

Then: 'Except for you, Private Palmer. Come and see us.'

He just went, 'Aw, get fucked.'

They turned around and said, 'Nah, only joking, mate.'

Maybe the last part of the test was knowing when to laugh.

FIFTEEN

We had four days off, including a weekend. The Regiment did everything they could to deflate any sense of pride or satisfaction we might feel. One of the things they told us before we went out was, 'Don't go down to the pub telling everyone you're in the SAS. You've done nothing. You've only done the first step. You've got another twelve to fourteen months of training ahead of you. All you've done is a course that tells us you might be suitable for extra training. Get that into your heads right now. This is where it starts. All you've done is walk in the front door.'

Try as they might to take the wind out of our sails, when we hit Perth we had a good time. We still didn't know each other well, but that's the way the army is. We were on an understandable high; it was also weird being back in society, especially in a city I didn't know, after three weeks in the bush. My head was spinning, and then I collapsed into sleep. Some of the guys racked out for fourteen or fifteen hours.

At eight o'clock on Monday morning, we were thrown straight into a Special Forces weapons course, the first stage of the twelve-month Reinforcement Cycle, or 'Reo'. My rank was now trooper, as it is for all enlisted men when they join the SAS, no matter what their rank was beforehand. Obviously for me, having been a private, this wasn't much of a comedown! But to level everybody off like this is an important statement from the Regiment, that we're all starting again from the bottom, no matter what we did before.

Reo gave me that first-day-at-a-new-school feeling again. We had to do a lot of reading for each course, and then lock it away and try to make room for more information. The SF weapons course ran for two weeks, before a six-week patrol course. The core of how the SAS operates is the five-man team. The Regiment began as a long-range recon group, dropping in behind enemy lines, gathering intelligence and getting out without ever being seen. It used to hang its hat on reconnaissance. You had to learn how to walk through the bush quietly, using cover and shadows. Sometimes you go as little as 500–700 metres in a day, often stopping and standing still for long periods. It's hard to walk like that all day, and takes a lot of patience. You had to learn the lay-up position (LUP), which was four blokes sitting with their backs to each other, the shoulder turned in, each scanning a 90-degree arc with his weapon. The patrol commander (PC) sat in the middle, receiving and dispensing information. It was good for me because I hadn't done a recon course, hadn't done snipers, hadn't been in the battalion for four years like the others. For me it was all new. I always had to work extra hard to keep up and was never anywhere near the top of the class. For the more experienced ones, the challenge was that the standards required were a lot higher than where they'd come from.

One key difference from the battalion, which I really thrived on, was that they made sense of each skill. In the battalion, if you were taught to move slowly in patrol, it was just a task you had to do. In the Regiment, you were told that it was because you were in a high-enemy-threat area, and had to take everything in during your scans. Being such a small element, you had to use stealth, cunning and awareness to be in front of the enemy's thought process. Everything was tailored to the scenario you found yourself in. In the weapons course, we did a lot of live fire, blowing up Claymores – 700 grams of explosives with ball bearings inside. I'd done Claymore ambushes in the army before, but these instructors made sense of it, explaining specifically how to protect ourselves. Likewise, in the patrol course we had to take our time to pick our route, scan our arcs, find the enemy fire positions, stick to all the shadows we could find – all useful skills in themselves but doubly enjoyable because the reasons for them were fully explained.

And it had results. At the end of each course we did a full mission profile (FMP), where we had to combine the skills we'd learnt into a complex jungle-war-fighting scenario. In a camouflage exercise, we had to walk through an area scanning the bush, and if we spotted anyone from another patrol, they had to stand up. Sometimes we walked on top of a bloke before seeing him. I remember thinking, *They aren't kidding, it actually works.*

There were funny moments on that patrol course. Silence being the be all and end all, in one of the patrols, a guy named Baz decided to do a loud fart. A DS came over and said, 'That was too loud.' He looked at the rest of the patrol sniggering and said, 'Flatulence isn't funny.' Baz had his name written down – 'Found flatulence funny while passing wind on patrol.'

It could be awkward if you were on patrol and your guts were falling out. The rule was, when you needed to do a shit you couldn't go more than one metre away from your LUP. You did it into a plastic bag and took it out with you. On our patrol, one guy did his shit and then dropped his plastic bag onto my pack. We started chucking it from bloke to bloke. This was after a rainy seven-day patrol at the end of the course. We were getting a bit silly because we were near the end.

But the lighter moments were a reaction to the ongoing tension. One of the big shocks on the Reo was when people started getting kicked off. The patrol course culled those who weren't picking things up quickly enough. They weren't sent back to square one, having to do selection again. They might get sent to Singleton for a twelve-week infantry patrol course, or have to go to infantry for a year, but they could come back and enter the patrol course the next year.

It was surprising who dropped out. We had this hard old bugger who never wore socks. He watered his boots in olive oil. Fuck, it stank. Everyone in his room hated it. On the patrol course, out of nowhere he said he was quitting.

I said, 'What do you mean, mate? You've done all this hard work to get here and now you're talking about pulling the pin?'

'Yep, but Donno, this isn't what I thought it was. I thought it'd be different.'

I thought, *Mate, why throw it away after all that hard work without knowing how it's going to turn out?* We didn't know how life in the actual Regiment was going to be. We were still only in Reo. But he was gone that afternoon. I guess there could have been other factors. You don't know what people have going on in their lives outside the Regiment. Another advantage I had was a very uncomplicated life outside, though that was to change soon enough.

We got instant feedback after the courses. A senior instructor (SI) said to me after the patrol course, 'We think you've done okay. Don't let this go to your head. There's guys that are good and guys that are really good. It's a long Reinforcement Cycle, so keep working.'

I was thinking, *I'm just happy I've got through another course.*

We did the Special Forces rope course, which was a lot of fun, over two weeks: how to fast rope, how to rappel with your pack on out of a helicopter, suspended rope extractions, roping off buildings. These skills reminded me of the books I'd read about the SAS's activities in Vietnam, such as Terry O'Farrell's *Behind Enemy Lines*, and again they were integrating it with scenarios that made it all the more enjoyable, and encouraged us to use our brains in ways the battalion hadn't deemed necessary.

The next course would be the basic parachute course, over in Nowra, south of Sydney. We'd be flying across on the Monday night, so we hit it hard on the Sunday night, at the Little Creatures Brewery at Fremantle. One of my Reo mates rang up a girl he knew from the signals section at work, and she was bringing a friend of hers.

At two or three o'clock in the afternoon, we were sitting back and he said, 'They're almost here, Donno.' I remember my eyes kind of skating over his girl and going straight to her friend. As she walked through the door a voice in my head said, *Mate, you're in trouble here.*

I'd never had that feeling before. Of course, she came and sat right next to me. Emma was a communications worker at the Regiment. I'd seen her a couple of times but hadn't spoken to her. A slim, tall blonde, she was a bit of a knockout. She was really funny, making me laugh by taking the piss out of the bloke I was with. We had a lot of laughs. But that voice kept saying, *You're in trouble here.*

The group was wanting to move on, but I just wanted to stay and get to know her better. For me, that was really out of character, to break ranks for a girl. She had to go to work the next day, but decided to come with us to this nightclub. She and I went up to the bar at one point for me to order a round of bourbon and cokes for all the others.

She turned to me and said, 'I've never done this, but I've got to go now. Do you want to come to my place?'

I gave her a look.

She said quickly, 'Nothing's going to happen. I just want to go back home.'

I looked at the eight bourbon and cokes I'd ordered. My mates were over to the side. I looked at the bourbons, looked back at her, at the bourbons, at her, and her smile was starting to freeze up.

'Nah, I think I'll stay here and keep drinking with my mates.'

The smile went off her face. 'Fine then, I'm going.' She turned and stormed off.

Once I was sitting with the boys again, I was telling myself, *Smart move. She'd be nothing but trouble.* But I was finding it hard to keep up with the banter. This conflict kept going in my head about that girl.

Around midnight, my mate and I were on our way home, going past the apartment where his friend and Emma were staying.

He said, 'Donno, let's pull up here and see what they're up to.'

'No, let's go. It's midnight.'

We were pissed and had to get some rest before flying to Nowra. But he insisted. I was really thirsty and found one of those huge water-cooler bottles on the ground floor of the apartment block. I picked it up and lugged it behind him up the stairs. It was about half-past midnight when he thumped on the door. Emma came to answer it. My mate said, 'Hey, we're staying here the night.' He nodded over his shoulder towards me and said, 'I brought this as well.'

Swaying about, with the water bottle on my shoulder, I walked in. 'Hey, how you going?'

She stood there and watched as I put it down in the lounge room and said, 'Where's your bedroom?'

She laughed. 'That's a bit forward, isn't it?'

'Nah, I need to go to sleep.' She showed me into her bedroom, and I passed out right there.

That was how we met.

*

Emma had been at the Regiment for about a year, having been in Brisbane and then Townsville, though not at the same time as me. She'd joined the military after high school, planning to stay for a year or two, and ended up in it for thirteen. Rather than take the career path to sergeant, she'd chosen to go to Perth to do a Special Forces signals course. She was in the support staff for the SAS, the group who set up and maintained communications for new operations. Within the SAS, there's a large group of support staff in various roles who don't have to do the selection course, a trial reserved for those who are to become frontline SAS soldiers, or 'operators'.

In the few hours we had together that Sunday and Monday, I remembered something Kelvin had said, up at Wooli, while we were sitting at his place after a surf. He and his wife were stirring each other up, talking about how you know if you've fallen in love. They were teasing me about being a free agent, and I was saying, 'Nup, not me, no family, kids just hold you back. I just want to surf for the rest of my life.'

Kelvin's wife said, 'You know when you know, don't you, Kelvin?'

'What are you talking about?'

'You knew when we first met that I was the one.'

'Nah, I didn't know that until I married you.'

I was laughing. When she went inside, I said to Kelvin, 'Did you know?'

He said, 'Mate, I knew within the first five minutes. Trust me, you'll know.'

I never believed it happened that way any more, and certainly not to me, but it did. The silly old bugger was right.

It was definitely good luck to fall in love *after* I'd joined the Regiment. It can be hard for people who form relationships, and then go into the SAS and find that their life is turned upside down. At least Emma understood what it meant to be with someone in the Regiment. Men who have a successful time with their partners are generally the ones who can communicate with them. If you don't talk to your partner, and you find yourself just saying, 'I'm leaving for a couple of weeks tomorrow, can't say where or when I'll be back,' and leave it at that, that's when you can have a problem. It's all about communicating.

That doesn't necessarily mean Emma accepts it. My friends would often tell me how awesome it must be to have a wife in the military; it's called going for the 'in-house discount'. But in the decade that's passed since we met, we've had kids, Emma's left the Regiment, and real life is not just an add-on to military life. It's a concrete, ongoing reality, and the demands of work over the next few years would pull me in the opposite direction. It's not easy, and while Emma's military background has helped, it's by no means a cure-all. The best way I can put it is to say she understands when work takes me away from home, but she doesn't necessarily accept it.

*

I wouldn't be able to see Emma again until after the six-week parachute course at Nowra. I'd only ever done a tandem jump before, and parachuting was a buzz. Guys were still getting culled, and some injured their knees or broke a leg, which could set them back twelve months. I was single-minded about getting through: I only wanted to do this once before becoming an operator.

We went to Townsville, where I could finally pack up all my stuff, and then moved over to Perth. I had four or five days with Emma down south, which was our time to really get to know each other. During those six weeks I'd been thinking about her a lot. It was amazing what an impression she'd left on me.

Meanwhile, the pace of the Reo courses was unrelenting: heavy weapons, demolitions and either a patrol signaller or medic course. SAS operators all have a basic trade, which is either as medics or signallers. There's little choice. They got a list and went down the line of us: 'Medic, sig, medic, sig,' and so on, splitting us in half. If you really wanted to do one rather than the other, you could kick up a stink or find someone who wanted to swap. I was happy either way. For me, I got a six-week signals course. Being a sig is an easier course but harder out in the field. Being a medic, the course is much more intensive, but out in the field it's easy unless someone gets hurt or sick. As a sig, you're working all the time. In a five-man team you're in charge of communicating back to base, which may be hundreds of kilometres away.

I got into some trouble towards the end of the survival course. We had to walk 30–40 kilometres to a base camp and then wait. We broke into ten groups of three, and walked all night. When we got there, instead of waiting outside, some of the guys snuck into the camp where the DS were sitting around the fire having a feed and a few beers. They didn't realise one of our blokes was hiding under a table. He snuck off with a five-man ration pack, which is quite a large box full of rations. He found the patrols and started dishing out food. In the morning, the DS found us hoeing into it. They almost went to the point of sacking us. We got a lecture about poor performance in getting caught – which was more of a misdemeanour than taking the rations. Some of those who got away with it also owned up, but they were told, 'We don't care. You didn't get caught.'

Guys continued to get failed on the close quarters battle (CQB) course, which included hand-to-hand combat. The standards were extremely high, and I was among the last three to get through the pistol-shooting component. Some are naturals, but I was one of the ones who took some time. The instruction these days is much better; during my course I was just told, 'Sort it out,' or 'Lock on, mate.' A big part of the course was not just shooting, however, but how to fight through a building to rescue hostages and kill terrorists. That part I really enjoyed, and still do. There's a lot of reward in taking down a building as a team. The quick decisions can result in life or death. You need a high level of situational awareness, or knowing where you and your weapon are in relation to your teammates, the hostages and the enemy. The principles I learnt on that course and the patrol course gave me the base level for understanding success and survivability in combat. A great quote I once heard, which rings pretty true in these environments, is: 'It is very noble to die for your country, but don't give it to him on a silver platter. Do everything you can to make him die for his instead.'

There was a phase of urban fighting, which involved complex scenarios with IEDs (improvised explosive devices), enemy fighters behind barricades and the like, partly based on procedures we'd learnt from the Americans. I was in my element moving between buildings and shooting on the move. I put a lot of pressure on myself and found my confidence increasing. It was hard, with a lot of PT throughout the courses to break us down, but by this stage I was confident I was going to get through. To give us a boost, they had formally posted us to the Regiment. Even though we didn't have our sandy berets, we were allowed to call ourselves SAS troopers now.

Late in 2004, I bought a house at Willagee, down the south end of Perth, and Emma and I moved in together. We weren't mucking about. In the Regiment I was paid far better than in the infantry, and having owned nothing my whole life, I overcompensated by buying a big four-bedroom place the pair of us rattled around in. It was fun, though, to have some time off. We had an orphans' Christmas with some others who didn't have anywhere else to go, and walked to the beach every morning with our new dog, a bull-mastiff-ridgeback cross Emma had bought from a pet shop. When I'd left Dorrigo, my old dog Lister had gone to live with the Beaumonts and then with a family in the Bellinger Valley, and had a good life until he died in 2009. This dog, though, was a menace – it got narky with Emma, chewed off part of the side of the house and gave us a bit of grief.

Back at work, I did a driver's course to drive army cars, which you had to do even if you already had a licence. We followed that with our patrol insertion courses. Again, there were specialties for insertion: you could choose between land, air and water. There was a myth that the wateries were the hardest blokes in the Regiment, but I just liked the idea of diving, coming off submarines and climbing up the sides of ships. Those days I'd spent watching Dad scuba diving, going snorkelling with him, and later, the time of my surfing obsession, had left me with a special affinity for water. The risk of becoming a watery was that they were known for having high standards, and for being punishing, quite judgemental, on their rookies.

The wateries' course started with two weeks of boating, which was hard because you had to de-service your kit every night to have it ready the next morning. The motto was 'de-service or die'. If you didn't keep it functional, it would break down on you in the ocean, which is a bad place for that to happen. So after days of PT, going out in big swells around Rottnest Island and learning all the boating techniques, we'd be up until one or two o'clock in the morning pulling apart and cleaning the engines and other gear. The DS would come up and say, 'Hurry up, you're in your own time,' and then make you start again if there was a grain of sand in there. It was like selection again.

The exercises themselves were challenging but fun. We did a parachute drop, taking our boats with us. We hit the water, swam to the rafts, unrolled them from their bundle or cut them from their pallet if they were already inflated, hooked up our fuel lines, pumped the rafts up a bit more, and got underway. We then had to do a 60–nautical mile transit to an island, and send a swimmer-scout to recce it and find a landing spot on the beach. This was all under the cover of darkness. When landing, we dragged everything up onto the beach, dug a hole and buried it. Then, with our pack and gun, we were off to conduct the task.

I was excited when we got to the diving phase. Much as I loved the water, I'd never scuba dived. The first time, it was a matter of coping with the overflow of information when I went under the water. We did two pool dives on air sets – compressed air breathing apparatus (CABA) – and our first night dive was straight into the ocean. It was overwhelming initially. The noise of the bubbles and the inky blackness and the thick shiny phosphorescence got my heart and breathing rate so high I was chewing through my air and had to check my gauge.

After seven days of that, we did our free ascent training in an 18-metre-deep pool. If you take air in at depth, as you rise the gas expands relative to the decreasing pressure. If you keep that air in, your lungs will explode. That's what had killed an SAS trooper, David O'Callaghan, during a training exercise in Bass Strait in 1982. We had to learn how to let it out slowly. It wasn't too hard, but was another hurdle: if you didn't master it, you couldn't progress. We followed that with closed-circuit breathing, which is using an oxygen cylinder, soda lime and a scrubber canister to recycle your air and create no bubbles. For us, trying to escape detection, it's an important skill.

We were taught how to navigate under the water, keeping our bearings, time and distance in a complicated exercise. Then, in the tactical phase, wearing body armour and carrying guns and climbing equipment, we practised going up the side of a ship or the pillars of an oil rig. We dived as a team, launching off our craft and swimming with poles, steel-wire ladders, grappling hooks with ropes and a set of Jumars (ascenders), and put ropes around a pylon in accordance with specific timings. At the signal from the PC, we closed our circuits, breathed out and came to the surface, making sure we didn't blow our lungs. We had our weapons up and ready to fight. Then we hooked our ladders onto the target and climbed up.

I loved that war-ish stuff, and it was a thrill to think we were going to go off and do it rather than spend our careers in a peacetime army. In 2005, though, the Regiment was in limbo when it came to assignments. Their work in Afghanistan had ended in 2002 and in Iraq in 2004. There was a big exodus of SAS troopers to the private security sector. The Regiment hadn't committed back to Afghanistan so when I came out of Reo in April 2005, we were in that in-between period.

But that was not on our minds when we had our beret parade. It was held in the gym at Swanbourne, and was run by the Governor-General, Michael Jeffery, who had been a commanding officer of the Regiment in the early days. I'd had a great year with the guys on my course. The Regiment used to keep patrol strength – maintain the same small teams – for years. Nowadays, it's much busier and patrols are mixed up, so you don't have that same continuity and camaraderie, which means the bond you develop with the comrades on your Reo cycle can be the strongest of your whole time in the Regiment.

I had Uncle Ken and Auntie Margaret come over, and was as proud as could be. I still had *The Sentinel* in my wallet, and the articles I'd collected from September 11. Now I was getting the coveted winged dagger badge. It was as if I could now stand my ground alongside that picture in my wallet.

I was pleased to have got to this point less than three years after turning up at Kapooka, although there was an embarrassing moment where my inexperience was shown up. Some others on my Reo cycle had done a lot in the army, including going to Iraq and Afghanistan. When we were called up to receive our berets, our military biographies were read out: 'So-and-so has been to Iraq, Afghanistan, East Timor', naming the units they'd been with. Then it was: 'Trooper Mark Donaldson. 1RAR. Enlisted 2002.' And silence. Walking the full length of the basketball court, amid the empty echoes of my inexperience, was something I'll never forget!

There was no silence at the crucial moment in the official photo we had taken in front of the Gratwick Club, the soldiers' boozer at Campbell Barracks, affectionately known as the Gratto. We were out on the lawn, overlooking Rottnest Island, lined up in a big group. The Governor-General and senior officers joined us. *Smile!*

It's not your average photo. Some of the people are making disgusted faces, the officers are cringing, and most of us are fighting back laughter. Julian, whose speciality in Reo was doing the loudest fart at the most inappropriate time – say, when a particularly disliked DS was giving a lesson, or out on that patrol course – had just delivered. I love that photo, which shows us all reacting. All except for one, that is. The Governor-General is completely unfazed, a serene smile on his face. He didn't say a word, just carried on. I guess that was his training kicking in!

SIXTEEN

Since joining the army, I'd often felt like I was on my first day at a new school, but nothing was quite like this. When I took my paperwork to 3 Squadron, my new home, I was told to grab a shopping trolley and go to the squadron Q store. When I got there, they said I could take whatever I wanted. Body armour, gas masks, pouches, boots, flush hoods, helmets, you name it; there was more in that Q store than in the whole infantry. The Q-ies at the battalion made you sign for everything, begrudging even a water bottle and warning you against losing one. Here, they were much looser about signing for things. They trusted you.

The flipside of being treated as a grown-up was that you weren't pandered to in any way. Each squadron had about seventy-five personnel, divided into three troops: land, water and free-fall. Within each troop, there were four patrols of five operators each, and also an officer, a sergeant and a signaller. On top of that, each squadron had another fifteen to twenty staff in operations support, intelligence, signals and admin. I was put into 3 Squadron as one of their wateries. I knew a few of the others from rugby, which I'd begun playing on weekends during Reo. Guys from work used to play for a local club in the Perth competition. Because they couldn't be regularly available, they played in fourth grade, but they were much better than that. The opposition used to hate it when the Regiment guys turned up for a game. That year, we went through undefeated and won the grand final. So knowing some in the squadron was good, but it was still 'Hey, Rookie', with the implied threat that you had to prove yourself or else. I was constantly on my toes.

3 Squadron was on call for domestic counterterrorism, which meant we were on very short notice to go anywhere in Australia. On the first Friday night, I was out getting pissed to celebrate finishing Reo; on the Sunday night we were called out for a national exercise and were put on a Herc to Adelaide. It happened that quickly.

The exercise, involving police, fire brigade, ambulance and emergency services, was held at the Edinburgh RAAF base and then at a warehouse in town. According to the scenario, hostages had been taken and police were nego-tiating. We were there to be called in for the worst-case scenario, the last resort. Our operation was based on the British SAS assault on the Iranian Embassy in London. I enjoyed being part of what was clearly a professional opera-tion in a different league. Emma was there too, having been attached to 3 Squadron as a signaller, one of the few times we could work in the same place.

We were about to head home when they gathered us in and said, 'There's an Australian who's been taken hostage in Iraq, and we're going to send two patrols over.' We were all excited, and Emma and I were asking each other if we knew who was going. In the end they picked one land and one water patrol, but not ours. The hostage was the businessman

Douglas Wood. Even though I missed out, it made me realise how quickly I could be on a plane to Iraq, or anywhere else for that matter. The ones who came into the Regiment after having been to Iraq or Afghanistan were more battle-ready. They knew the feelings they'd get when they went outside the wire. Inexperienced, I just wanted to go and be part of it. The whole reason I'd joined was to be in this group and go away, get in a fight, and test myself and see how I handled things under fire. No amount of training is going to simulate the real thing. For me that keenness to get into a firefight, just to see how I'd go, was building. I thought I was ready. I just wanted to have a go. When I look back, all I can see is a young, naïve kid who thinks he's ready but really doesn't have a clue what's waiting for him. That's not a criticism of junior soldiers; it's just that being in combat changes you and tests you in ways you can never anticipate.

*

Late in 2005, my PC told me I would be needed for a personal security detail (PSD). The chief of army, prime minister and defence minister were going on separate trips to Iraq and Afghanistan, and the government had already sent one of the SAS squadrons back into Afghanistan. Things were heating up.

I was stoked to have been chosen, and rang Emma. She was happy for me, but with mixed feelings, because we'd just got some news of our own. She was pregnant. I got into my training. It was a quick build-up period, and we had to practise skills with some new fellows from other squadrons. I was getting more and more excited until, two days before I left, Emma had a miscarriage.

If you haven't anticipated it, or been close to someone it's happened to, it's very hard to comprehend what a trauma a miscarriage is. Emma was ten or twelve weeks pregnant, and of course I'd heard how common they were, but nothing prepared me for the grief she was feeling. She didn't want me to go away, and it was difficult. I was trying to say, 'This is something I've worked for for a long time, and they're depending on me.' She thought I was choosing work over her. I didn't see it like that. They'd asked me to go, and if I turned it down, I thought that would be it, my career would be over.

We eventually worked our way through it, under the pressure of a 48-hour deadline. I went away, feeling I had let her down but unable to do differently. I wished I could have stayed around. But the timing wasn't mine to control, and I was a newcomer; I didn't feel I could ask to stay out of an operation. Looking back, maybe I could have, but being a rookie I was highly keyed up and didn't feel I had the power to make a personal request.

The first PSD was for the Chief of Army, General Peter Leahy. Two weeks ahead of him, we flew in a chartered passenger jet into a controlled Kuwaiti air base. I looked down on thirty or forty big concrete bunkers left over from the first Gulf War. Every one of them had been hit by a bomb of some description. I thought it was good that they'd been left there, as a stark reminder to inexperienced soldiers like me that we weren't here for a harmless adventure.

When we stepped off the plane, we were hit by a wall of heat. I'd never experienced anything like it. I had felt the heat in Townsville and out in remote Western Australia in the summer, but this was the driest heat I had ever been in. The hot wind mixed with the searing earth was bad enough but when it gusted hot, dry sand into all open spaces it was close to unbearable. We were bundled onto a bus, air-conditioned fortunately, and were shouted at by an army guy. The place was ringed with American checkpoints, and we had to wait in two-kilometre lines. Every vehicle, military and civilian, was being checked. It was our first impression of the size of the American operation.

We zipped into Kuwait City in our own cars for a look around. There was nothing around the base but sandhills as far as the eye could see. The Kuwaitis drove like madmen. We were going 140 kilometres per hour on a freeway, and cars were overtaking us easily, including a ute with a camel standing in the back!

Our two weeks of reconnaissance and training included a few days at a rifle range run by Sandy, a crusty US soldier who'd been there since the first Gulf War. He was a classic southern-states American, chewing tobacco the whole time, setting up the targets for us. Our exercise involved being ambushed. We were driving as a two-car packet in a couple of American Chevys, big V8 town cars. The top priority was to get the VIP out to the safe house, and those of us who were left had to fight our way out.

We ran the drill as usual, a dry run first, without bullets, and then a live fire exercise. I was driving the first car, which got hit. I pulled up where I was supposed to, and the VIP got moved to the second car. I went around to the back of the first car as the second reversed up to get the VIP out of there. It reversed, and then stopped with a jerk. Then it sped off. I was firing at targets with a machine gun.

All of a sudden people were yelling out, 'Stop! Stop! Stop!'

When someone yells 'Stop!' on a range, you know something's gone wrong. I turned and looked. The second car was 30–50 metres away and I could see someone under it. By the time we got over there, they were calling for a med kit. The guy I was with was saying, 'Fuck, fuck, fuck.' Sandy came running over, asking what the hell was going on. The driver of the second car had jumped out to look underneath, and now he was just sitting down, in shock, with another bloke looking after him.

We took a look and saw our warrant officer, Dave Nary, trapped under the car. I could instantly tell it was bad by the position he was in.

After getting the jack out, we tried to lift the car so the medic could have access to Dave. We tried to chock up the jack with blocks of wood so it wouldn't sink. We dug into the sand to get some access. The medic was checking Dave's vitals, but said he couldn't feel a pulse. We called for an AME – aeromedical evacuation – and the chopper was on its way.

The AME landed through some purple smoke. An American doctor jumped out and climbed under the car. A few seconds later he came back out and said, 'That's it, he's dead. There's nothing I can do.'

Every time we tried to lift the car to get him free it just wasn't working. In the end one of the senior men said, 'Leave it, that's enough.'

We just sat around and started trying to come to grips with it. We got Dave's body armour off him and put his gun to one side. The driver, who was badly shaken up, was taken away from the range. Eventually they lifted the car with a forklift and cut Dave out. He was very experienced and well liked, and we were all rocked. When we got back to our accommodation I helped one of the guys pack Dave's gear so we could send it home to his family. It is never a nice thing to do. It was not the last time I would find myself doing it, either. We hadn't even done the task and someone had died. No one had died on a PSD before, either in the real thing or in training.

A decision was made not to bring us home or swap out the team. They replaced Dave with a new warrant officer, and we carried on. When Peter Leahy arrived, he took us into a room and said, 'I understand you guys have gone through some stuff recently and I appreciate what you're doing for us. I'm sure he was a good man and he'll be respected appropriately back at home.' He kept it low-key, and it was good to have such a senior person still trusting us to look after him.

*

The type of PSD we were doing wasn't overly difficult, but with a VIP of that stature, if something went wrong it went wrong big-time. The replacement warrant officer, Fergs, went down the line shaking everybody's hand, and when he shook mine I felt him slip me something. It was two packets of cigarette papers, courtesy of Emma. I'd started smoking again, after a break of several years, since I'd been in the Regiment. That's not uncommon, but it might seem anomalous, considering the emphasis on physical fitness. Later I gave up smoking – to take up dipping, or chewing tobacco, with a vengeance, but I only did that when I was away. The things that you get into during a war can be unnecessary at home. Over the years, I developed a whole series of habits, such as growing a beard, taking a lax approach to personal hygiene, listening to certain music, and developing a highly questionable sense of humour, as well as dipping, that I wouldn't dream of bringing into my home life. When you're away in a combat zone you become almost a different person, as a way of dealing with the stress and fitting in with your mates, so that coming home isn't just a matter of adjusting to the needs of your family, but also of switching back to your non-combat self.

Six to eight of us were in the detail to go ahead of General Leahy to Tallil Air Base in Iraq. We linked up with the Australian battle group that was already at Camp Smitty, near Samarra. This was where I ran into my old sergeant from infantry training. We tried to blend in, but we stood out, being new faces without name tags or Australian flags on our cams. The base was enormous, surrounded by checkpoints with a lot of procedures to do with unloading weapons before getting through the gate. I felt they were overcomplicating it with three or four weapons-readiness processes. No wonder they had so many unlawful discharges. Then again, a lot of people were coming in and out who didn't touch weapons much of the time, and that could be quite dangerous.

General Leahy was going from one secure base to another in a Bushmaster, a big armoured vehicle, and we had to stick right behind him wherever he went. Because I suffered from motion sickness, I threw a headset on and got up into the hatch with the gunner. I wanted to see the landscape, too. Iraq was a lot dirtier than Kuwait, with rubbish on the side of the road and less infrastructure. There were open sewers, mongrel dogs, walls riddled with pockmarks. Kids were throwing stones at us as we drove past, though generally the roads were pretty good and everyone knew to get out of a military convoy's way. The women were fully covered. What was eye-opening to me was that little girls of ten or eleven could run around like normal, and then at puberty they were covered up. By the river there were kids with a donkey and a big flat cart. They were whipping the shit out of the donkey, which was bellowing in pain. I remember thinking, *You wouldn't get that in Australia. These kids must have grown up in a tough environment.*

The key problem we had to watch out for was an IED followed by small-arms fire. I was scanning around, watching vehicles coming alongside, taking note of parked cars and passing this information to the guys below. I was thinking, *This is what you do your training for.* Everywhere, I was seeing good spots from which to shoot up a convoy. This culvert – they could hide in there. Those long reeds – they could get away through those. All these possibilities were going through my mind.

General Leahy had to go across the Euphrates into Samarra for a meeting, and then he wanted to see an abattoir where the Iraqi Army used to torture and kill prisoners. It was now being secured by Australians and reopened as an abattoir, putting life into the local community. We had to go up a very tight street. I was out of the hatch, with buildings very close on both sides, and I said on the radio, 'If anything happens in here we're stuck. We can't turn the cars. We'll have to reverse out or break into a house.' We came out into a big roundabout, where the abattoir stood. I was sitting on the roof while the chief went in, and was looking down an alleyway towards some kids in their early teens mucking around. A power pole with thick wires was in my way, and I was only catching glimpses of them. They were near an Iraqi police post, a makeshift hut with some sandbags. One of the kids looked a bit like he was holding a gun.

I said to my mate, 'Is that an AK–47?'

We agreed it didn't look right. It might have just been a toy gun. I was waiting for them to do something. I wasn't on a hair trigger, and wasn't that nervous that I might have fired; it was more that I couldn't quite believe that this was happening. Was it a real gun? Was I now in a world where kids would shoot real AKs at you? Suddenly anything seemed possible. Then they ran off down an alleyway. I thought, *You could get yourself killed playing with toy guns here!*

*

The chief was going from Iraq to Afghanistan. We flew back to Kuwait and then on to Uruzgan province, where the Australian contingent had its main base in the town of Tarin Kowt. Uruzgan has about the size and population of the Australian Capital Territory, but Canberra it ain't. The population is 97 per cent rural and almost 100 per cent illiterate, farming in the green belts that run down between the towering mountain ranges and barren *dasht*, or desert. More than a kilometre above sea level, Uruzgan is strategically positioned between the former Taliban strongholds of Kandahar and Helmand provinces to the west, and Pakistan and the tribal areas to the east. Tarin Kowt is the capital of the province, and we would operate there and in three other areas, around the towns of Deh Rawod to the west, Chora to the north, and the Khaz Uruzgan area to the east. The north of the province was more mountainous and desolate as the land began to rise towards the Hindu Kush, while the south and west were more flat and open, with plenty of farmland in symmetrical gridded paddocks that resembled, in my mind, the wheat belt of western and southern New South Wales.

With the focus of the War on Terror shifting from Iraq back to Afghanistan, Australia was just starting to take responsibility for Uruzgan. I was excited to be going to Afghanistan, even without the slightest hint of how important and familiar the country was going to become. When we landed in Tarin Kowt, the wind was blowing from the east and the first thing that hit me was the stench from the rubbish tip outside the base. A strong smell of burnt plastic got into the nostrils and stayed there. When we ventured out into the town, Tarin Kowt had that south-Asian urban aroma of stale water, rotting garbage, food spices, sewage and diesel fuel. Even though it's not a big city, a smoggy diesel smell always settled over TK, like the old diesel vehicles I remembered from the 1970s.

It was November and there was snow on the mountains, while the streets had turned into mud and cold slush. The base, on the southern side of the city, was primitive: green army tents and only ration packs to eat aside from one hot meal every second day. The base was about half the size of the town itself, and at that point contained about 2000 personnel: American Special Forces, the Australian SOTG, and a small Dutch contingent.

There was a feeling we were in a fortress. The base's perimeter was made of HESCO barriers: big cubes, about head high, made of galvanised metal caging. They were filled with dirt, which was held in by a fine mesh, and then each cube was blocked along and linked together around the perimeter, with barbed wire along the top. At intervals there were wooden overhead guard boxes, sandbagged, with machine gunners inside. All of the forward operating bases (FOBs) around Afghanistan were constructed in much the same way.

Some of my mates from Reo were already there, and told us about a big contact they'd been in in the 'badlands' around Bagh Koshak, where they were attacked by a large Taliban force. I was fascinated to hear their stories. One guy had had his earmuffs shot off. A rocket-propelled grenade (RPG) had hit the radiator in their car and not gone off. One of the blokes had bullet holes in his car seat, which had been made as he bent down to pick up some ammunition. Even hearing it second-hand, it felt like we were in the thick of things. I was all eyes, watching the senior operators, picking up hints, wanting to absorb some part of their experience. But ultimately I knew there would be no substitute for getting outside the wire and doing it myself.

We flew up to the American air base at Bagram for the chief to have some meetings, then back to Kuwait. General Leahy thanked us, and gave us a coin commemorating our service. He mentioned again his appreciation of our professionalism after Dave's death.

Our next VIP would be the Prime Minister, John Howard, on his first trip to Afghanistan to visit the troops. I went on a reconnaissance to Kabul, which was very different from Tarin Kowt. It was just three of us, and we flew into Bagram. We hung around the base feeling like backpackers, looking for a hut or somewhere to crash. All we had was a sleeping bag and essential personal items. In a funny way, I felt like when I was younger, thumbing my way around New South Wales and North America. Who would have thought being a bum would set you up for this sort of stuff?

We eventually got a lift with some Americans in a HiLux heading into Kabul. A year and a half later, there was no way in hell you'd do that. There were shops out the front of the air base, where hawkers and hustlers prowled the footpath urging people to come in and buy. The Americans were allowed in there until a suicide bomber came in and blew himself up.

The roads were bad and the traffic eye-opening. There were HiLuxes and Corollas carrying ten times the number of people they were built to take, and 'jingle trucks', colourful, highly ornamented lorries overloaded with people and cargo. We were shown some burnt-out Russian tanks from the 1980s, in spots where, it was explained to us, the Mujahideen had realised they could neutralise the tanks' firepower and ambush them. It was like having a history lesson, seeing the wrecks still there.

Kabul was very busy, with no road rules that we could make out. You had to get used to it quickly and go with the flow or else you'd get frustrated. It was much more westernised than Tarin Kowt, with short-haired men in jeans and leather jackets rather than in turbans and traditional dress. There were apartment buildings, hotels and advertising signage for local products like their telephone network. Everywhere we came across big posters of the Lion of Afghanistan, the assassinated war hero Ahmad Shah Massoud, and the current president, Hamid Karzai. We were shown a run-down picture theatre and streets where all the retail was concentrated on one product. For example, there was Chicken Street, Carpet Street, Tailor Street, and Pots and Pans Street. Women sat in blue burqas on the side of the road, begging with their kids. There was a lot of poverty and a lot of security, with civilian contractors standing at the front gates of buildings ringed with barbed wire.

Our planning included establishing primary and alternate routes for the prime minister's convoy. One alternate was a dirt alley behind some houses. On a wall were bullet marks and a large rust-coloured stain. We were told that this was one of the places where the Talibs used to execute people who'd broken a law.

Sometimes we felt vulnerable, driving around in a soft-skin Pajero. Unable to access the airport from one of the alternative routes we'd been checking out, we ended up driving through a paddock into a grassy dry watercourse. A couple of kids were hanging out at the back of their houses. I said, 'This is a dodgy road to be trying to enter an airport by.'

That was when we noticed white-painted rocks beside the track. Alarm bells were going off. I said, 'This isn't going to be good, man.' White-painted rocks meant there were mines around. There was a system of white and red to show you where to steer to avoid the mines, but the Taliban often painted red ones white or turned them around to cause confusion.

A young boy came running out of his house, dodging the painted rocks, waving and shouting to us, trying to get us to stop. We pulled up, and he told us not to continue down the road. He was miming explosions, making a noise and throwing his arms about. We thought we should get out of there. One of the guys said, 'Let's give him something for his troubles,' and flipped him an Australian dollar coin, showing him the kangaroo on the front. The boy stuck it in his pocket and ran off. One probably useless dollar for potentially saving our lives.

I was trying to absorb every sight, smell and sound during those recces. Once we got stuck in a heavy traffic jam, which was complicated by there being no traffic lights or policemen. Whether Afghans are in the right or wrong, their paramount value is never losing face. One local had T-boned another, but he wasn't taking a backward step, and the two drivers were going to town on each other. Kids wove among the stationary cars asking for money, followed by men who'd had their legs blown off. A little boy was following us, banging on our window for the entire duration of the traffic jam. We stayed well out of the incident. Even if we got into an accident ourselves, our instructions were to slip them a hundred bucks and get out of there. The last thing we wanted was to be part of a big scene.

A couple of days in, the prime minister arrived and jumped into his car with some of us and a couple of his Australian Federal Police security detail. We'd had some delicate negotiations with the AFP. They wanted to run the show, but they didn't have cars, didn't know their way around, didn't even know how to get to President Karzai's palace. Even with the reconnaissance we'd done, they didn't want to be in our hands, for some reason, so we let them get another car and look after themselves.

We had the opposite problem with the big media entourage following the PM. A reporter blew up because no one with a gun was coming in his car. I said to him, 'We don't have to worry about you. You're not our problem.'

'But what if something happens to us?'

'The only guy we're worried about is John Howard. The rest of you can find your own way.'

They didn't like that at all, but we weren't there for them.

It ended up being a ridiculously large convoy. Our part was only three cars, but we were followed by about a dozen vehicles carrying the entourage. First up, the American lead car took us the wrong way out of the airport gate and down a back alley. Our radio was going off with people saying, 'What the fuck are we going this way for?' We decided to go with it and stay prepared. We knew this way. It went past the wall with the bullet holes and the stains.

We took the PM to a military meeting and then to President Karzai's palace. Outside, we chewed the fat with the AFP. One of them looked at me and laughed. 'How come the smallest bloke's got the biggest gun?'

I had the machine gun, and a cigarette in my mouth. I said very sarcastically, hamming it up for all I was worth: 'Usually because the smallest guy is the toughest.' We all had a laugh.

The prime minister's visit was quick. The same day, we got him onto a plane to Islamabad in Pakistan. He had a chat with us on the flight, thanked us and said, 'I hardly knew you were there.' He also mentioned the fatal incident in Kuwait at the start of the trip and said it was good to see how professionally we'd handled ourselves.

When we were flying over the mountains back to Kabul, I jumped in with the pilots and watched the snow. I was frothing, looking at the lines and taking photos. I wrote Emma an email saying I was in a place with lots of mountains and snow, and when we got out of the military

I'd open the extreme skiing resort to end them all, where people could pay lots of money to ski and get shot at at the same time. We'd run the resort and hire locals to take pot shots at the guests.

*

In the entire PSD with General Leahy, Mr Howard and the Defence Minister, Robert Hill, we didn't have any security incidents, so the whole thing was a success. The nearest we came to any trouble was when Senator Hill was meeting the Iraqi defence minister in a big open football field where people started showing up from everywhere and things were getting too loose for comfort. The Iraqi minister's personal bodyguards were tooled up a lot better than their down-at-heel countrymen: jeans, big boots, bomber jackets, over-shoulder gun holsters, silver-chrome AKs, white T-shirts and aviator sunglasses. They looked like they thought they were in a Hollywood movie. Their guns were on instant, fingers inside the trigger guards. As far as we could tell, they were just local thugs with money, and we weren't confident in their training.

We told the minister we had to wind it up and leave. It wasn't violent, just potentially so, with the mob mentality and these heavies with their chrome weapons. We got the minister back to Tallil on the British Merlin helicopters, famous among the military for their luxury and cost. The seats reputedly cost $50,000 each; 'Merlin', they joked, stood for 'most expensive rotary lift in NATO'.

After a month away, we were back just before Christmas. We sat down with Dave Nary's wife to tell her how he died. It was an extremely hard thing to do. Though nowhere as difficult as the emotions she would have been going through and dealing with at the time. Emma and

I again hosted the military orphans. She and I were trying for a baby again, and starting to plan a wedding. But things were up and down. She was frustrated because she wasn't getting pregnant, and because all I was worried about, having learnt that our squadron was going to go to Afghanistan in May 2006, was gearing up to go away again. It's an occupational hazard that I didn't understand at the time. Once you know you're going, you begin to disengage mentally from your daily life. You want to maximise the time you have together before you go away, but your head's not really there. Emotionally you can go a bit cold and you don't pick up on it, whereas your partner does. So, for instance, if Emma came home and said something like, 'I nearly had a car accident today,' my normal response would be to enquire what had happened, and where, to agree with her that Perth drivers are crap, and to ask if she had given him the bird. But in the days before going away I'd just say, 'Oh, really.' That's the level of interest I would show. I wasn't doing it willingly or consciously, and I never thought mentally preparing myself to go away was more important than family life, but there came a point where I could be in transit between the two headspaces. It was part of a new reality we both had to come to terms with.

Emma discovered she was pregnant again in February, and was upset that I didn't get as excited as she was. Again, it's something that afflicts expectant fathers in every walk of life, but I didn't see it. I was thinking, *I've got into the Regiment, I'm doing what I want – now how do I deal with this?* I'd worked so hard to get to this point. But neither did I want to let her down. Things were tense, then they were good, and then tense again.

By April, we just needed a circuit-breaker to take the stress out of things. We cancelled the wedding. It was disappointing to have to do that, but with the wedding taken out of the equation, things settled down again between us. We could look forward to the baby's birth later in the year. But first, I had to get through my initial full-scale deployment to Afghanistan.

SEVENTEEN

Even though it was May, the heat was like a punch in the face as we stepped off the ramp of the C-130 Herc in Tarin Kowt. This would be a different Afghanistan from the one I'd experienced on the PSD. The first night, I could hear the sounds of the town: tooting horns, the whine of motorbikes, and the ever-present rumble of buses and lorries. Someone was yelling and someone else was whistling; now and then a policeman's whistle blew and a siren went off. It never went quiet.

Our brief was pretty simple. We had to drive out in our LRPVs (long-range patrol vehicles, or basically tooled-up armoured Land Rovers) and find someone to fight. That sounds a bit flippant, but the intelligence was that in 2006 the Taliban were reorganising after a couple of quiet years. More than 4000 people were reported to have died in the conflict in that year, ninety of them from NATO forces, the most since 2001. The estimated number of armed attacks had trebled, from 1500 to 4500. The squadron that handed over to us told us plenty of stories about fights they'd got into, and how they'd handled them.

We got our vehicles sorted, a big job for me because I was the driver and signaller for my patrol. We had two LRPVs per patrol, with three operators in each, plus whatever interpreters, signallers or other support we needed. I was by far the least experienced of our patrol. The PC had done fifteen years in the Regiment, and the 2IC was a soldier from a British unit. The sniper had been to Afghanistan before with 3 Squadron, up in the north. Even among the three of us who were there for the first time, the other two had been to Iraq and had spent a lot of time in the army. I was by a long way the most junior.

Our orders for our first task were non-specific: just to drive into a certain area out of Tarin Kowt and see what we could find. I packed what would become my routine gear for a patrol of twenty-four hours or less. I had six or seven mags of thirty rounds each, so that was 210 M4 rifle rounds in my webbing. I had a pistol with two mags, and enough food for twenty-four hours – two tuna sachets and a Mars bar, or a couple of muesli bars. The ration packs might have beef stroganoff in a little sealed bag. That was enough for me. Among the other mandatory gear was two litres of water, a basic medical kit to patch up wounds, and some fluid bags to deal with a bigger trauma wound. I had a tourniquet that had to be accessible using either arm, a radio, a spare battery, and specialist gear such as rubber latex gloves, plastic bags to collect pocket litter and other evidence, handcuffs and at least two blindfolds for possible detainees, and an explosive charge.

We left in the middle of the night, wearing our NVGs; soon the moon made it bright enough not to need them, which was a relief to me, because driving in NVGs gave me headaches. The guys were on edge, having been told that there was a good chance we'd get into a fight.

The bulldust on the roads, which had a kind of goat-shit-and-fur animal smell, kicked up in massive plumes. We had to steer away from the dust from the vehicle in front, to avoid being engulfed. The desert roads were rutted and rocky, with plenty of offshoots where drivers had avoided mud holes or a rock scratching the diff. When we got into the hills we were driving on goat tracks, scraping the sides of the cars, doing three point turns, trying not to roll down hills or flipping the cars – it was very hairy. One squadron in the Char China area had taken seven hours to go one kilometre, in a flat fertile area on top of a plateau in winter. It was so soft and boggy, they had to winch each other forward all the time.

Our procedure was to find a hide spot on top of some hills and watch a village. We had an Afghan interpreter, or terp, with us to listen to the chatter on the local ICOM radios. The terp was routinely with our headquarters element, listening to the radios and passing it on to our boss. The best terps did a literal translation, word for word, while some others tried to interpret what they saw as the meaning and consequences of what they heard. We didn't want that, and encouraged them just to repeat what they were hearing. Most of the time that was just, 'Ahmed, are you hearing me?' 'Yes, Mustafa, I can hear you. Can you hear me?' For long periods, they would just keep contact with each other. Then, when they were preparing to fight, there would be a lot of bravado. They gave us codenames such as 'onions' or 'potatoes', and called their weapons stuff like 'watermelons'. So when things heated up, they'd say, 'Go and get the big watermelons, come to Akhtar's place, and we'll get rid of the onions.' They boasted about how they were going to attack and rout us, which put us on edge, but it was usually exaggerated. Then after a while we got complacent, because they were often threatening and doing nothing. Sometimes their preparations would peter out because getting organised was too hard for them. But it was dangerous to get complacent, and we had to take every threat seriously.

We would wait for the ICOM to spike, watch patterns of life, and see if suspicious types were running around with weapons or doing things they normally wouldn't do. We were also mapping the routes through the valleys and passes, figuring out where we could get vehicles through and where to avoid.

Not much happened until we caught up with American Special Forces at a FOB (forward operating base) near Deh Rawod, west of Tarin Kowt. Deh Rawod was a big open valley, essentially the gateway from Uruzgan province to Kandahar province. The scenery was impressive. On the edge of the town was a huge, battered, sphinx-like formation. It was said to have been a castle built by Alexander the Great. The Americans' intelligence was that a ferry was moving Taliban across a nearby river during the night. We planned an ambush and got geed up. This was going to be awesome, hiding in the weeds in the water, just like Vietnam. There's a famous SAS story about a patrol blowing up a vital Viet Cong tractor, known as the 'Tractor Job', and everyone was talking about this as the 'Ferry Job'.

As we got set up, our squadron's other troop was up in Chora, north of TK, and we'd heard about them getting into fights in which Matthew Locke got a Medal for Gallantry and another Australian got hit in the neck by an RPG. We were spewing to be on the other side of the mountain range, missing out. But we had the Ferry Job all planned. We were like Melbourne Cup horses trained for this day. It was the epitome of what we did: water ops, using all our skills and knowledge to tackle a problem.

And then it was called off. Our OC on that trip was very risk-averse. Headquarters were sending questions on the radio: 'How do you know they're going to be Taliban and not just locals with guns?'

Well, the intelligence we'd got was that they were Taliban. If they weren't, we'd be able to tell. The Taliban had a certain look – the turban, the eye make-up, the way they carried themselves. The Americans working with the local forces were certain they were Taliban.

But the questions betrayed headquarters' timidity, and they called it off. We were shitty as hell. We didn't know if the Squadron HQ was having trouble leading two troops, or if they didn't rate us as a troop. This was what we'd come here for, and to be pulled away from it was extremely frustrating to say the least. To have that chance taken away by anything was bad enough, but to have it taken away by our own people was shattering.

I think it was all down to inexperience. The command element were on their first trip. They had grown up in a peacetime army, and had had a troop in a couple of contacts. They were scared of risking us. On our side, what angered us was the lack of trust. We weren't idiots; we weren't going to blaze away at anyone.

As disheartened as we were, though, we had to be careful not to start blaming everyone else. Morale had to be preserved. So we had to rise above it and push on to the next job.

*

The tantalising near–Ferry Job set a bit of a tone for that 2006 trip. Our patrol was sent up north past FOB Cobra, to mountainous terrain where the Taliban had some important supply routes. We lay up behind a hill for nine days over-looking the villages. When we were out for long periods, we took sleeping bags when it was cold or just silk liners when it wasn't; some guys had swags, but I preferred just to sleep on the ground with my webbing rolled up as a pillow. I generally fell asleep pretty quickly at night, listening to the pining of jackals in the distance.

During the day, on the ICOM we heard the Taliban spotters telling their bosses they knew we were up there, but they never came looking for us. The scenery was quite dramatic, with burnt-out vehicles lying alongside high twisting mountain passes. The eerie thing was, no matter how empty it seemed, there was always someone there. At night, we could see Taliban spotters flashing their lights to each other. They were sent out with a radio, a hundred batteries, some water and naan bread to live like dogs for as long as their bosses paid them. If they saw a coali-tion convoy or helicopters, they passed the word up the valleys. It was hard to get in there by car without them seeing us coming. At night they would give themselves away by flashing signals with their lights. On occasion we would observe them for a while and when we were happy that it was indeed a spotter and he was alone, we would pump a few rounds up towards them, but not much happened.

We did see some Taliban coming together for a *shura*, or meeting, in a village. Some commandos, who we'd had attached to us for their mortar capability, came up and fired a few rounds, and a JTAC (joint terminal attack control-ler) called in some fast air to drop some bombs. There was one suspicious-looking man who squirted from the site on a motorbike. He was being chased with mortars. On the Taliban radio network we could hear the motorbike whin-ing in the background, and we saw him weaving up the side of the river. He got away. It was a brief moment of excitement.

The frustration was mounting. We wanted to achieve military objectives, and for the most part weren't able to. I might sound gung-ho about our desire for contact, and it's a characteristic of the untested soldier to want that first challenge. Among your peers, it's a way of earning your stripes, and we felt that we came out of that trip with a name for being the troop that hadn't been in the main fights. It's our professional mindset: this is what we're trained to do, and we want it to happen.

Further up that valley, we received information that a MVI (medium-value individual) was in a village. To get 'eyes on', we took an extra sniper from another patrol and started what turned into a very hot five-kilometre walk up a hill. As soon as the sun came over the peak, it was on us all day. Once we were up there, we stayed for three days and nothing happened. We were organised in two groups: an LUP and an OP (observation post). The LUP was for food and water, admin, recording any observations in logbooks, and signals. I was constantly working, passing back photos, information and other details, including a sketch on the computer of the layout of the houses. When it was time, we would crawl the few yards between the LUP and the OP to do our jobs.

To rest, we lay in the dirt behind a little wall, but it was almost impossible to sleep in the heat. Now and then we would hear dogs barking or the jingle of a bell on herds of what we called 'Beyoncé sheep', for their particularly prominent rumps. We had some parachutes we cut up to use as a sunshade. We got them after a resupply in the field; god bless the Americans, because the pallets had a few *Playboy* magazines in them. We were on only two litres of water a day, lying there and getting fried. We would drink the water to keep hydrated, but it was like turning on the hot-water tap at home and trying to drink from it. You wanted to spit it straight out. It wasn't refreshing in the slightest. They were long days. We had to do everything on our backs or stomachs, crawling or shimmying from place to place. Before or since, I've never known such heat. Then, at night, a welcome breeze whipped through the valley. If I was on piquet I would drop my pants, lift my shirt up and let the wind cool me.

Boredom was a problem, and we would sit and let our minds travel back home. I thought a lot about modifications I'd like to do to the house or garden. Or, with some others, we'd whisper about places we'd like to go on holidays, and places we had been, or just make up games. For me, it being my first trip, I was too busy and mentally active to get too bored. I was constantly occupied with trying to get the communications to the main base up and maintained, and to support other patrols and the rest of the troop. Every time the PC wanted to send something back I had to be ready. Or if something came in, I always had to check it in case he needed to know something. If I missed an urgent message, it could jeopardise the patrol's position. The PC would have to wear it if the sig had been lazy and not watching the radio.

After three days of inactivity, we were packing up to leave in the morning. Just then, two suspects came out of the house we were watching. We were about 1800 metres away, and watched them through our binoculars. They got a phone out, and were holding it up to the sky, walking around trying to get reception. Finally, after all that waiting, we confirmed that they were the two targets. We scrambled into position and called the snipers in. The JTAC got an A-10 Thunderbolt overhead – an awesome piece of machinery that carried GBUs (guided bomb units), and a

30-millimetre cannon. Because it was an old style of plane, it had to be talked onto the target in a detailed way. It had one big limitation: when it came for the run-in, if the 30-millimetre cannon fired for too long, the strength of its recoil would force the plane back and stall the engine. So they could only come for shortish sweeps.

The two Talibs started walking towards the house. The jet came in, dropped a bomb, and fired its cannon. They missed, and the pair began running. Our snipers took a shot and only just missed. The targets got to the house, and then the jet came around again and blew out the whole side of the building. That was a great sight for us. Of course we had a technological advantage; we happily took it. Always bring friends with guns to a gunfight.

Another Talib was running back and forth, trying to get away from the snipers, who were pinning him in. The plane came to do a gun run. The noise was incredible – it's one of the best sounds you hear over there, a loud throaty groan as it lets rip.

At that point a group of women and children came out of the other houses and started waving. We called a ceasefire. A suspect had slipped in among the women and had picked up a kid as a shield. He had that many women around him that our PC decided not to engage him. He ended up walking off with them: the price of our rules of engagement, which the Taliban already knew how to exploit.

We packed up, and wanted to do a BDA (battle damage assessment), but our HQ thought it was too risky to go into the village. This was frustrating again, but it turned out that the three targets we'd ended up getting were significant Taliban fighters. As a first real contact, it was invigorating and exciting, and it was good to know that we'd achieved a result.

Back at FOB Cobra, we debriefed with the Americans, who had some fresh food for us. After being out for a couple of weeks, we were pretty dirty. I'd started chewing my 2IC's mint-flavoured Skoal tobacco, and my cams were filthy. Driving along, I had to spit the stuff out, and my whole shoulder soon wore a disgusting dark brown stain, as did the side of the car. When I was on piquet, I spat into a water bottle. I would always be leaving bottles filled with spit on my mate's gun turret, because it drove him crazy but entertained me. Unsurprisingly, I was looking and feeling like a complete grub.

There were a couple of uneventful patrols north and east of Tarin Kowt before we went to the Baluchi Pass area for a couple of days. We picked off a Taliban spotter with a .50-calibre round, and his comrades left him to be chewed up by a dog. They had very different customs from us when it came to looking after their dead and wounded. If I was beginning to get the idea that life in Afghanistan was cheap, the main people I put that down to were the Taliban themselves. They had a recklessness about their own lives, and those of their comrades, that shocked me at first. Soon, though, I got used to it, and wary of it. If they didn't care whether they lived or died, that made them all the more dangerous.

On one hill, they were trying to mortar us but were falling well short. We had the advantage, being able to see them and having superior range. They were actually firing from inside their village. They seemed to lack all understanding of the advantage they'd given us. But once again, our commanders wouldn't let us go into the village, fearing that we'd either hurt some innocent people or get hurt ourselves. Again, we felt that the trust wasn't there.

Out of FOB Anaconda, named after the famous battle between the Americans and Al Qaeda in 2002 – I'd read

Sean Naylor's book about it, *Not a Good Day to Die*, in Kuwait the previous year – we went up the valley of Ana Kalay. We drove two cars to an Afghan National Army (ANA) compound, and although we heard some ICOM chatter from enemy fighters threatening to come and hit us, nothing happened. I would get to know that valley very well two years later. In 2006, it seemed a bit sketchy but was more or less in friendly hands.

By the end of the trip, we were getting very frustrated, especially knowing that our squadron's other troop was still getting much more action. We went to conduct another OP in support of friendly call signs. It required us to use one hill for a helicopter insertion, but at the last second the Chinook's crew wouldn't land or let us jump. The helicopter itself was making straining sounds like it was about to crash. It was kind of heavy because if it had crashed, the steep nature of the terrain would have made it difficult to recover us and the helicopter. We had to walk the hill instead. I weighed 73 kilos and my pack and rifle weighed 79 kilos. I had three radios and batteries, seven days' worth of food, 20 litres of water, and extra machine gun rounds. I don't mind that, but it's tough to carry when you've been expecting to come by helicopter and still think you could have. And in the end, when we came to an impossible place to get through without ropes, the PC called the whole thing off and we walked out. The next night, another helicopter insertion was aborted when the pilots said they'd seen people moving around near the HLZ (helicopter landing zone). That was just the way it was.

We did have a better outcome on a patrol near Baluchi near the end of the trip. We were getting mortared, and saw about twenty enemy fighters on the side of a hill. The JTAC called in a 2000-pound (900-kilogram) bomb, and the whole hill looked like it caught fire. Flames poured out, a massive fireball. A couple of nights later we did a BDA around the enormous craters. The ground was burnt, a car was incinerated, nothing had survived. It's impressive firepower. It was hard to tell how many had been killed in the strike as it had been a few days and the Taliban would usually remove the bodies before sunrise the next day. But when you're ducking mortar rounds and at a disadvantage on lower ground, you tend not to think of the men firing them as people like us, with families and homes; they're a military force trying to kill us, and at the end of the day one force is going to defeat the other. Them or us, one or the other, is going to survive this fight. We were grateful that we had the firepower to enable us to be the men who walked away.

As I prepared to come home, I had to stash these thoughts at the back of my mind, away from my home life. Afghanistan had become a central part of my world, but not *the* central part. It was the first time I'd been away for such a long time, and readjustment would be difficult. We didn't have the internet in Afghanistan, so I couldn't send photos, but Emma had been sending photos in the mail as she grew from not having much of a belly to having a big soccer ball. It was a sobering contrast to reflect on: while our job was about killing or being killed, the essence of war being that brutal reality of the fragility of human life, I was going home to see one precious new person come into the world.

A week or so after that fight, we were on a flight home, and a fortnight after I landed in Perth our baby was due. I wanted to go for a 14-kilometre walk around Mundaring Dam. It was the type of thing I liked doing to decompress after a trip, and Emma was stubborn enough to want to come with me, even though she looked about fifteen months' pregnant. I can still see the walkers on the track giving me dirty looks – imagine the type of man who'd make such a heavily pregnant partner go through this!

Three days later, Kaylee was born. I was there, which was fantastic and emotional. It was something I had not really processed and yet here I was, in the hospital about to see my daughter arrive into the world. To be frank, I had no idea of how I was going to crack this new mission. All I could really do was try to be there for her when I could. It would have made my mother extremely happy, that's for sure. Emma reckons I fell asleep in the birthing suite, watching TV. I dispute that: I was resting my eyelids, saving my energy for the big event.

Taking Kaylee home, like any young parents we said we would still go out to dinner and do all the things we'd always done. A couple of weeks down the track, we realised Kaylee had a stronger will than either of us. I was surprised and still am at how much will and resolve a little human can have. So life changed.

But the other life, the life of world affairs that the Regiment was responding to, wasn't going to stop for my convenience. Kaylee was born in October; in early November I was told I would have to go to East Timor for three months to do a security detachment for the President, Xanana Gusmão. Neither Emma nor I was really happy about it, but at least this time she had a focus. With Kaylee in the house, Emma would be too busy to dwell on my not being there, and compared with the previous time it was probably easier for her. But as I've said, she didn't resign herself to it willingly.

Luckily for all of us, the three-month detachment was cut short at two weeks. We accompanied Xanana Gusmão from his house to events, tagging along to help his personal security staff. He went to Dili's main football stadium to hand out medals to freedom fighters one day, and we saw it as a high-threat environment. At the end of the presentation, a couple of women started getting up and shouting at him that they should have got medals. His PSD crew got around him, and the crowd started firing up. We got him out of there, and that was the most exciting thing that happened.

Two weeks into our stay, the SAS suffered a terrible day in Fiji when a Black Hawk helicopter collided with HMAS *Kanimbla* while trying to land on it. Two men were killed, Josh Porter, from the Regiment, and helicopter pilot Mark Bingley, which hit all of us pretty hard. At the same time, we were told the East Timor operation was being shut down, and were brought home in time for Christmas. Xanana Gusmão thanked us for our help and gave us ceremonial scarves, but I have to say, as much as we were happy to help him, it was quite a deal better to be back home for Christmas.

EIGHTEEN

Early in 2007, there were rumours about squadrons going back to Afghanistan. I was warned that I'd be going back, but for something different, not just war fighting. It would be the first time I would go away as a father, but the pain of leaving Kaylee wasn't as acute as it would become in later years. In 2007 I was excited that our operations were ramping up and that we were gaining experience in combat. In another compartment of my mind, and heart, I was on a high that Kaylee had been born, but she was still a baby and her bond with Emma was stronger than it was with me, and if I was happy about our family situation as I went away it was partly for the selfish reason that Kaylee was now giving Emma a daily focus.

The 2007 trip was an alternate mission set near Kandahar, the former Taliban capital in the south of the country. Due to operational security reasons I can't say too much about it. What I can say, though, is that we nearly got locked up in a civilian jail, which would have been hairy, until the Brits came and talked our way out of it. Unfortunately, that's about as much as I can say about the operation.

Kandahar was much more traditional than Kabul. You didn't see people wearing Western clothes. It was turbans or skullcaps for men, and full burqas for women – sometimes they would wear high heels, but that was the most you could tell about who was under them. The old city, on the southern side, was very slummy, with tight little streets of hard-packed earth, garbage and raw sewage, and women begging in the open. It seemed much poorer than Uruzgan.

The city was busier than Kabul, and more volatile. It was in that year that a lot of IEDs were starting to go off. These homemade roadside bombs would change the tactical nature of the conflict. Trying to drive around wasn't easy at any time. If you were caught in a traffic jam, which you didn't want, it felt high-threat. Out towards the west of the city, where the Canadian and US troops were based, there was constant danger and a visible Taliban presence.

There were also incongruities, such as a Gold's Gym. We had an ongoing bet of $100 for anyone who did a single run into Gold's Gym, did a hundred push-ups, and came out alive. Nobody took it on.

We befriended a trader in the markets who showed us photos of himself in bodybuilding competitions. He said he could get us anything we wanted, and just to test his claims we asked if we could have a black bear to keep as a pet. He said he had one but it was up at Mazar-e-Sharif. When he couldn't get it – or a lion cub, which we also requested – we asked for a Russian desert tortoise. We got two from the marketplace, but they could climb up walls, and one kept escaping. We got another. When they escaped, people brought them back to us. With a female one, Trixie, we painted on her shell: MY NAME IS TRIXIE. PLEASE

RING THIS NUMBER FOR PICKUP. Every week or so we'd get a call from someone asking us to pick her up. Trixie doubled up as our barmaid. If someone wanted a drink at one end of the bar, we stacked the cans on Trixie's back and laid down a piece of cucumber at the other end. Sniffing the food, she would reliably carry the cans down.

We also got a Kandahar fighting dog we called Barry Dawson, after the character in the Australian Cougar bourbon TV advertisement at the time. Barry was a good little dog, but unfortunately got run over.

So we had a bit of time on our hands.

When I returned home after five months, I didn't have to be on-team, meaning in readiness for hostage recovery either domestically or internationally. Emma, Kaylee and I spent a beautiful summer together in a little cottage we'd bought in Fremantle. The downside was that Emma suffered a couple of miscarriages, which got us both down. We had such joy with Kaylee, we were determined to add to the brood.

In the Regiment, though, family life is always subject to sudden disruption. One day just before lunch, they called five of us into the office and said, 'There's a job in East Timor, the prime minister's going over. They want a quick response for protection.'

I rang Emma and said, 'Can you get some jeans and collared shirts and underwear out for me?' I went home for lunch and said, 'I've got to go away.' I couldn't give her any idea where, or how long I would be. I went back to work, and by then it had changed. Alfredo Reinado, a military officer who'd gone rogue, had just tried to assassinate the East Timorese Prime Minister, José Ramos-Horta. They wanted a whole troop to go over and pick up Reinado's number two and three. In the space of an hour, we were scaled up from a five-man outfit to an entire troop with a different job. We flew out that night on a C-17, landed in Dili the next morning, and went to our base. That's how quickly life could change.

We were under the command of the army CO, Major General Mick Slater, who gave us three days to get our stuff sorted. We said we would be ready in two hours. I think he was shocked, and impressed, that anything in the army could move so rapidly.

It's that informality that I love about the Regiment. The romance, or anachronism, of being allowed to be a non-conformist while in the military was what had appealed to me ever since I'd read about Special Forces. We don't quite have free rein to tell everyone to do as we say, but our standards are kept so high that we're entrusted to make our own decisions. It's a sacred contract – we have to justify that trust – but it always makes you aim up and be the best you possibly can. There's no incentive or comfort in sinking down to doing the bare minimum.

In Dili, the official intelligence on the suspects we were chasing was unclear. A couple of our blokes had been chasing Reinado on their previous trip to Timor, and they'd found a few good contacts in the local pubs. Someone phoned a number, and the same guy still had that phone. He gave us new intelligence, which intel were sceptical about, but it was first-hand and much better than they had. It's a credit to the Regiment operators who'd done it outside the official chain.

But the job turned into a fizzer. One night we went into Dili and our informant grew confused about which house the target was in. We dismounted and walked through people's yards. We felt like ghosts, sneaking through their lives without them being aware. We climbed up into the second storey of this house, but the man inside turned out to be the wrong one. In any case, our target gave himself up and we were home within six days. But it was an illustration of the changeability of our lives. We'd been told it could happen that suddenly, and it did. You go to work for a normal day and find yourself in Dili by nightfall.

*

The SAS was changing fast. After decades of long-range reconnaissance, it was being turned into a more aggressive force. That suited me. If we only did reconnaissance, I doubt that I or others like me would be so drawn to the Regiment. When we went out to Cultana, near Whyalla in South Australia, for a week and a half's training before leaving for Afghanistan in 2008, we were told that there would be a push to do more targeting: going after enemy networks and/or individuals. We had to prepare for more night work and getting our CQB (close quarters battle) worked up as a team. We would build intelligence then execute a plan based on it. This was the start of the 'Find, fix, finish, exploit, analyse' period. Most of my SAS generation had been wanting to do that for years, and were pleased that the system was catching up with our way of thinking.

Working in the Regiment was now very fulfilling for me, and I had a sense of really fitting into a group of like-minded people for the first time in my life. For once, the army had lived up to its promise. The Regiment pursues excellence. There's always something that's not quite 100 per cent for you to improve on. That was my own internal drive, which before I'd been feeding through surfing and snowboarding. Now I had a whole world of people around me who lived the same way, who were competitive about getting better, and who offered me every positive encouragement to do so.

At Cultana, they introduced working dogs into the Regiment. My mate Blue, a big tall bloke with a shaved head and covered in tatts, had used dogs in Afghanistan in 2007. In 2008, we would be integrating the dogs fully into our work. I helped Blue with the training, renewing my love of dogs. These weren't bomb-detection dogs, but combat assault dogs (CADs). We were using them in an offensive role. We were training them so we could send them into a room or out into the fields to find enemy fighters lying down or in ambush locations. The dogs' role was more like the way they're used by military police, but adapted to our needs. We used a Belgian shepherd sub-breed, the malinois (pronounced MAL-IN-WAH). Their work ethic suited us better than that of the German shepherd. They were smaller and didn't gas out. German shepherds work until they're tired, whereas the malinois will go on forever. And they needed to, since they might be asked to trek over many kilometres and then sprint long and hard to run someone down.

For this trip, my role had changed too, and I was in a new patrol. I was a scout now rather than a signaller: up the front of the patrol and more involved at the sharp edge of what it was doing. I couldn't have guessed how sharp that was about to become.

NINETEEN

When we did the handover at Tarin Kowt with 1 Squadron, they told us that the big change was the proliferation of IEDs. The enemy had also grown in number. The previous year had been cold, and a bad harvest meant the peasants were more open to offers of money and threats of coercion to join the fight. The Taliban, realising we had an advantage over them in firefights, laid the IEDs on the roads we used, at choke points, and on the high overwatch positions they knew we favoured. Just before our arrival, 1 Squadron had been hit in a wide valley we called the TK Bowl. An IED had ripped through the base of their LRPV and wounded an Afghan terp.

Another change was that our patrols were taking more Afghans with them: ANA soldiers we'd trained up as well as the terps. After hearing about the number of IEDs, we agitated for a change in our transportation. The six-wheeled Land Rovers weren't well enough armoured underneath to keep up with the IED threat. We also wanted to be inserted more frequently by helicopter. This argument wouldn't be settled until the following year when we would finally get the helicopter support we wanted.

In July our patrol was sent on a seven-day driving loop from Tarin Kowt to Chora in the north of Uruzgan, stopping at a government building called the White House (just a whitewashed house), which would become the centre of FOB Locke, named after Matty, our Regiment comrade who had been killed in 2007, nine months after he won the Medal for Gallantry. We would then come back through the Chora Valley. This would be a 'famil', or familiarisation patrol, to drive around certain villages, sneak into them at night and see what was going on. We were opposed to this, most of us having been to Afghanistan at least once before. With the danger multiplying, why were we doing a famil rather than going straight into specific targeting? It seemed an unnecessary risk. Everything was a lot more pressurised than in previous years, and soon we had more than enough action on our plate.

On the patrols, we could feel how the tension had increased. Driving out of Tarin Kowt, we felt like aliens. Men sat in their shops or at tea houses, smoking and watching us. Beside a roundabout near the base, there was a two-storey hotel that we nicknamed the Taliban Hotel because it was full of guys who looked like Talibs, sitting there and watching us malevolently.

Outside the town, the land smelt soggy and wet as the farmers flooded the paddocks to feed the poppies, a muddy turned-earth smell, sort of cabbagy, very strong in the green belts. One night we were sneaking down a road near a *shura* house where some men were gathering. We came through a cutting, which threw a shadow onto the road. All of a sudden the blokes got up from their *shura* to take a toilet break. We dived into the shadow, crowding against the hard rock wall of the cutting. The men were only a few paces away, taking a piss, without knowing we were there. A funny thing about the Afghans is they have a weird sixth sense when someone is looking at them. They feel it. One man stopped washing his hands and peered around suspiciously, but didn't see us in the shadow. The patrol turned out to be uneventful: we got in and out without detection.

Just before we left the FOB the next morning, one of my mates came up to me.

'Is this yours?'

He was holding a piece of jewellery. Emma had given me an amulet with the image of St Christopher, the patron saint of travellers. 'Promise me you'll wear it,' she said, before my departure. I'd promised, and put it around my neck.

Taking it back from my mate I said, 'Yeah, thanks, my missus would have killed me if I'd lost it.'

It was a good omen for a bad day. We set off with two engineers down the road heading south of Chora. The green belt flared out to the west and came back in at the Baluchi Pass. It was quite an exposed area, and we could see the piles of rocks on the roadside that the enemy used as indicators when they were setting up IEDs. Or they would leave a plastic bag in a tree, which looked like rubbish but actually told them where the bomb had been left. Being in the front car, I didn't like it at all. There were fresh diggings everywhere. I said to Adam, my PC, 'This blows, mate.' He agreed.

If we could keep moving fast, our speed would give us an advantage. The enemy couldn't have IEDs set up all the time, because they would blow themselves up. They had to duck in between our patrols, set them up, and get us coming back. If we moved quickly, we could beat them. But because we were stopping at every lump or bump and sending out the engineers, we were losing our speed and making things easier for someone to set up an IED ahead of us. We decided to go a bit faster, and pick a path around the fresh diggings and indicators instead of stopping at every one.

We came to a cemetery on a spur line, and the engineers got out and swept over the top of the hill, where we would drive up to the higher ground. As we came down, I stopped at a divot that had been dug in the track marks left by other coalition vehicles that had gone through there, avoiding a choke point. I said to Adam, 'I don't like the look of that divot, let's drive around it.'

The message got passed back on the radios to the other vehicles: 'Turn right, don't follow the deeper tracks, follow our tracks off to the right.'

The next two vehicles did that, without any problem. We paused on a mound to hold security while they came through. I was looking back. In the fourth car of the convoy were our troop sergeant, Deano; a JTAC; a terp, and sig Sean McCarthy manning the .50-calibre gun mounted on the back. The terp was in the tray by himself. I didn't know Sean extremely well. He was a sig rather than an operator, but he was frequently out with us and the information he provided was critical. He was a good guy, who got along well with everyone. Some signallers feel a bit apart from the operators, but Sean was good mates with Blue and some others, and blended in easily.

The three cars that had already been through, weaving to the right of the divot, had left deepened track marks. Maybe for this reason, the driver of the last car got confused and followed the earlier tracks. As the car came through, there was a massive bang and a mushroom-shaped cloud of smoke. *Oh fuck.*

Deano was thrown so high he was doing somersaults in the air. A tyre flew a couple of hundred metres. Bodies were getting thrown out everywhere. Our first instinct was to race back, but we had to restrain ourselves. This could be a classic ambush, the enemy laying an IED and waiting for us to converge on the damage before hitting us.

The whole village had come out to have a look. Masses of women and children started leaving towards the south, the surest sign that something bad was happening. After setting up security, some of those closest charged down the hill towards the car. A couple of bodies were lying there. The car had hit an IED right in that divot we'd veered away from. They were only a metre or two out from being in the safe tracks. Their front tyre had set off a pressure-plate charge. IEDs were typically made of two metal plates which, when pressed together, completed the circuit. A battery pack with wires connected the plates to a detonator in the actual charge, the explosives, which sent out a mass of rudimentary metal, often just saw blades and pieces of machinery. This one was made of two anti-tank mines stacked together.

What was new and lethal was that the charge was offset from the pressure plate. The enemy had figured out that a lot of their IEDs had exploded right under the wheel of a car, which would disable the vehicle but not injure anyone. If they offset the charge, as they had here, it would blow up under the passengers, not the engine or the wheel. This one had blown a hole directly under where Sean was standing.

An AME was called for, but it took forty minutes to get there from Kandahar. Some Apache gunships came overhead and shot at a few Talibs in the mountains. The patrol first-aiders and the medic were doing their best to look after Sean, who had been torn in half. He also had a fractured face. One of his arms was severely broken, which hampered efforts to get an IV line in. The terp had lost his leg from the knee down, and his other leg was badly broken. The AME came in and got Sean, Deano and the JTAC, who'd been blown out of the car too and had some shrapnel wounds. The medics kept Sean alive until the AME came, and he fought for about an hour. They lost him on the helicopter.

We stayed at the site for the rest of the day while some regular army came up from Baluchi with a flatbed truck to take the damaged LRPV away. One of them said to the medics who'd worked on Sean, 'Why the fuck would you drive through there?' It was pretty inconsiderate, and he nearly got bashed out in the field.

Some locals zoomed down to the bombsite on motor-bikes, probably Talibs seeing the results of their work, and we detained them before sending them to the FOB for questioning. We were angry and frustrated. We sat in the sun all day holding security, and only when we got back to a safe position were we told that Sean had died. We were pissed off that they hadn't informed us straight away.

Looking to catch the people who'd done it, we walked the four or five kilometres back to the site that night, and created an event with some gunplay to draw them out. It didn't work. We wandered around looking for suspicious characters, and only left as day was breaking. When we returned to the FOB, which was a pretty rough, dusty place, everyone was ratshit.

Still without much sleep since Sean's death, we moved to the next FOB further south with some intelligence about a Talib target. We were pissed off that one of our mates had been killed, but were not acting with vengeance in mind. We had to focus on the next job, and the immediate legacy of that incident was to heighten our awareness of the IED risk. We crept through the green belt, sensing danger. We weren't taking any chances. When we came across farmers working in their paddocks, we hog-tied them. We couldn't let them go, as they might have been Taliban or might go and alert the Talibs to our presence. It was a precaution to tie them up, and they generally accepted it, even putting their wrists out to be tied the moment they saw us. They were questioned and released once the operation was finished.

We got to the double-storey building where we'd been told the target was. It was midsummer, and in the heat the Afghans slept on the roofs. I was the first one up the ladder. I had a pistol with a suppressor. It was like being the first to breach a ship on the water exercises I'd done: you feel very vulnerable in case there are sentries up there. I breached the edge of the compound keeping as low a profile as possible. The rooftop was clear and I signalled for the others to follow.

We went inside to have a look. People lay sleeping on their beds of woven reed mattresses raised on blocks above the floor. Whole families shared one bed. The NVGs put a slight green glow under our eyes. A woman woke up and looked at us – that sixth sense again. She sat up, peeked out from a blanket over her head, and mumbled something to herself. Our terp said she would have thought we were evil spirits, humanoid shapes with green eyes, and was probably saying a prayer to make us go away. She lay back down and put her head under her blanket.

Our other patrolmates were sneaking around the compound looking for evidence of enemy threat. We didn't want to lose our element of surprise. We eventually woke the target by poking him in the face with a muzzle. We had found that if we did that, there was rarely any resistance. We did some immediate tactical questioning – where were the weapons, the bombs, the other fighters? – and had him sent back to the FOB.

*

In early August we did a job in the area between Chora and the Char China Valley, a rat line for Taliban coming in and out of the area. Their leader up there was the big IED maker in that area, with five or six bodyguards.

We flew to a FOB and had a heinous all-night 20-kilometre walk to get to our spot before first light. Nearly everything we did was at night, so it was no surprise that we got very good at nocturnal operations, with the technological advantage of the NVGs. All the same, they required a lot of training to work with. NVGs draw in ambient light and create a green-tinted image from it, but you only have a 40-degree field of vision. Getting into firefights, you need to be aware of where your mates are. You lose a lot of depth perception, because the NVGs are made of two monocles that you have to set to a certain focal distance. On these jobs, you would set them so everything was clear 50 metres away, but anything closer than 5 metres was fuzzy, and you only saw outlines of blurred shapes. Trying to open a door handle or do fine skills clandestinely, moving tactically, you had to adjust your monocles to get a closer focus. If you were walking, you'd lose balance with them because you'd trip over logs or rocks or aqueducts you couldn't see. You had to make your movements deliberate – moving your head around to see your mates. And they were a nightmare to drive in. I struggled with headaches if I was driving in NVGs, from looking through two monocles and the stress of trying to drive inside the tracks. I was often popping Panadol to keep these headaches at bay.

We had to walk so far because it was better to be dropped at a distance from the target and walk in to avoid any compromise from the enemy, who could hear helicopters and vehicles if we brought them too close. The rocks were very loose underfoot and I couldn't get a good rhythm going. With insertions, we tended to go bold early and slow down as we got closer. Our approach became increasingly slow and stealthy, with communication by hand signals or lasers or moving our rifles a certain way to tell our mate what we were going to do. We'd been trained for this kind of ordeal, but some Australian infantrymen who followed us overheated and had to be taken out. We had to delay even longer while waiting with them for their evacuation.

A surveillance Predator was passing us information about where the enemy was. It's pretty amazing technologically to think that an unmanned aircraft sends down pictures that can be beamed to us in the backblocks of Uruzgan. We came across some dwellings with animal pens and lots of stacked hay. All we could hear was the animals and the trickle of streams. We heard that some Talibs were possibly sleeping in a paddock, information passed from the Predator. Our JTAC got on the radio to ask the Predator to sparkle those men with an infrared beam, visible to us through our NVGs but undetectable by the targets, even if they woke up. It was very cool to see a beam come out of the sky and guide us in.

As we were getting ready to enter the target house, a man on the western side started moving away through low reeds. He picked up some others on the higher ground and they tried to squirt. Luckily we had a patrol around there, which saw them. The JTAC called in a Hellfire missile from the Predator. They were pretty sure they got them all.

Everything had gone loud with the crack and boom of the missile, so we had to work quickly to take the houses. We didn't find any people in them. We cleared the animal pens and saw a lot of women in there. They came out reluctantly, and among them was a man dressed as a woman. The size of his feet and hands, and the absence of bangles, gave him away. With the way he was trying to hide something and himself under the dress, he was lucky he didn't get shot.

There was a weird urgency about the place. I couldn't quite put my finger on it, but it's as if I could feel a kind of electricity in the air, a low buzz that I could sense without seeing, like there's one of those outdoor fluorescent mozzie-zappers around, charging things up, but out of view. It's a sinister, tingling feeling. We cleared another building and saw the reeds moving in the low ground, as if two people were trying to escape. We took off into the reeds, yelling at them to come out. A couple of our men were about to start shooting when two kids, eight or nine years old, came out with their hands up. We were angry – if someone's running away it's a pretty good indicator that they've got something to hide, and we could easily have shot them. We told them to piss off back to their house. The professionalism and restraint was a credit to our guys.

The target and his PSD weren't there, but they'd left their motorbike, which we decided to blow up. We put it in an outhouse with some weapons he'd been using, and put a charge on it. Our charges were used to make explosive entry into a target building but were versatile enough to be used as cache destruction, so were ample for a motorbike. We were only about eight metres away when it went off; we'd seriously underestimated the impact of this explosive. The whole building erupted, taking out the back half of his house, and burying his tractor. We'd overdone it a bit, but felt satisfied that we'd created a nuisance for him.

After walking five kilometres to the extraction point, we squeezed into the waiting Bushmaster. We were dog-tired. As on the selection course, when you're that tired you'll laugh at anything, like madcaps. We had a megaphone that the terps used to call people out of their buildings. Our 2IC at the time was falling asleep, saying how tired he was, and one of the operators, Joel, picked up the megaphone and yelled 'WAKE UP!!!' right into his ear. The 2IC was so pissed off I thought he was going to belt Joel. Most of us found it funny. That's how tired we were.

Among all the work there were moments of comedy as well. One day back at the base we were doing some medical training with the troop medic. One of the guys was very sick with gastro and couldn't stop vomiting. The medic was going to give him some Maxolon to try to subdue the vomiting. As it was coinciding with medical training, one of the signallers asked to give it, under the medic's guidance. The medic got the dosage ready in the syringe and prepped the patient's buttocks for the injection. The medic gave a run- down on how to administer the medicine – he described holding the syringe like a dart as it was easiest to control that way. The signaller's medical prowess was questionable. As it came time to insert the syringe, he literally took the medic's advice as gospel and threw the syringe into our mate's bum like he was at the pub trying to hit a triple twenty! As it went in, very easily and very deep, the patient obviously got a shock, yelped, and his leg muscles contracted in response to the sudden foreign object. Because of that, the syringe was bouncing back and forth and then went dead straight. The rest of us onlookers couldn't believe it and instantly hit the floor rolling in laughter and pointing at our mate's misfortune. It was the little things.

*

Now that we'd had a few weeks to digest the loss of Sean McCarthy, we were keener to do some aggressive targeting. It wasn't for retribution so much as acknowledging that the threat had grown since the previous years, and that we had to work harder to eliminate it. After a few days' break in Tarin Kowt, we did a job down south where we found a cache of weapons and IED-making materials, and were then put onto a job chasing Objective Spear.

Spear was the codename for a Taliban organiser. Tracking him down was a task shared between us and the Americans. We knew Spear's bosses were in Pakistan, probably in Quetta, but they needed deputies in Afghanistan like him to help them travel when they visited, to pass on orders, and to facilitate their operations generally. Our squadron had planted some letters in likely areas telling Spear we were chasing him, which might have spooked him, and received intelligence about his bed-down location. We had done a few night operations with the objective of frightening him into moving to a vulnerable area, and they seemed to have worked.

On the night of 8 August our troop got the call. We jumped into Bushmasters, which made our packet a lot smaller – one team could go into one vehicle, making us smaller, faster and more secure. The Bushmasters were big trucks compared with the LRPVs, and much better armoured. Since Sean's death, we'd pretty much dispensed with the LRPVs.

Before leaving we ate spaghetti bolognaise for dinner in the mess, and I got a touch of 'TK belly'. As we trundled along, I was vomiting out the side of the Bushmaster. The medic gave me some Maxolon to stop the vomiting, but I still felt pretty lousy.

Our plan was to have a recon team of five or six, including me, go out in front of everyone else across the *dasht* and see what was going on. At the vehicle drop-off point, another crew would form security on the Bushmaster. Our team set off thirty minutes early, sneaking past tents in the green belt, darting down little alleyways in villages, scouting a route for the main group. We found the target house inside the village and circled it. A sentry was sitting outside with a lamp. We found a different entry point and told the guys behind us to come in from the north, not the east as planned. We wanted to contain the place before going in, keep things quiet for as long as possible.

We all got into position. The roof team went up and got eyes on. It was a nice silent approach, and we didn't wake anyone up. We found the target, and poked him with the suppressor. As he woke up he had two or three guns on him. Again, it was a lot calmer than waking them up by jumping on them and wrestling them.

I was in charge of finding evidence in the house. Still feeling like dog shit, I started vomiting again. I got on the radio and was halfway through saying I needed another fifteen minutes, and my violent vomiting was broadcast to everyone on the ground. It was all I could do not to vomit on the evidence, which, incidentally, was of high importance. There were dual-tone multi-frequency boxes that the Talibs used as a remote control system for IEDs, plus other makings, including pressure plates. It was important to learn what we could from this evidence. Also, it became the basis for prosecuting and locking these suspects up. Most of the targets we detained would later claim to be innocent farmers. When we created a database of fingerprints, and collected evidence in standard police-style fashion, it was easier to get convictions. Importantly, following this procedure showed the Afghans that we were using hard evidence rather than word of mouth or a hunch, giving them an example of the rule of law.

We got back to the vehicle drop-off point, waited till first light and drove to TK. I was still sick, and fell asleep. Blue was on a high because Richa, our combat assault dog, had shown his worth as well. During the detention of one of the objectives' bodyguards, there was a bit of a tussle and the dog was valuable in taking him down. When I woke up from my sleep, Blue had laid chips all over me and the others were laughing and taking photos. The usual thing. But it was a good job: in TK, it was confirmed that we'd captured Spear, the number one Talib in Uruzgan. Strategically it was big. Without him overseeing it, the rest of their operation would be disjointed, which could cause infighting – which was what we wanted.

*

A couple of days later, on 11 August, our squadron was on the eastern side of Uruzgan, near Kakarak, searching for an IED maker who was running free. We planned to take a Bushmaster to an overwatch spot, make them think we were staying there for the night, and then drive into the green belt and drop off the patrols who would set up the ambushes, hoping to catch the IED maker in the process of planting his handiwork.

The targeted area was a known Taliban compound, what we called an enduring target, meaning they weren't necessarily there at any given moment. This is opposed to a time-sensitive target, which is when the person is in a place for a short time, and a dynamic target, which is a suspect who is moving around. If the IED maker wasn't at this enduring target, we would still blow it up a bit, to make him feel insecure, knowing that we knew about it. It kept the pressure on the enemy and denied them freedom of action, which allowed us more opportunities to get them. As well, it allowed other military units and agencies to conduct their work in relative safety.

Our ambush-setting patrols were dropped off in different places. I was in the front Bushmaster, on the back rear right gunner's hole. An engineer in the turret, with a gun, guided two other bomb-detection guys sweeping out the front.

Just before midnight, we came over a little rise. We were following a line to the side of the road, where the engineers deemed it safer. Another road came in from the side and there was a vulnerable point at a dry aqueduct. There was a pile of rocks with a stick at the top of the hill overlooking it, suggesting enemy presence. It was suggested we clear a lane and drive around the aqueduct.

For some reason, I decided I wanted to be at the front of the truck. I walked across the top of the Bushmaster, where we had our swags piled up. I sat on the swags behind the engineer, Dinger, in the front turret. The engineers out the front signalled us to stop and began digging away. They deemed it okay and moved on. There was a little rock wall on the side of the secondary road. We crept forward, crept forward, and the next moment . . . *BOOM!*

I remember a loud crack and then a ringing in my ears. I felt weightless, out of control. I couldn't see anything – it was pitch-black. In my head I thought, *Shit, we've hit an IED.* I was tumbling and spinning in the air. I wasn't so shocked that I didn't know where I was: I was totally under the control of the blast's momentum. I felt myself reach the apex of my flight. My stomach just floated as I stalled in the air. Then – *I'm coming down. Holy fuck, I must be a long way up – I still haven't hit the earth.*

Then – *Bang.* My face, wrists and knees hit metal. I bounced and did another somersault before hitting the dirt face-first. My rifle was still in my hand. Everything was black. All I could hear was a hissing, wheezing, grating sound. I must have bounced on the Bushmaster's bonnet. I went to roll to the side, thinking the vehicle was still moving and might run over me. My legs went out from under me and I rolled into an aqueduct. I stumbled around, and then lay in the dry watercourse, waiting to get shot at. I heard voices on the radio in the Bushmaster. I grabbed my dick to make sure it was there, grabbed my legs and arms, did a full check. I was more numb than sore, though soon my wrist began to throb. I had about 20 to 25 kilos of gear as well as my own weight. Later I figured out that I'd come down from about seven metres in the air onto the bonnet, then done a full somersault onto the ground.

The immediate danger was an ambush. When an IED has gone off, you do a five-metre scan and then a 25-metre scan to make sure there aren't more explosives around. The Talibs often set mines or other IEDs around the first one to get more blokes as they rush in. We were very conscious of that, so the others were going through that procedure as I lay in the creek bed. I heard my PC on the radio telling everyone to sound off, or check in. Another of our patrol, who had also been in the vehicle, had landed in the crater left by the blast. That would have been hot as hell. He said he felt like he was on fire. They assessed the IED to be 30–40 kilos of explosives – enough to move the big vehicle about five metres.

Our first responders from the van behind us rushed in. We were very light on for people, because we'd dropped those patrols off earlier. Our operators with the dog found an enemy fighter hiding behind a wall with a mobile phone, and detained him. A medic checked me out. My NVGs had been blown off my helmet. I said, 'If you could find them, that'd be awesome.'

The driver lay next to us in the aqueduct, wide-eyed, saying, 'Holy shit!' Then he looked at his weapon and said, 'I guess I should go to action, eh.' That is, get his weapon ready to fire.

I said, 'Yeah, that'd be a good idea.'

Our drivers were regular army guys from the Armoured Corps who usually drove tanks, but we were using them as our Bushmaster drivers. They did a good job.

I was bleeding a bit from my knees and my wrist was sore. My mate who'd also been thrown out of the Bushmaster had injured his back, and was put on a stretcher with a cannula in his arm, but he was lucky not to have ball-bearing holes through him. There were plenty of those holes in the Bushmaster. I was lucky too. If I'd stayed in the hatch at the back, there was a good chance I'd have been taken out.

We had a mobility kill, as our vehicle had lost its wheels. Some of the other patrols got around us and pushed some Bushmasters around for security, and they called in an AME. My patrolmate had to be stretchered out. I said I was okay, but they insisted I go too.

We were waiting for the American Black Hawk to come in from Tarin Kowt. As the Hawk finally approached, a strobe was dropped on the dirt to mark out the landing zone. The helicopter's descent created a brown-out, a huge cloud of dust the pilot couldn't see through. That same day there had been dust storms around Kandahar, which meant AME Red, or no flying. The pilot pulled out and tried to come in again. Again he couldn't get it. For the third attempt, he came in from a different angle. I was watching through my NVGs, which the medic had found. The Black Hawk's rotor blades looked like a huge phosphorescent disc; I could see the static electricity.

He came in really hot, about 10 metres from us, into a paddock that had been ploughed into long parallel ruts. At the last moment, I thought, *Holy fuck, he's about to crash*. His wheels hit a rut and flipped the entire machine. The main rotor got flung over towards us and the blades dug into the ground, tearing up and flying everywhere. Now only about seven metres from us, the helicopter was being ripped apart. I could hear the shearing of the blades and the whipping, whirring sound of bits of rock and metal flying past us. The dust blasted out in a blinding cloud. As the main rotor stuck, the body auto-rotated and the tail rotor spun around straight towards us.

Everyone was yelling out, 'Run!' Some of us turned back into the dust cloud to pick up the injured guy, who, we remembered, was strapped to a stretcher on the ground. But he came barrelling past us with the stretcher still attached to him, sprinting away with the drip hanging out of his arm.

As the dust settled, I went closer to the helicopter. It was slowly shutting itself down and gave out what sounded like one big sigh before shutting down completely. The pilot was sitting in the cockpit. The Americans liked to dress up, and he had a helmet like a centurion in ancient Rome, with a brush running down the top of it. He was sitting there, just saying 'Fuck! Fuck! Fuck!' and smashing his helmet on the dashboard.

They called it a 'hard landing', not a crash – an interesting euphemism. It looked like a crash to me. A blade was found 100 metres away. One of our guys in another Bushmaster had been sitting there next to an antenna. As the helicopter crashed, he ducked and a flying piece of blade sliced the antenna in two. Another piece of blade or rock put a massive dent in the bin at the side of a Bushmaster the same distance away.

It was only luck that got us through. I couldn't believe it. I'd been blown up by an IED and then, forty minutes later, nearly had the rescue helicopter crash on top of me. The engineers had found a second IED in the small wall next to our blown-up Bushmaster, set up to hit any first responders to the initial incident. This would have caused a lot more damage if it had gone off. Our technology had enabled us to block the remote signal that was sent to set it off. The whole scenario resembled the type of elaborate game they might have played on us in training: 'You've been blown up, and you're being AME'd out. Get ready for that. Now – oh, it's changed again, your helicopter has crashed.' If they'd put us through this in training, we would have said, 'Don't be ridiculous, things never change that fast.' But that was exactly how it had happened.

Our mission was aborted, and it was now about getting out of there. Everyone went into an all-round security set-up. We had to wait till morning for a downed aircraft recovery team (DART), to come up with a Chinook from Kandahar. Being injured, I got to fly to TK first for a check-up before they went back out and picked up the downed Hawk. The other boys had to wait out there another eighteen hours for coalition partners to come and prepare the Bushmaster so they could load it onto a truck and take it away. By then, they wouldn't have slept for two days. It would have been hard for them to set up a decent defensive perimeter for that length of time, knowing they were exposed. As it happened, when the recovery team came to lift the helicopter it flipped again and dropped into the dirt, causing more damage. Then the Chinook took it over the blown-up Bushmaster, and nearly clipped it, only missing by a metre. That would have brought the Chinook down too.

Unknown to me, the next morning some personnel in cams turned up at our house in Fremantle. Emma panicked. They said, 'We're here to let you know there's been an incident overseas. Mark's been out on a mission, there's been an IED explosion, and he was all right. But then a helicopter went to get them and crashed, and we don't know any more.'

These things are indescribably hard on your family. Emma was in a terrible state, thinking, *Thanks a lot! What do I take from that?*

Very soon after, I was able to ring her up and tell her I was safe. But it wouldn't be long before she would get another visit from army personnel.

TWENTY

The nature of the conflict had changed, and the way we did business changed in response. Each year I went back to Afghanistan between 2006 and 2012, the enemy had adapted their TTPs (tactics, techniques and procedures) to ours, and we then adapted our TTPs to theirs. In 2008, it was getting a lot more heated and confrontational.

In the hospital at TK, the doctors found I had a pitted patella, or dents in my kneecap. They suspected I might have broken a bone in my left wrist, and I was really worried they'd send me home. Luckily the X-ray showed it wasn't broken, and I put up with it for the rest of the trip. Every time I fell over, which was quite a lot on night walk-ins, with the little walls and aqueducts that we couldn't see, and the unbalancing weight of gear I was carrying, I seemed to fall on that wrist and jar it again. I wasn't going to let anyone know how bad it was, and it wasn't putting others in jeopardy, so I just put up with it. It was in a plastic cast for my first couple of days out of hospital, and after that I taped it up.

We had a couple of successful night jobs, including one where we picked up a suspect when he was fully nude with his wife, trying to make another baby. We picked him up just after he'd finished. He was a local government leader who was double-dealing for the Taliban. We were getting good at sneaking into their villages, streets, homes and bedrooms without being detected until they got a nudge to the head with the suppressor on the end of an M4 rifle. It got inside their planning and their mentality, and they hated us.

After that one, towards the end of August, we flew by Chinook to a place called Paygolkar to go after two targets codenamed Longbow and Javelin. Javelin had been saying he was going to take out Prince Harry when he went over there, and they were supposed to be important Taliban commanders.

Our insertion was a six-kilometre walk, mostly downhill, but I kept slipping on the loose stones and falling onto my injured wrist. It was a dark, moonless night. The farmers had just cut their corn, so with our NVGs we could see a fair distance under the trees to their apple and almond orchards. They also grew opium and marijuana, the cultivation of which was all out in the open. Most of the area had been harvested. We had to hold tight while the other two patrols were taking down the first target. A squirter tried to escape from them, but their dog got him. A burst of radio traffic let us know he was in their control.

We saw a light come on in the house we were targeting. I was up the front with the other scout, Joel, and the PC was offset to our left. We saw a sentry sitting on a wall. As we approached, a farmer walked up and down in a field, grooving a gutter to move water. We stayed out of his field of view and moved up on either side of the sentry. We stopped about five metres away. He had a blanket, or *patou*, over his shoulders.

The PC said to the farmer in the local dialect, 'Don't move, put your hands in the air.'

Just as that happened, the sentry stood up. His blanket fell away, revealing a chest rig with an AK. The PC shot him and he dropped off the back of the wall. Joel and I pushed to the wall and found him just as he was reaching for his gun. I shot him in the head as I popped over the wall, and Joel put a couple of shots into his body.

We cleared his weapon, taking the magazine off, and rolled him over to make sure he was dead. We sat and waited to see any movement in the target house. We had suppressors on our guns so our shots hadn't been loud. Nobody moved. We surrounded the compound, and when we entered, only some women and an old man were in there, asleep. When we woke them, the old man said the owner had left earlier that evening.

We said, 'Who's the guy out front with the gun?'

'He's from Pakistan. He's only just come. We don't know who he is.'

That sounded dubious, but it might have been the truth. A year later, we went to that exact spot, approaching the compound down the same road, and I thought they might have a sentry on that wall again. As I focused on it, I saw a metallic reflection in my NVGs from a light source. I was at a high level of readiness, but when I got closer I saw that it was sticks in the ground with bits of rag and metal stuck to them. It was the grave of the fighter I'd shot. They hadn't buried him, but piled rocks over him and marked it. He still lay where he'd died, a year on, so perhaps he was a foreigner.

The other patrol took out another Talib, who had a satchel full of long-range .762-calibre rounds and a rifle. The dog had alerted the team and he walked straight into them. Rightly, they took no chances. He might have been another sentry. But the main target had got away before we'd arrived.

As light rose, we walked about two kilometres and waited for extraction. I looked around at the arid landscape; in that area there were a lot of green, red and pink minerals in the earth, giving the land a rosy tint in early morning and late afternoon. Physically, Afghanistan is a beautiful place, which contrasts strongly with what's going on in the war, and with the material poverty of the people. It seemed unfair, almost, that all this shit was happening in a land that was physically so stunning.

I thought about shooting that guy. It wasn't the first time I'd shot at people, but it was the first time I'd been up close and shot someone dead. When we got back to the FOB and were chatting about the task we'd done, I had an unexpected moment, wondering who he was. Was he really from Pakistan? I wondered if he had a family back there. Did he have children, like I had? How were they going to tell his family what had happened? But then I thought, *It's his choice and that's that.* He could have shot one of my teammates first. He could have shot Joel or me if we'd got to him a moment later. If he'd shot me, I don't think he would have been sitting around that night wondering about my family. He would be happy to have killed me. I never gave it another thought. I reconciled myself with what I'd done, but it was a surprise to go through that spell of introspection. I was always so focused and keen, I thought I would have no trouble with moments like this. We're trained to achieve military objectives, which in effect means trained to take human lives, but this is never as simple or straightforward as it sounds.

*

It was at the end of August that they sent our squadron up to FOB Anaconda, to join the Green Berets out there. We didn't think they were trained to the same level as us skills-wise, but we had a lot of respect for their willingness to put themselves on the line.

We told them about the target we were after up there, the Taliban's successor to Spear. We had a bed-down location for him, and three patrols set off together for a six-kilometre walk-in at night. We planned to nab him and be back before daybreak.

Taylor, the replacement for the guy who was blown off the same Bushmaster as me, came in straight off his Reo cycle. We nicknamed him Rabbit, after the unfortunate new recruit in the movie *Super Troopers*, which we'd been watching a lot. Taylor had to carry a 12-kilogram telescopic ladder on his backpack, and kept stumbling around in the dark. Strung out in a kind of extended Indian file, our patrols had to cross a full aqueduct, the chilly, silty water chest-deep. I got across. The muddy, crushed-grass smell reminded me of running around Dorrigo as a kid play-ing wars in the creeks, or going fishing with Dad. There were actually little fish and mud-dwelling crabs in these aqueducts. I turned back and saw Taylor take a couple of steps before losing his balance and going completely under. Louis, behind him, reached in and straightened him up and got him out. I was laughing my head off.

'How you doing, Rabbit?'

'I'm fucken freezing my arse off!'

We were only about 400 metres into the infiltration, and he had a long, cold night ahead of him climbing over walls, pushing through scrub, while trying to stay stealthy. We eventually got to the house and climbed onto the roof with the ladder. It was empty. The intelligence was wrong, or our target had skipped out.

We went up some muddy terraced paddocks and through a village. The air was thick with pollen from the maize.

The crops were mature, and it tended to get into my nose and make me sneeze. Which isn't always ideal at night. When we were pushing through the fields themselves, I found it hard to breathe.

They call the SAS 'phantoms of war', and I felt like a ghost as we drifted through these people's paddocks and houses, their personal property, without them knowing. As we walked past a house, fifteen to twenty of us looked through the window to see a whole family sleeping inside. Next house, there was a man sleeping on his porch, none the wiser to this large group walking through his life. It was surreal.

On the way back, poor old Taylor kept walking through the other patrols looking for us. I was saying, 'Come back, come back,' but he couldn't hear me. He said later, 'Fuck, I was so embarrassed. I walked up to the head of the line and they said, "What the fuck are you doing here?"'

If I'd been outside the wire within a month of completing my Reo cycle, I would have been no better. He was a good soldier, and it was a testament to his ability that he'd been sent so early. He was about to have that ability tested to its limit.

TWENTY-ONE

We went back to Anaconda. As there were no choppers to take us back to Tarin Kowt, we asked the Americans what we could do to help them out. They told us of some trouble areas and it was planned that we could slip out of the FOB at night to set up some ambush positions. The Americans would go out as bait in their cars the next morning, the enemy would set up to ambush them on their way back, and we would be waiting for them.

We walked out at night and set up. The Americans drove up in convoy; the ICOM talk told us the Talibs were being ordered to move into their positions in the green belt and ambush the American convoy on its return. Hidden in the higher ground, we saw three enemy fighters walking down the road with AK-47s and other weapons. Our guys shot them. The ICOM was crackling and our terp heard that they were going to send a car down to have a look. Five minutes later, a grey HiLux came down the road. We were thinking, hopefully, *Stop, stop!* We thought it would drive past, but it pulled up. It was full of Taliban fighters, and as they cracked the doors open we could see their weapons. The patrols in close proximity opened fire and ended up killing them all.

Their ICOM sparked again. They were going to send another car and sure enough, a van soon came along the road. It pulled up when they saw the dead fighters from the HiLux. Three men jumped out to have a look, and we could see another cache of weapons inside. So our snipers began shooting them too, until one of the snipers saw a woman inside the van. Our rules of engagement (ROEs) were clear on women and children; we stopped shooting. But the Talibs were also aware of our ROEs, and one of them was hiding behind the van, using it and its occupants as a shield. Eventually, our snipers did well to shoot him and not anyone inside.

Another fighter squirted to a half-built hut near the intersection and tried to do a runner to a place with more cover. He didn't make it. We ended up with about thirteen enemy fighters lying near this intersection and two cars full of holes. The woman got out of the van, and a man on a motorbike came in from the north, picked her up and took off.

That was it for that particular job, which had gone off like clockwork. The Americans came in to do a BDA, cleaning everything up and taking what information and equipment they could for intelligence-gathering purposes. We walked back towards Anaconda and linked up with our other patrols. We heard some fighting to the east. The patrols that had hitched a ride with the Americans were in contact. It lasted about twenty minutes before some fast air came in with bombs to put an end to things. An advantage of fighting alongside Americans was that the fast air came in pretty fast!

We had left thirteen dead men behind us, but I had no sympathy. They had more than thirteen weapons, and any one of them might have had a round with my name on it. Whether it was this contact or any other, the feeling is always the same. I viewed these tasks, once we'd achieved them, with a mixture of relief and satisfaction. To put it very basically, I'd got through another day without being seriously hurt or killed, and we'd eliminated thirteen men who were hell-bent on doing that to us.

As often happens, however, there was a catch. When the BDA had taken place, a dead child was found in the back of the second vehicle. Our medics checked out the situation and confirmed that the child had been dead for some days. The woman might have been the mother, taking the little boy or girl somewhere for burial and catching a ride with the Talib fighters. But when headquarters learnt that a dead child was involved, there was an investigation. To me, it was a reminder of how different life was here in Afghanistan, that a mother could be taking her dead child into a war zone with a group of armed men who were quite likely going to get into a fight. There were always messages like this, telling you that life and death were seen through a different lens in Afghanistan.

Two days later we would attempt a similar job in the non-permissive Ana Kalay Valley, east of Anaconda. After a few of the patrols had walked into the valley during the night, we loaded up our five-car convoy on the morning of 2 September. Barry was with us after a gastro attack had stopped him walking with his own patrol. Our convoy included a total of thirty-six people: two SAS patrols plus Americans and Afghans. The Americans made the important decision to overload their cars with ammunition. We were silly enough to rag them out for overdoing it.

It was very quiet on the ICOM as we crawled along beside the dirt road to avoid IEDs, with the Australian and Afghan engineers out minesweeping. We came to a knoll in the valley, north of the green belt. Our patrol dropped in behind it for cover, while the Americans drove towards the green belt. The rest of our patrols had gone up to the north. We wanted to squeeze the Talibs up to that end of the valley, where they could either show their hand and attack the Americans or drop further and further back into the mountains towards our patrols. There was a pass out to the *dasht* at the top of the valley, and we were happy if they chose to escape through there because they'd have no cover. The Americans did their thing and cleared through a village, essentially spooking the enemy fighters to the north, which allowed the other patrols, who were already in position, to be able to effectively engage them.

Things still seemed quiet. We collapsed our position on the knoll to link back up with the Americans.

When the decision was made at around three o'clock to drive back through the valley, we had the discussion with the Americans about staying out versus going back to Anaconda. Adam, our PC, was in favour of staying and using our night advantage, but the Americans were determined to go back, in part because the Afghan soldiers in the convoy did not have the technology to stay out at night. After some discussion about cutting the Americans loose, we stayed with them.

The return trip started smoothly enough. Driving along, we got word from the terps that the enemy were going to ambush us, but they didn't. There was just one farmer out there ploughing his field.

I've described how, when we were the last car to come out through the next shallow pass, we got hammered, the rounds raining in on us. I grabbed the 84-millimetre rocket-launcher, bailed off the back of the vehicle and moved off to a flank to fire it. One rocket was in the tube and I stood up, waiting for someone to tell me where to shoot – what we call a target indication. I was given a rocky outcrop about 600 metres away and put a rocket up there. I ran back to the car, got another rocket and ran back. These launchers leave a big dust cloud from the back blast when they fire, so the enemy immediately knew where I was. Lots of rounds began kicking up the dust around me. I loaded and fired another one. Taylor grabbed a rocket, ran it out to me, and I put it in the tube and fired it. While I was doing so, he ran to the car to get me another one. More rounds were coming at us all the time.

The rockets have a tongue-and-groove seating, and in the heat of the moment Taylor misaligned the next one. He was jiggering around with it.

I yelled, 'Hurry the fuck up!'

'Yeah, Donno, I'm trying!'

Later, I felt bad about shouting at him – Taylor was only three weeks out of training, basically, and was already in this big contact – but at the time we were fighting for our lives.

In that initial period, one of the Americans, Joe, had been hit, a round passing through his arm while he was setting up a 60-millimetre mortar. He was put into a car to be taken care of by a medic. It was far too dangerous for an AME, even if it had been necessary.

Unable, so far, to get rid of the enemy who'd been shooting at our position, I decided to set up the next rocket for airburst. The launchers had a dial on the top, with a timer, so I set it to go off at 500 metres, a distance short of the target. When it does an airburst, it sends a cone of shrapnel towards the ground. As if you were choosing a shotgun over a standard rifle, the difference was a trade-off between the concentration and the spread of the fire. I'd fired six rockets without stopping the enemy fire, and now the air-burst rocket seemed to have an effect – the rounds stopped coming at us. I could not say whether it was because of our rockets or just the weight of fire that we sent back at the enemy in those initial stages.

After that airburst rocket, the shooting went into a bit of a lull. Some of our guys, at 45 degrees to my rear right, were still firing back. I put the rocket-launcher back on the car, which was manoeuvring into formation to get us going again. We pushed back to the rear side of that knoll we'd come down. That first contact had gone for about twenty minutes, with quite a lot of metal flying around. I'd done a mag and a half from my rifle as well as the seven rockets, and passed that information up to Bruce, so the PC could know how much firepower we had left.

The odd shot was still coming through. Bruce had a Minimi, a light machine gun, and was taking a couple of pings at an enemy fighter who was poking his head around a corner of a building.

With a moment to breathe again, I was laughing with Taylor. 'How's that? Three days outside the wire and you've been in a contact, you bastard!' Some SAS operators had been there for years without anything happening.

Then Bruce had a stoppage on his Minimi. The casing from spent rounds had expanded and become jammed in the breech, and he couldn't get it out without clean-ing rods. He yelled out to me, and I took my Leatherman multi-tool from my belt and threw it across the 20-odd metres to where he was.

Suddenly, it was on again. A volley of rounds cut straight through our patrol, four or five bullets coming between me and Taylor. We turned around, realising that this firing was coming from behind us, on the high ground to the north. We were pinned down on three sides.

We moved around to the south side of the knoll, facing up to the high ground. All the machine gunners in the cars turned and put rounds up there. Bruce was cursing because his Minimi was still stuck, and for the first time I started weighing up how many Taliban there were. There must have been a fair few, considering the amount of fire we were receiving from the three points they were attacking us from. I have to say, we felt exposed. We were going to need a lot of luck to get out of this.

The American F-18 gave us a break, and we ran back to the vehicle. Another of the Americans had taken a minor hit, and one of the Australians had jumped into their turret to take over the gun. Despite the casualties, the Americans were still insisting on trying to get back to Anaconda. We grabbed a drink of water and I apologised to Taylor for yelling at him. He shrugged it off. 'Don't worry, it happens.' He was good about it.

The jet came again, and put a 500-pound (225-kilogram) bomb onto the area I'd been firing at with the rocket-launcher. It made a massive boom and the ground erupted, which gave us a really good feeling. A bomb that size, accurately targeted from above, is loud and big and makes you feel like you've got the advantage. It's an awesome thing to see. The pilot then hit another building where they'd been shooting from. We thought that would be it.

If only! They soon started shooting at us again, and it was heavier now, from the green belt. About a kilometre thick, the green belt had plenty of cornfields, trees and buildings for them to hide in. We piled off the back of the vehicle again and tried to find out where they were. I thought, *This vehicle is my cover – but it's also their target.*

Some machine gun fire came in again from the ridge line to our north. Those gunners on the ridge line were closer to us now, about 200–300 metres away, closer than when they first hit us from the rear, back at the start of the ambush. The green belt was, in parts, a lot closer. Rounds started hitting the car we were supposedly hiding behind, except now we were on the exposed side. We ran around to the south side to take cover, but got more fire from the green belt. There were five of us huddling in, copping it from both sides but trying to give some back.

Bruce ditched his jammed Minimi and picked up an American SAW (section assault weapon), the same type of gun. We were all shooting back into what we thought were likely positions, but with no real chance to assess it we couldn't get an accurate fix on them.

The fire was too heavy on the south. Three RPGs had just slammed into the ground 15 metres in front of the vehicle so I decided to move to its north side. While moving to that side of the vehicle, I picked up what looked like the enemy's location on the ridge line to the north. I jumped onto the back of the tray and talked the machine gunner on to its location. I remember saying to him while he was shooting, 'Left a bit . . . Left a bit . . . ON TARGET!' and he sent a 50–70-round burst into that position. During that time there were bullets pinging and skimming off the car and the tray we were on. We could hear and feel them snapping just over our heads and we were constantly bobbing and weaving. Directly after, we swung back around to the south again due to the weight of fire from the north. The PC yelled out a target indication, so me and the gunner engaged from the back of the vehicle. The fighter managed to snap off an RPG and it whooshed over the top of the vehicle.

Just after that our PC was shot through the wrist. I had at this stage jumped back off the car to join Bruce and Taylor. The PC dropped his weapon, repeating, 'I'm hit! I'm hit!' It was hard to tell how badly he was hurt, but there was blood around his wrist. We pushed him into the back of the Humvee. He stuck his arm out the window and asked Rob, one of our SAS snipers, to patch it up.

The cars were moving slowly, desperate to get out of there but also giving cover to those of us who were running around them and getting chased by bullets kicking in from both sides. One of the guys doing the same as me for the car ahead of us was Barry. I heard him yell that he was hit and saw him hobbling, trying to catch up with his car. He'd taken a bullet in his leg. Then, as he scrambled to get to his car, he got hit in the other leg and went down. He was crying out to his car to pick him up. Dinger, the Australian engineer, jumped off to help Barry and came close to getting hit himself. He started to apply tourniquets to Barry's legs. Eric was on the radio talking to the aircraft and scanning the ridge line with his binoculars.

We were immediately behind them, so we pulled up alongside to provide cover and pick them both up. Barry was the medic, but one of our scouts, who was trained as a medic, jumped off to help Dinger with Barry. A few of us who were uninjured pushed away from our car and lay in the ditch.

As 2IC, Bruce took control. He and I were lying in the shallow ditch, covered by those two football-sized rocks. We were completely exposed to the southern side. From the ditch, some of the guys were getting fleeting glimpses of the enemy as they changed position. They were moving a lot. It was difficult seeing them in the green, but our boys were firing off a few shots.

Air support was crucial, and in the distance we could see some Chinooks, heavy transport helicopters, doing a resupply to the FOB, which was about three kilometres away. Chinooks can't look after themselves, so they had a couple of AH-64 Apache gunships escorting them. The Apache is a pretty fearsome weapon, and generally the Talibs would get down and stop fighting if those helicopters were anywhere nearby. So our JTACs were straight onto them. 'Come over here, we're troops in contact! We need you to put in some fire.'

The Apaches were manned by Dutch crews, who had more passive ROEs than we did. But still, their ROEs didn't exclude giving protection to troops in contact, so we expected them to come in and place pressure on the Talibs in the green belt or on the ridge line at the very least. They flew over us very high, at about 5000 feet (1500 metres). The enemy kept firing at us, and the JTACs passed this up to the Dutch crews. I remember yelling, 'What the fuck? We've got to get these helos down to put some fire onto them!' But the pilots kept replying to the JTAC that they couldn't see anyone shooting at us. The JTAC said, 'Come lower, just a flyover, to get them to keep their heads down.' We put a massive burst of small arms rounds, grenades and a rocket into the ridge line to mark the position for the helicopters, but they just wouldn't acknowledge that the enemy were there.

To make matters worse, Eric our JTAC was shot under his left arm, the bullet cutting through his chest and organs and coming out just above his right hip. He went down as well. Lying in that ditch, with our mates around us getting hurt if not worse, I saw the Apaches fly back to the FOB. I worried we might not get out of this alive. I thought, *Fuck, well, we're on our own here. Bunch of useless pricks. We are going to have to get out of this ourselves.* We were all angry, but it had happened now, and it didn't matter one bit what we thought.

Strange as it seems, Bruce and I had a chat about making a strongpoint in an abandoned compound on the edge of the green belt, but we agreed that the Americans would want to push for home, even with the casualties we were taking and the risk of more.

Meanwhile, the medics stabilised Barry and Eric as the cars began to push off. They said they wanted to move Barry into our car. I ran around to help transfer him, but just as I got him into our car it took off. I felt extremely exposed, running along in the open with rounds pattering in the ground around me. Nobody could have been more relieved than I was when I reached the relative safety of the next vehicle and pushed around to the northern side with Bruce and Taylor. I felt safer there for a few moments. But the car in front was copping a barrage of RPG rounds. I don't know how we avoided a mobility kill on that vehicle. I said to Bruce, 'They've got this spot dialled in,' and we ran off to the side to a coffee-table-sized rock to create a diversion. The rounds followed us and it didn't seem like such a great idea after that. It was pretty hairy, but it did give the car enough time to move through that zone.

During that phase, Rob, Carl – the PC from the other Australian team – and another American were all wounded. Carl was actually under the car in front of us after the first RPG went off; he had already been hit in the ankle. More rounds were coming in, and he could see the bullets ricocheting up into the undercarriage, inches away from him. The car took off, and he held on to the axle. It dragged him along faster than he could hang on, and when he let go and found himself in the open he was showered with gunfire. He was racing to catch up to the car when he was hit in the hip. The car slowed down, but he couldn't get back on, because he couldn't lift his leg. He limped around to the side of the vehicle. He saw some enemy fighters up in the hills and took a few shots up there, but then another round came and slammed into the breech of his weapon. The momentum smashed it into his face. His gun saved his life – he would have been hit in the neck or face – but it was ineffective now. Moving to the front of the vehicle, he jumped on to the bullbar and found a suit of armour of sorts, wrapping his face up in the tow chain for protection. He'd been shot in the ankle and the hip, and if he got shot in the head he'd be done.

What followed was the most intense phase of the battle, for me anyway. Bruce, Taylor and I ran in circles around the slowly moving Hummer, trying to drake-shoot the enemy positions, but we were draining our ammo and taking more fire than we were dishing out. Some others were trying to do the same around the other vehicles, but I didn't know exactly how many, and who was doing what. An hour and a half into the ambush, we were now getting hammered relentlessly. I took that round that went through my pants without realising how close I'd come to being wounded. But a miss is a miss, whether it's an inch or a mile. Then I had that period of deafness when the .50-calibre machine gun above my head overwhelmed my hearing. Taylor got shot in the head, receiving a gash that came extremely close to taking his life. He was and still is the luckiest man I have seen in combat. As Napoleon said of his generals, better to be lucky than good.

We were tantalisingly close to the exit-point of the valley when that RPG went off in airburst above the car in front, separating Sarbi from her handler, David, and sending the Afghan terp flying into the dust. Bruce and I had that brief discussion about what to do, and I took off.

TWENTY-TWO

As I ran out towards him, I didn't realise how far away he was. Would I have acted differently if I'd known he was 80 metres away, and not 20 or 30? I hope not. There were a lot of rounds following me, kicking up around my feet and chasing my legs. When I got to him, he was lying face-down. A pool of blood was already staining the earth around his head. I started hitting him on the shoulder to see if he was conscious. He didn't say or do anything, but he was alive.

I stood up and did some more drake-shooting back at where the enemy was firing from. I bent down, grabbed him by his webbing and started to drag him. The incoming fire was so heavy the rounds created an effect like when you're in a thunderstorm and the drops are falling into a puddle, kicking up everything around them. I've never experienced anything like it. After I'd dragged the terp for another 20 metres or so, my legs began to really burn. The car was getting further and further away and I thought, *I'm not going to be able to drag him to the car.* I got him up onto his feet.

He started to come to a bit. His face was covered in blood with bits of flesh hanging everywhere. His lip was split; his entire jaw was a gaping wound from where it had been hit by shrapnel. His whole face was a big, bloody, jelly-like mess.

I got my arm underneath him enough to half-carry, half-drag him. I didn't quite get him into a fireman's carry. He was kind of walking, kind of dragging his feet. He was trying to talk, his voice coming out in a gurgly sound. All I could make out was the word 'eyes.'

We kept moving, overtaking Sarbi's handler, David, who was also covered in blood. I said, 'Keep fucken running, mate.'

'Okay.'

'Are you all right?'

'Yep.'

I don't remember being scared, exactly. For the most part I was just thinking, *I've got to get to that car in front. I can't fall behind.* My mind was constantly processing my options and making rough calculations of the odds. I saw holes in the dirt – just divots, basically, not even big enough to lay an overnight bag in – and thought, *Should we try to get down in there for cover?* I did wonder if we were going to make it. There was a moment when I thought, *If I get hit here, we're totally screwed. We'll be such an easy target if we stop moving.*

Luck was on our side. We got to the cars, finally, but I couldn't get my bloke in. There was a big metal plate at the back, with a small gap through which you could get onto the tray. It was hard enough getting yourself up there, let alone someone who's wounded. I sort of leant him against the car and tried to lever him up. The car was still moving and taking rounds. Another RPG whooshed over the top of us.

It was hopeless trying to get him onto the back. I dragged him around to the left-hand side of the vehicle, but could not get the door open. I shifted back around to the right-hand side and had a few goes of the door. After a couple of attempts I got it open. I got the car to slow down so I could push him in there. I got a bandage for his head, stuck a first-aid dressing into his facial wounds, wrapped the bandage around his head as the car was moving along, and then shut the door and jumped out to the side.

By now I was pretty fingered. Bruce had dropped back somewhere in all that and it was now just Taylor and me. The road passed through a shallow cutting, and I ran along leaning against the car for support and protection. As it sped up, Taylor and I had to sprint again to keep up. I shouted, 'Come on, mate, we've got to get on this car!'

I managed to grab a piece of the antenna on the back. I chucked my rifle on and dragged myself up. I looked back and saw Taylor still running. I grabbed his gun and he was able to climb up, with blood all over his face from his head wound.

There was carnage in the tray of this Hummer. The American, Joe, was lying there with his arm bent unnaturally. The Australian engineer, Dinger, was there. He'd been shot in the leg and the hand.

I said, 'Are you all right?'

'Yeah, I'm all right.'

I asked if he had any ammo, and he started passing me some mags. The small machine gun on the back wasn't going. Up above, one of the Aussies was in the turret on the .50-calibre. I lay down on top of the guys in the tray, my legs overlapping with Taylor's, and started firing my rifle.

Down at my feet, an Afghan who'd been shot in the face was trying to sit up and tell me he'd been shot. I kept telling him, 'I can see that, but if you sit up you'll get shot again.' In the end I got the shits and put my foot down on his head to keep him from standing up. 'I know you've been shot in the face, mate,' I shouted, 'but there's nothing I can do about it!'

The fight had been going on for a constant three hours. The enemy fire we received was relentless. We seemed so close to the clearer ground where we could take off for the FOB, but we were right out in the open and copping a last blast of very heavy fire. Taylor and I decided we had to get some helmets on. He started rummaging around. There was an American dog handler, Gregory 'Rod' Rodriguez, who'd been shot in the head and killed early in the contact. He was lying in the back of the tray.

Rod had a helmet on, and I started to try to get it off his head, which was difficult. Finally I did, and there were bits of his skull, his hair, his brain matter and quite a lot of blood in it. I grabbed handfuls of it, scooping bits of his brain and tipping it out. I don't have the world's strongest stomach – I've had a lifelong problem with motion sickness, and I'll never forget how revolted I was when Dad butchered that lamb in front of me – but the solemnity of the situation, the recognition of what I was doing, overrode all of that. I had to detach myself. To Joe, I said, 'I'm really sorry I'm doing this to your friend.'

In his Californian accent and cool as a cucumber, he replied, 'It's all right. Do what you've gotta do.' I was grateful for his attitude. It was a terrible moment that I've thought about a lot since. I've never mentioned it when telling this story previously.

I scooped out as much as I could and put Rod's helmet on. I could feel his blood rolling down all over my face. I was flicking bits of his brain from the end of my nose. The smell was pungent, almost like pure alcohol.

Taylor looked at me and said, 'You lucky bastard, you've got a helmet.'

I jumped up onto the machine gun at the rear and drake-shot through the green belt to likely enemy positions. The engineer was passing Taylor and me all the mags he could find. After being outnumbered, firepower-wise, with the rifle, I felt a surge of strength to be using the machine gun, but after several dozen rounds it had a stoppage. I went through the drill to fix it – cock the weapon to see if any link or brass ejects from the gun, then refire. It failed to fire again, so I checked the gas setting at the front . . . the gas system had been shot right off and it was peeled apart where the round had struck. I swung the gun, on its swing arm, off the back of the vehicle in frustration and lay down next to Taylor. Because we were on top of the others, we were quite exposed. Rounds were still flying in and hitting the sides of the vehicle and the ground around us.

Picking up my rifle again, I started shooting left-handed across Taylor's back. I didn't realise his shirt had come up, and my gun was getting very hot as it lay across his exposed skin.

'Fuck! Fuck!' he shouted.

I thought he'd been shot, but realised my weapon had burnt him.

'Sorry, mate. Sorry! You're not shot, you're just burnt.'

It's no exaggeration to say that we only just made it. The car had been going in the wrong direction for a while, and had needed to do a U-turn, putting us in the way of even more fire. The guy on the .50-calibre, our biggest weapon, was down to his last hundred rounds.

The sun was setting. When we'd turned around at three o'clock that afternoon, we'd been about four kilometres from the FOB. It had taken three and a half hours to get the 3.5 kilometres before we stopped taking fire. In other contacts I've been in, there have been bursts of fire interspersed with lulls. This one felt constant, throughout all those hours, with very minor breaks. There was always someone, from one of the three points, shooting at us.

It had been radioed through that we were pretty fucked up and had casualties. We cruised into the entrance of the base, through the gates and inside. At the medical aid post, Taylor and I jumped off. They had stretchers laid out ready for the casualties. We had to get everyone off the vehicles and look after them, grab more ammo and get the vehicles up on the ramps and defend the walls. The FOB was pretty undermanned, and if the enemy had known how light-on we were, they might have kept attacking.

We had a drink of water, for the first time since the beginning of the ambush. I nearly vomited, from the dryness in my throat and the sudden flush of water in my stomach. We got our body armour off and went back to the car. The tray was full of blood. We got all the wounded out, laid them down and got a triage going.

Barry had been shot through his legs and had tourniquets on. His wounds were really quite bad and he was in a lot of pain. Basically the round that hit his lower right leg tore a large part of his calf off, smashing the tibia and severing a lot of the nerve that runs to his foot, essentially disabling the amount his foot could be moved or felt. He was told that he would lose a lot of the use of his foot and have a permanent limp. His left leg was hit through the thigh and blew a large chunk of meat out of there as well. Strangely, the left leg turned out to have a more difficult road to recovery. The scar tissue that was built up in his leg bruised the sciatica nerve. Even though it was further from the foot it took a lot longer for that to heal as opposed to the nerve in the right leg that had to grow back. Miraculously he would eventually get the majority of movement in his legs back and return to fight with us again after three years of rehabilitation. He is truly remarkable.

Eric was in a bad way as well. He had many internal injuries and also had a long road to recovery. Now he is a dad and also recovered enough to pass all the tests and serve with the Regiment once more.

There were thirteen wounded, including US and Afghan soldiers, but amazingly, Rod was the only fatality. Carl, who'd been shot in the legs and hip, was filling out some paperwork to help the medics at the hospital in TK when they got there. I said, 'Are you okay? Do you need anything?' and gave him a hand. I came across Rob, the Australian sniper, looked at his holes and got some first-aid dressings out to help patch him up. I asked him if he needed any morphine.

'No,' he said, 'I'm okay.'

As a bit of black humour, I said, 'I'm no good at this, Rob, but I'll do the best I can patching you up.' He didn't say too much.

David, the dog handler who'd lost Sarbi, was lying there on the smooth river stones that covered the ground in the FOB. We had to cut his pants off to see if there were any more entry or exit wounds. He had quite a lot of shrapnel wounds that looked severe. Lucky he had his sunglasses on because they protected his eyes: surrounding them, he had a sort of facial tattoo of minor shrapnel wounds.

The first AME helicopter came in. We dragged some ammunition off and slung it to one side. The Black Hawks were fitted out for medical treatment, and we squeezed the worst-hurt Americans and Australians across the deck on their stretchers.

In the FOB, the medics were still working on the Afghan interpreter on the table. I went in and had a look. They'd lost him once and brought him back. They were holding him down, trying to get a breathing tube into his throat. He regained consciousness and started crying out, so they had to tell him to calm down. He was grabbing at his face and their arms. They got him stable enough to get the tube in. He was on the third AME flight out, alongside David the dog handler, who had an IV line in his arm just in case. The terp lost consciousness again on the helicopter. They stabilised him, brought him back, and got him to TK and then to the hospital in Kandahar.

I haven't heard anything of him or seen him since. I assume he's living in America now. I heard a rumour that he'd gone back out as an interpreter and got shot in the face again, and survived. But I don't know how true that is. It may sound strange that I've never followed him up, or him me, but these things are not generally personalised in your head. I helped out a US Afghan who was bravely working alongside us to improve and defend his country; from his point of view, his life was saved by the Australian Army. And there's every chance he didn't even know who we were or where we were from. It's our roles and actions in that larger picture, and not our names, that carry the weight.

*

Darkness had fallen and we were sorting out all the wounded guys' weapons. Taylor's head was still bleeding, so I sat down with him and washed his wound. Funnily enough, he'd started to have a bit of a headache. It had gone that close I could see his skull in the graze. Still blows me away how close he came to not making it home. We had a bit of a laugh, and a nurse stuck some staples in his head.

People kept asking me if I was injured. I wasn't, but they kept asking. Someone asked if I'd been shot in the head, and I kept saying, 'No, I'm all right.' Eventually one of the Americans said, 'You might want to go and clean your face up.'

I went into a bathroom where there was a mirror. I took a big sigh, and fell forward, leaning on the sink. It was the first pause I'd taken since the whole thing had started. All the adrenaline drained out of me. I could rest. Then I looked up at the mirror and saw all the blood and gore stuck to my hair and face. It was Rod's, from his helmet. Now I understood why people had been asking me if I'd been shot. I just felt completely drained, as if my insides had been scrubbed out by steel wool. I washed my face and went back out.

Bruce had managed to make it back on one of the other vehicles. Now he and the other guys who were not wounded were calmly running things for us, redistributing more ammunition. The cars with their machine guns were up the ramps, guarding the walls. SAS patrols were yet to come in through the gates after extracting themselves from the mountains. The plan had been for us to go back out and pick them up, but after it was derailed these patrols had had a tough walk across a lot of open area. They didn't get back until one or two in the morning.

When we finally got to sit down, an American came out with a bottle of bourbon. We were sucking on that and going over what had happened in the day. Someone said, 'Check your pants out.' That's when I realised they had a few holes.

Some of the late-arriving patrols came in and sat with us. They'd heard our contact through the afternoon, but the terrain had stopped them getting there. One of them said, 'Shit, that was a long walk!'

One of the others looked at him and said, 'Fuck, are you for real?' It was inconsiderate, I guess. I don't know if it was an example of the SAS humour being taken too far.

I had a word with Bruce, who was pissed off with me for running out and saving the interpreter. He thought it was a stupid risk. The chances of my getting wounded or killed, and then placing others at risk, were unacceptably high. I didn't agree or disagree with him. I'd just done what I'd done. It wasn't simply a case of the training kicking in. We'd trained for a man down, but there'd never been a scenario for 'What do you do if an interpreter or support staff gets hit and he's 80 metres out in the open?'

I just felt it was the right thing to do. There's no short answer for why I did it. I guess the long answer is everything that's in this book.

*

We tried to sleep as best we could. I couldn't, at first. I jotted some stuff down in my notebook. One of the older men had said, 'Write something down so you don't forget.' I was reading *Scar Tissue*, by Anthony Kiedis of the Red Hot Chili Peppers, and was near the end of it, so I decided to finish it. I finally slept at about three in the morning.

We got up pretty early, after three hours' sleep, and went back to the command centre where the troop sergeant had been up all night.

I asked, 'How's it all going? What are the assessments?'

The Americans had flown over the ambush area with a Hercules AC-130 gunship, blown up some bunkers and shot some enemy fighters through the green belt as they were reassembling at night. In total, they said there were about seventy EKIA (enemy killed in action). I found that hard to believe, thinking the number might have been closer to fifteen or twenty. It came out later through intelligence channels that my guess was about right, with about the same number again wounded. It's hard to do a battlefield count in a scenario like that, when we never got close enough to do a proper count.

Nine of the thirteen Aussies who were in our convoy were wounded. I saw Barry later in Tarin Kowt before he was sent back to Australia. When I saw how fucked up his legs were, that was emotionally tough. Eric was put into an induced coma and didn't wake up until he was in Germany. A battle-field in Afghanistan one minute, then a hospital in Germany. Of the four of us who were unhurt, two had bullet holes in our gear. One guy had had a round travel up his sleeve and go out the back of his shirt without touching his body.

I was sitting on the roof of the makeshift Command Centre, and noticed that a mate from one of the other patrols was staring at me a lot.

'What the fuck's wrong with you? Why are you staring at me?'

He said, 'When we came in last night, all you guys, your eyes were like pinpricks, it was like you were all on heroin. Now they're back to normal.'

I said, 'You got any dip on you?'

We had a dip and while we chewed our Skoal I told him all about it. You realise, in that situation, that the rea-son some soldiers die and others don't may not be up to you. Sometimes you're lucky, sometimes you're not. Where we'd been, it was like being in a storm and not being hit by a drop of water. There are ridiculous amounts of luck involved. Bruce, Taylor and I might have improved our odds by moving all the time. If we'd stood still on the back of the vehicles, maybe things would have been different. In fact I'm certain that our continual movement had a lot to do with our survival. Everyone was getting a lot of fire, and it only took one round to make the difference. You can what-if until the cows come home. We were well trained. Some of us were fortunate and others just lucky.

The vehicles we'd been in needed some attention. The thick, bullet-proof glass on the windows had been cracked from multiple strikes of small arms rounds. The armour plating on the body of the vehicles had holes punched through them in some spots. This led us to believe that the enemy were using armour-piercing rounds, which were not very common and showed a good supply chain. We had to wash out the cars. There was blood, bits of brain matter and stuff coming out of the back of the tray Taylor and I had been in. It was a grisly task. I cracked on with it, but was feeling really bad for Rod, thinking his mates should have been doing this, not some bunch of Aussies, strangers washing his gear for him. I thought, *If it ever happens to one of us, let's make sure it's us who looks after his stuff.*

But the Americans did hold a ceremony for him that day. They put his boots on the ground and stuck in his M4 next to them with a bayonet. They read out his service record. His dog kept circling where his boots were, and then sat down beside them. It was like he was sitting at Rod's left hand, as he was supposed to. He lay down and put his paw on Rod's boots. A lot of the personnel were in tears. I felt like I'd been scorched, inside and out.

TWENTY-THREE

There was little time for a breather or to really digest what had happened. Later, when the award came, I struggled with telling people outside work about what had happened. I didn't know if I could do it justice. When you're in the Regiment, people don't always need to know what you do and how you go about it. Sometimes I felt they'd be better off not knowing. What we do can be so brutal, it will shock people, and maybe turn them against us, unless they understand the full context. And it takes so long to explain it, you begin to wonder whether only those who were there and were trained for it *can* understand. It took me a while to figure out that the Victoria Cross overshadows those reservations.

What would rile me up was when armchair critics said, 'You're the SAS, you should never get ambushed.' That kind of critique might have applied to the old SAS, who were doing reconnaissance, not aggressive targeting as we were. When you're putting yourselves out there in this way, it's not up to you whether you get ambushed or not. Success is a matter of how you respond.

This is what happened to us. Maybe it shouldn't have, but it did. Sometimes too much importance is hung on success and failure. What is success anyway? Sometimes it's going out on a job where everything goes your way and you achieve your objectives. But at other times, it's when you're ambushed and escape with fewer fatalities than the odds suggested you would. This is another kind of military success, of which Australians have always been proud. Think of Gallipoli, for example.

Two days after the ambush, Chinooks came to fly us to Tarin Kowt, where senior staff from our headquarters patted us on the back and told us we'd done a good job. We saw Barry and Carl in the hospital, and they were carrying on in good humour. I tried to hide how upset I was feeling to see them knocked about, and went pretty quiet. I might have been feeling a bit of survivor's guilt, like it was unfair that they'd been wounded while nothing happened to me, but I was also anxious about how much I would miss them for the rest of the trip.

*

It was turning into a big trip for me in many ways. I mentioned earlier I had read *Scar Tissue*, a book that reminded me a lot of my own wayward years. Maybe it was a combination of the feelings stirred up in me by the book, and the closeness of death I'd experienced during the ambush, that made me write an email to Emma saying how sorry I was to all the people I had hurt in that time, how if I had the opportunity I wish I could apologise to them for being so destructive of myself and the relationships around me, especially my family. I also told her how I didn't want to waste any more time with us putting the wedding off. Life was too short and I knew she was the one I wanted to marry. Looking back, it was as if the very intensity of the trip was also making it a time of change and growth for me as a person.

To top it off I'd rung Brent to check in with him, and he told me that they were reopening Mum's cold case and starting to follow some new leads. I felt a small ray of hope, wondering if it was possible to find her after all this time. But then I pushed it out of my mind as it was logically impossible. It left me wondering if I would ever get some closure, some explanation of her final moments – though I wasn't sure if I really wanted that. It was complicated. Finding her would give us finality, but would also underline that she really was gone forever. The news was a heavy weight and I felt bad that Brent would be shouldering it alone while I was out of the country. As I said, a big trip in many ways.

*

We were losing four or five personnel from our troop, and received two replacements, including a new PC. The method of dealing with a big event like this, which I agree with, was to keep us busy and not to dwell on it for too long, so it was only another three or four days before we had our next job, just outside TK. It was a tricky one, with poor communications. We drove out to the vehicle drop-off point and began a five-kilometre walk-in through some houses in the dark. Just as we were getting going, a big beam came down from the sky and two Hellfire missiles screamed through the air. We asked the JTAC what was going on. He was calling back to headquarters asking the same. We got word back that the Predator had had a chance to exploit the targets and had done it without telling us. Potentially we could have been almost there. There were also about three platoons of ANA positioned for an ambush up the road. We hadn't been told they were there, and could have walked straight into them. After what we'd been through, it was frustrating and almost enraging when we felt we weren't being taken care of.

The missile strike didn't get the target anyway, so two nights later we were doing the same job again. Our PC was sick, so Bruce took over. We got through a creek and over some open ground into a complex maze of small buildings. We saw a sentry on a roof. He wasn't looking at us but back towards where we'd come from. We snuck past him and let the others know he was there.

We came to a small road cutting across us. The first patrol element bounced across it, and we were the second: Bruce, Joel and me. Just as Bruce was coming across behind us, a big burst of AK fire erupted from a house down that road. Bruce had to launch behind cover. The rounds only just missed his legs. Joel was in a ditch behind a mound of dirt. I'd got myself behind a building. There was some open ground between us and the green.

I yelled out to Bruce, 'Do you want me to come back across? Give me some covering fire and we can get the patrol all in the one place?'

He didn't think I should. He was 30-odd metres back. As a patrol, we'd been split up, and there was lots of confused talk coming over the radio. This Talib with the AK kept popping his head up and putting in good fire at us down the road. He must have had a metal plate in front of him, because when our guys were returning fire you could see and hear it pinging off metal, and he was still firing.

One of our patrols flanked around. I pushed up to the corner of a building. Joel and I were 50 metres apart and he was in an exposed spot, being fired at by the AK up the road. He also had a big set of double doors behind him, which he had to watch to see if anyone came bursting out. He had to lie on his back while feeling all the rounds hitting around him.

We saw some lights starting to come towards us through the green – it looked like more enemy fighters with guns. I helped the first patrol fire at them, and then they managed to throw some grenades to put an end to the Talib shooting from the building. That gave us the chance to reconsolidate as a patrol. Bruce was passing us some quick instructions. Our mission had been compromised, so we had to get out of there. The target building was still a way off and surprise had been lost. Just as we were about to leave, two RPG explosions went off near us. They didn't whoosh like the ones in the open valley, but made explosions somewhere to our front.

We formed a defensive strongpoint in a building before pushing back to the vehicle drop-off point. We had to cut through that urban space, expecting something to happen at any moment, covering each other across alleyways, putting all our training to use. It was all about angles and cover. When the rounds had come down the road, I was calm. After the big ambush, just with that chunk of experience, it was almost as though I was a different person from who I'd been five days earlier. If I could make it through four kilometres of rolling ambush, a couple of shots should be all right.

Allegedly it was an off-duty Afghan policeman who mistook us for Taliban that had initiated the contact on us. I found it hard to believe that a lone policeman would open up on a large group of armed personnel at night. Regardless of whether they were Aussie or Talib. We'd only been back at the barracks for ten minutes when we were told that some Afghans had been shot in the exchange, among them Rozi Khan, a good guy apparently. We were pretty miserable, saying, 'Fuck, we'll be shut down for the rest of the trip.' His death got into the news. A friendly fire incident was a big deal, but the way we saw it, they shot at us, so they were enemy. You have to defend yourself. As I hope my account of the incident shows, you can't necessarily tell who they are when they're shooting at you. You just fire back and try to survive. Your training kicks in and you have to act fast. I thought that in the circumstances we reacted in the proper way. It happened too quickly to do otherwise. As I said, though, we knew it would bounce back hard against us, and the last thing we wanted was to knock out one of the Afghans who could be relied upon. Without a doubt, the Taliban would pounce on this and use it for propaganda, telling the people that we, not they, were their enemies. We certainly felt bad and apologised for the outcome, but we couldn't apologise for having been placed in that situation.

*

We did a couple more small jobs to round out the eventful trip. We had learnt a lot of lessons. For me, I suppose the tactical lesson was that movement in a gunfight, whether it's quick or slow, keeps you alive. We became masters at working at night. Instead of being loud and blasting holes in walls to make entry, instead of yelling and crashing through assaults, we used suppressors and silent assaults to keep noise down where possible, and caught the enemy off guard. Psychologically, I felt I'd come through the hottest kind of challenge and my thought processes had held up. The success we enjoyed on that trip was proof that the training worked.

There was talk that some people might get medals, but there always is, and they always do, even if it's officers getting their obligatory DSMs (Distinguished Service Medals) and DSCs (Distinguished Service Crosses). We had spoken about the ambush in the first couple of days or so, but once we were doing jobs again, our minds were on the next mission, not on what had taken place before. It's the way things are. You have to focus on the next job.

As we cleaned up on the last day, we had a couple of drinks in our room in the base at Tarin Kowt. Each SAS squadron has its own emblem, and ours was a bull. Back in Australia, while I was out shopping with Emma one day, we'd gone past Bras N Things and I'd seen a G-string with a bull's head on it. I'd thought, *That may come in handy one day*.

I'd wanted to crack it out earlier in the trip for morale, but the right moment didn't arrive until the end. I got a bit overconfident, wearing the G-string and shaking it in front of everyone. I pushed my way into every room to show them up close and personal how good it was. I got the feeling it was well received! I busted in on Deano, the troop sergeant, while he was asleep. He says he's still disturbed by the memory of waking up and having this bull's head shaking around in his face. It's been over in Tarin Kowt until the end, up on the wall, the 3 Squadron G-string. Every trip, someone has got it on. It became a tradition.

I can't put into words how much I was looking forward to getting home. I was emailing Emma how much I'd missed her. I just wanted to hang out with her and Kaylee. I couldn't tell her yet about what had happened, but the excitement of seeing her soon was overwhelming.

The army is still the army, though, and we had to go back through Kuwait to get dicked around by military morons obsessed with ticking boxes. It was frustrating being told you had to have your hat on a certain way walking to the mess, or to take your thongs off and put your boots on. Coming out of country, living in the field, having been in war fighting, you have a gutful of the fact that these people will get the same campaign medal you're getting. They can get McDonald's and Green Beans coffee whenever they want, and you can't help resenting that. Those few days were frustrating, but in the end I realised it wasn't worth worrying about. Besides, one of our replacements had decided to get a facial at a salon on the US base. When he came out he looked like a Russian doll! His eyebrows were plucked and waxed so slim he looked ridiculous, and his face was red raw, which gave the rest of us endless hours of fun.

TWENTY-FOUR

I wish Dad had told us more about his days in Vietnam. It feels like a big silence. He didn't even tell Mum very much about it, and whatever Brent and I eventually found out was through relatives, or his mates, or even through my schoolfriend Murray.

His silence about Vietnam has made me determined to share as much as I can of my experiences with Emma – and eventually, when they're older, with my kids. When we're going on a deployment, we're told that we can't tell anyone where we're going. But afterwards, I didn't think it was fair not to tell Emma what had happened. She might as well know what I do. I wanted her to understand what the trip was like. She had had the military come over to the house telling her I'd been in the IED explosion, a helicopter crash and an ambush. It definitely wasn't fair that she should know this much and not the full story.

So when I got home, I sat her down and explained what had happened that day in the ambush. When I'd been longing to see her again, I'd been missing a person I wanted to share this stuff with; I hadn't been missing someone I was to keep secrets from. My mates who were there with me, I could share it with them, but I wasn't going home to them. They were my military family. Emma was my real family.

She was upset to hear about it, and funnily apologetic – she said she felt bad that while I was doing that, she was at home spending my money. We laughed about that and started planning to get married. We got it done quickly this time, without letting the stress of preparations get the better of us. We had a celebrant do it in a park in Perth with a small number of friends. We didn't even have family there. Brent wanted to fly over, but it would be one-in, all-in with the family, and I said it would keep things simpler if it remained low-key.

Over Christmas, I loved hanging out with Kaylee. I'd take her to a café and have scrambled eggs with her, letting Emma have a sleep-in. Kaylee was walking and talking and had grown up a lot. It was a summer of enjoying being married and a father. Around 6 January, I was at the gym. The outgoing CO of the Regiment, Dan McDaniel, was in there doing a workout. He came up and said, 'Look, I'm leaving. I just wanted to say congratulations on your last trip. Your squadron did a great job increasing our knowledge, being professional and pushing the boundary of where you're trying to get to. And I want to congratulate you personally on what you did.' I was a bit taken aback to be noticed by the top man. I just thanked him and wished him well on his next posting.

Two days later I was heading to the café with Kaylee to get her an ice-cream. The CO rang to say the Chief of Army, General Ken Gillespie, wanted to speak to me over lunch the next day.

I said, 'Ah, okay. Am I in trouble?'

'No, you're not in trouble.'

'Can I bring anyone?'

'You can bring your wife. Wear something appropriate.'

I got the ice-cream and went home and told Emma, and she said, 'What's all that about?' I said if I wasn't in trouble it must be something decent. I kind of had an inkling that it was an award, but didn't think any further about it. I thought it might have something to do with that trip as a whole. We'd been incredibly busy. We were going out up to four times a week, an almost unheard-of tempo at that time.

We sorted out a babysitter for Kaylee, and when we got to the Blue Duck Café in Cottesloe, the CO and chief of army were in a corner, having sealed off the whole back end of the café. After some small talk, the chief said, 'Well, we may as well get to the point. Have a read.'

He gave me a piece of paper with a short paragraph mentioning the Victoria Cross of Australia and my name and number. That was all I took in at first. There was a one-paragraph citation stating what I had done that day.

I sat back and breathed out. 'Okay, all right.' Emma was patting and rubbing my back as she was reading it over my shoulder.

'What do you think of that?' the chief said.

'Yeah, pretty good.' I turned to the CO and said, 'What does this mean for work, if I get this?'

He gave me a bit of a look. This probably wasn't the way I was meant to react. He said, 'If this happens, there might be some aspects of work you won't be able to do. But other-wise, it shouldn't change much.'

I said, 'At least that shows me my career path.'

General Gillespie started on his spiel. The gist of it was, 'If you do accept this, be aware that we're at a time when the army needs heroes, and needs to communicate the good things we're doing over there.'

I turned to Emma and said, 'What do you think?'

She shrugged and said, 'It's up to you.'

The chief said, 'I don't know everything that will happen, but it will change your life. It will be really big. There hasn't been one for forty years. I understand your reservations, but trust me, the army will be there to support you as much as you need.'

I said, 'What about going back overseas on operations?' The common idea was that once you got that award, you were done as a soldier. They would keep you in cotton wool because politically they couldn't risk a VC getting killed.

He said, 'We might cross that bridge when we come to it.'

I said, 'I'm going away in six months so we'll have to cross it pretty soon.'

He said, 'You might not get back over this year, but that doesn't mean you won't in subsequent years.'

I thought, *No, it's non-negotiable. I need to go on doing my job and going back over.*

The chief gave me a bit of paper, showing me where to sign my acceptance.

'Are you going to accept it?'

I said, 'I've got a honeymoon starting next week to New Zealand for two weeks.'

'You should be able to do that. Nothing will happen before late January, early February.' Only he, the CO, special ops commander of Australia, the chief of the Defence Force (CDF), the minister for defence, the prime minister and the governor-general knew about it so far.

General Gillespie explained that it still had to go to the Queen for her sign-off. I thought that would take a while, so the honeymoon was safe.

I signed the paper.

The whole exchange was a bit surreal. On reflection, I don't think I was trying to be ungrateful or defensive. I was still a very junior member of the Regiment, and cared deeply about progressing as a soldier. The last thing I wanted was to be cotton-woolled. But this was probably a screen for the feeling that I wasn't worthy of such a huge honour. It was almost like I wanted to protect my status as a humble trooper, because that was what I was and what I wanted to continue to be. I was in shock and denial about the whole thing.

General Gillespie said I would meet the Queen, the governor-general, the prime minister and many other dignitaries. I knew what the Cross was, of course, but I didn't *really* know. He said it was the first one under the new system, the inaugural Victoria Cross of Australia, and the first VC for an Australian since nearly forty years earlier, when Keith Payne was awarded one for his actions in Vietnam. As he explained what a big deal it was, I thought that no amount of preparation or training in Australia's elite unit could prepare you for sitting at that table and being told this is what the nation wants to bestow upon you.

As it sank in, I started to feel awestruck. I definitely felt unworthy. This would increase later, when I read about other VC recipients and went to the Australian War Memorial. I'd thought the VC was for changing the tide of battle, but there are plenty that haven't been for that. They've been awarded for many different kinds of one-off acts of valour, including saving the lives of others. Once I understood the diversity of acts that had been recognised, that feeling of unworthiness lifted a bit.

On the other hand, feeling unworthy of a Victoria Cross never really leaves you. When I met other VC recipients, none of them thought they were worthy. When they spoke of the acts that had earnt them the award, they all said they did what they thought was the right thing at the time. Someone had to step up and they were the ones.

I also felt embarrassed in front of the imaginary audience of my mates who had been there that day in Afghanistan. I wasn't the only one fighting there, and others did more important things than I did. I was the one who was singled out. The last thing I wanted was to feel, or for any of the others to think I felt, that what I'd done was over and above the collective effort. Especially Bruce and Taylor.

After some more small talk, food and coffee, Emma and I made a beeline for the Ocean Beach Hotel across the road. We had a beer and said cheers to each other, and had a laugh. 'Well,' she said, 'meeting the Queen, eh!' We never thought we'd be sitting there at lunchtime with that sort of news. And then we had to go home and let the babysitter off.

We packed for New Zealand, but it soon became clear that the Cross was bigger than my honeymoon. The higher-ups talked about sending the prime minister's plane to Queenstown to bring us back, but in the end they said, 'It's happening next week, you'll have to postpone the honeymoon.'

The three of us flew to Canberra six days before the event. When we landed, Kaylee, who was still only two, cried out, 'Mummy, yay, we're in New Zealand, we're in another country!' People were looking at us strangely, as if to say, 'What have you been telling your child?'

I provided a list of people I wanted to invite, and as soon as they were notified, they began calling me to ask what it was about. I couldn't tell them, which with my family was difficult. I also wanted to talk to my mates from the patrols who were out that day in Afghanistan. They were the ones who wrote me up for the award. I wanted to make sure they were happy. But I was told not to talk to anybody. I just had to make sure Emma and Kaylee were treated well.

After all, I was in damage control over not going on the honeymoon!

There were all sorts of things to juggle, and I was doing my best to keep up. I requested that if my mates from the squadron were to be pulled up from their holidays and brought to Canberra, they could at least be allowed to come in civilian suits rather than their military polyester uniforms. Then there was media training. Sometimes there were light moments. At one meeting, where we sat in a circle with a great number of important officers who all had their piece to say during a long hour and a half, the deputy chief of army started speaking and Kaylee, who'd put up with it all while sitting on Emma's lap, turned around and cried out, 'Mummy, can you please stop the boring man talking!' And put her hands over her ears.

Emma and I looked at the Hall of Valour at the War Memorial, helped out by the tour guides. I bought a book on Victoria Cross winners. Emma said, 'I can't believe you're going to be up here with these blokes.'

'I don't feel I've done what they've done,' I said.

She laughed and said, 'The funniest bit will be when your face comes out in the paper and the guides will realise you were the bloke wandering around like a tourist.'

I talked about how much I wished Mum and Dad could have been there. Then I laughed and said, 'I bet Dad would have kicked my arse for doing what I did.' Regardless of how Dad felt he was treated when he came back, he was proud of what he did in Vietnam. He showed that by wearing his slouch hat everywhere. He had his green army shirts forever. He was proud all right, and would have been proud of me. As would Mum.

Emma reminded me how life is full of these moments, when you miss your parents. Kaylee has already had plenty of occasions when she's wished I was at special parties and events, instead of away in Afghanistan.

It was good to be thinking about Mum and Dad, as I would over the next few days. I'd learnt that lots of guys in the Regiment had changed their direction in life after some type of hardship or trauma. You can either use it as an excuse for everything that goes wrong or turn it into your driving force.

When my extended family came, we were given Campbell House, the officers' quarters at the Royal Military College – Duntroon, the night before the ceremony. The army put on a dinner for us and looked after us really well. Ross and Val, Margaret and Ken, Kenny and Julie, and Brent and Kate and their two children came down. Even at dinner, they were still saying, 'What are we here for?'

I could only reply, 'Wait till tomorrow.'

Afterwards, I asked Brent and Kate to stay around. Kate was very excited about how clandestine the whole thing was, but couldn't guess why they were there. Brent said, 'It's either you've killed Osama bin Laden and have to spend the rest of your life in hiding, or your squadron is getting a big award.'

I explained what we'd done and said I was getting the Victoria Cross. They were really excited, which made me feel great. Brent shook my hand and with pride in his eyes said, 'Congratulations.' It was almost as good as having Mum and Dad there. But yeah, I wish I'd been on the Osama bin Laden job too!

*

Six days of preparation did nothing to ease the nerves on the big day. We went to Government House and greeted people arriving, and then went into a back room where the

Prime Minister, Kevin Rudd, and the opposition leader, Malcolm Turnbull, came to meet me.

We went into the big hall, and I felt the heat of the cameras and media people, who didn't know who I was or what was going to happen. The dignitaries came in, the trumpets sounded, and we sang the national anthem. I felt numb and overawed – all this for me?

They read out the citation, and I stood in front of the Governor-General, Quentin Bryce. She didn't have a microphone on, and it was one of the first major awards she'd given out since starting in the job. It was a big day for her too! She said some really nice things, and I could see in her face how proud she was of this person she'd never met. I said, 'Thank you,' and she pinned the Victoria Cross on my chest.

Nothing prepared me for that moment. It was like she was pinning an emotional weight to me. Not a burden, just a lot of swirling emotion. It had a magic to it. It's just a piece of cannon, but I could feel all the stories that went with it, the 150 years of history; the honour was a physical thing that coursed right through me.

Camera flashes went off. I just went with the flow and sat down with Emma. The prime minister got up and made a speech, welcoming 'Mark, your beautiful wife Emma, and your wonderful, wonderful, wonderful . . . child.' Kaylee's name and sex just wouldn't come into his head, no matter how hard he struggled. Malcolm Turnbull gave a really inspiring gee-up speech, talking about smashing the insurgency and not taking a backward step. My mates up the back, extremely hung-over after a long celebration the night before, were clapping and cheering.

The most moving part of the ceremony, for many people, was after the CDF, Air Chief Marshal Angus Houston, had made his speech. He put his hat on and came over to me.

I stood up. He saluted me. It's such a powerful thing that the CDF would salute the lowest rank in all the military. Whenever we've had a hat on since then, he's always saluted me first. He doesn't have to do that, and there's nothing saying he has to. It's an Australian tradition, that's all. As they say, one medal for valour will move more people than any number of stars on a general's or an air marshal's shoulder.

I sat down, and everyone else in the hall was standing and applauding. Emma stood up and moved away so I would have the limelight alone. You can see in the footage how uncomfortable I am with being the centre of all that attention.

That day was the start of a six-month whirlwind. There was a media doorstop and a blur of dignitaries. I was getting quite anxious to see my family and the boys from my squadron. Barry was there, on crutches still, and the boys were suitably informal at the lunch that followed. I was at the head table, with the governor-general and prime minister, struggling to keep up with the protocol. I just don't get it. I'm not from that background. Part of me would have preferred to be with the boys, who had two tables of their own and were starting to drink the Government House cellar dry. There was a break in proceedings and I went over to their table. The PM sat next to one of the fellas, and said, 'How are you going?'

'Good, Prime Minister, how are you?'

Rudd said, 'Aren't you hungry?'

'Yeah, I'm starving, Prime Minister, but I'm really hungover and feel like I'm about to throw up.'

Then another bloke showed up with his plate full and stood above the PM.

'You right, are you, Kevin? You're in me fucken seat, mate!'

Kevin said sorry and got up. My mate shook his head and tut-tutted and sat down to eat. The PM was at a loss for words. Maybe he didn't realise they were taking the piss.

As per protocol, the governor-general left first, and I escorted her. One of the boys yelled out, 'Hey, Quentin, are you going to come and get on the piss with us later?'

She turned to me and said, 'They're a cheeky bunch, aren't they?'

Another of them said, 'We know where you live. We'll be over later!'

She found it very funny.

That night I had 260 messages on my phone, a lot from people I didn't even know. The governor-general, who had found out about our postponed honeymoon, was flying to Afghanistan the next day and very nicely offered the Queen's Suite of Government House, staff and all, for Emma, Kaylee and me for a whole week. 'There'll be no one here,' she said. 'Treat it like your own.'

The next morning, we found they'd left a teddy bear with a note on it for Kaylee. We had a great week. The chef kept saying, 'What do you want to eat?' We'd say, 'Oh, don't worry, we'll just go down to the kitchen and make a sandwich.' He said, 'We're working anyway, you might as well have us make something.' So when I said, 'Oysters'd be nice,' they brought thirty-two fresh oysters in different styles. We cracked a beer. There's a picture of one of my mates, Kaylee and me in the suite with the massive bulletproof glass window and the view down towards Yarralumla, living large. It was incredibly generous of the governor-general. When I've seen her since, she's greeted me like an old family friend.

We decided to hand the medal to the War Memorial, and the army helped me through the media barrage. I was given a great mentor, Steve 'Patto' Paterson, who'd been in the Regiment and was doing some reserve time. He was a sounding board for all sorts of issues, and helped me through it all with constant wise advice.

In February, we finally got to New Zealand and fell in love with the place. I managed to fit some work in, going to Auckland to meet the NZ SAS and Willie Apiata, who had received a VC for actions in Afghanistan as well. Willie is a cool, cruisy bloke, and over a beer we swapped stories. It was important to me to share the experience with someone who'd been through it. He showed me a room with gifts – a lot of Maori tribes had given him some prized patus, which were used to deliver a fatal blow to the head. 'I only let people who've been actual warriors hold these things,' he said. They were made of stone, jade, whalebone. One was stone, but felt cold and wet. Another felt very hot. One that looked heavy felt light. Each seemed to have its own kind of personality. I felt honoured that Willie, a bloke about my age but from this warrior culture, trusted me and passed on an experience I'll never forget.

*

So many things went on in that first half of 2009, I have to restrict my account to the highlights.

Among the many invitations, one of those I was keenest to accept was to Dorrigo for the RSL's ninetieth anniversary. It blew me away how proud they were that I'd come from their town. The father of a girl I went to school with, a hippie sort of Vietnam vet, had made a hinged wooden book with a carving of the Dorrigo war memorial on the cover and a full carving of my face inside, with an inscription of the VC and the date. He'd made it by hand, and presented it to me in front of the RSL members. I didn't know how to handle it, I was so overwhelmed. I mumbled some words of thanks and told them how Dorrigo had made me who I was.

Later, I asked him how long it had taken. He said, 'I love my wood carving, mate, it only took me a morning and a bit. I just got up really early one morning and felt proud of ya and smoked a really big joint and carved this out for ya. Ya'll have to come out to the farm one time.' He said he had carved designs and faces and totems into a lot of fence posts around his farm. One day I'll go and see them all.

No doubt a few people in Dorrigo were surprised at what I'd done. They generally said it was the cow shit and the mountain air that had made me what I was. I got letters from Vaughan's parents, and from Jamie Bleakley, whose dad used to coach us at soccer. My friends from my North American period got in touch. Drew said he'd googled my name and couldn't believe what came up. He wasn't alone.

There were notes of recognition from people that blew me away. PACOM, the Pacific commander of the American fleet, sent me his hat. The US General James Mattis, who had commanded the first push into Afghanistan, sent me a letter. But alongside those, the things that most affected me were letters from kids in Australia to say thanks. In Canberra, a lady came up in the street and said she was proud to meet me. She suddenly started crying and gave me a hug. She said her father was a vet who hadn't talked about the war. It was pretty moving, happening out of the blue on the streets of Canberra. Seeing how it affected others was what brought the magnitude of the Cross home to me.

I wanted to help Legacy. Meeting old diggers was an absolute privilege. I got to meet POW survivors from Changi, vets with two Military Crosses from different wars. I met Georgie Palmer from the 39th battalion at Kokoda and got him to sign a photo for me. The World War II vets spoke to me differently, soldier to soldier. Those who have seen combat have a more subtle approach, but are also more direct in the way they talk about it. You're sharing an experience, and you enjoy mutual respect.

Meeting Keith Payne on the day of the ceremony was a high point, as was going to Geelong to meet Ted Kenna a week later. Ted, who was the last World War II VC recipient in New Guinea, was about ninety, and when I first walked into his house, he had a smoky look in his eyes. His daughter and wife were sort of interpreting his croaky words for me. He'd got shot in the face three weeks after his VC action, and the first time he saw this nurse in the hospital, he said he was going to marry her. By the time he got out they were engaged, and here they were, more than sixty years later. He joked about smuggling alcohol to the front, and trudging through the jungle hung-over. His eyes lit up. The smokiness went out of them and he was young again, back in the 1940s. It's those little things that are the most enjoyable – talking to a veteran and seeing that reaction. I get more out of that than from making a speech to a thousand people.

When Ted died a year or so later, I was overseas, so it was a privilege to have met him. I'll never forget, at one point, him turning to me and saying sharply, 'Don't ever let it go to your head. That's the only thing I can tell you about it. Don't let it go to your head.'

As we left, he settled back down into his chair and the smoky glaze went back over his eyes.

*

The tug-of-war inside me was starting to build up after a couple of months. There was no road map for this. There wasn't a template that could be followed or used to navigate how to deal with such an amazing honour. Keith Payne had done his bit, but that was nearly forty years ago. Society and media, especially social media, has changed a lot since then. I don't think anyone expected another VC to be awarded. So we basically made it up as we went along. I learnt a lot and had to develop a strategy of deciding when and what to do. I enjoyed going to Kapooka and Singleton, re-creating the ambush in a 'Lessons Learnt' seminar. I loved doing school events. I felt positively honoured to be taken to the War Memorial for a behind-the-scenes look at some of the treasures in the archives, such as letters from Simpson and World War II POWs. Even so, I never got used to being this VC guy.

One day Emma and I were walking into Army Headquarters at Russell Barracks, Canberra, and an army officer saluted me going through the turnstiles. I was just wearing jeans and a T-shirt. I said to Emma, 'Who was he saluting?'

'You, you idiot!'

But there was also the pressure of being a so-called celebrity. *Backyard Blitz* requested to come and fix up our house. (Emma nearly killed me when I said no.) *Men's Health* wanted to stick me on the cover. I was invited to hundreds of cocktail parties, which wasn't my world anyway, and sometimes all I was meant to do was be a celebrity 'name'. When I pushed back against that, Patto stepped in to play the bad cop. He knew where I was coming from. The army wanted at least one good news story to come out of Afghanistan, when all the media were running with was the roll call of the latest fatalities. I was pushing back a bit because I never thought an SAS trooper was the right type of person to be doing that kind of hearts-and-minds work in Australia. We don't ask for praise, we get on with the job, we're anonymous – that's the fundamental ethos of the Regiment. It looks for humility in soldiers. To go from that to being put on the front page, on radio and TV, and getting letters was bizarre and went against the grain, and I felt the pressure.

Patto and Brigadier David Mulhall, the Chief of Staff of Army Headquarters, were key influences in helping me deal with that. First, I had to accept that you don't choose the Victoria Cross, it chooses you. It can be awarded to anyone who is deemed to meet the requirements, regardless of whether that person comes from good stock or has the right family bloodlines. The truth is many recipients are ordinary people. An Australian VC recipient once said that everyone has a VC moment inside them. What makes it so special is because it can be awarded to any rank. I had to remember that I represented something much bigger than myself. So if I blew someone off and came across as an arsehole, they would remember something bad about the Victoria Cross. I had to remember, from my experience with that lady in Canberra, that it might be an amazing experience for someone else, which you can destroy by acting badly. People may forget what you said or what you did, but they will always remember how you made them feel.

The burning issue for me, even more so in mid-year than when I'd first asked the question of Ken Gillespie in that café at Cottesloe, was whether I would be allowed to rejoin my squadron. I really wanted to do another trip as a scout. If I missed out on 2009, the way our rotations were working, I wouldn't be going again until 2011. My concern was that I would never get back to being a soldier. My career was still young; I had a lot of things I still wanted to do. Everyone was telling me, 'That's it for you, you're never going back. They'll wrap you up in cotton wool, the politicians won't put you at risk. You'll be like Keith.'

There was a tradition behind this belief. 'Diver' Derrick was a VC who went back in World War II and then got killed. There was a bit of public backlash about it. Ray Simpson went back to Vietnam after winning his VC, but was put in a less hot area. Keith was wounded and had a stomach ulcer, and by the time he was better Vietnam was over. The other two who won the Cross in Vietnam died in those contacts. The circumstances are always different, so there was no law about VCs not being allowed to go back to war. And the inner me, the deviant, was saying, *If you tell me I can't do something, I'll go do it.* I made it my mission. It was hard on Emma and Kaylee, who would have been very happy for me to be in cotton wool, but I was so determined, I said I would just show up in Tarin Kowt of my own accord, and they would have to take me in.

I put the argument to my superiors that if I couldn't be a soldier over there, why had they spent a million dollars training me? I hadn't done enough time or got enough experience to go into a training role, which I didn't want to do anyway. If they weren't going to send me back, I threatened to get out of the Regiment altogether.

Emma would have been happy enough for that to be the case. She never wanted me to go back, and had a hard time dealing with the way people celebrated what I'd done. She looks at it as the day I could have died and not come home. She doesn't feel happy about the celebrations. She's happy for me, but it's a different day for her. She doesn't remember it with good feelings. And she's right. People don't think about how close you came to dying. Whether it's a VC or MG (Medal for Gallantry) or SG (Star of Gallantry) or no medal at all, the difference might be a couple of millimetres between that and not coming home at all. So for Emma, what people are celebrating is only that tiny margin from what, for her, would have been a lifetime of grief.

But I was on a mission. I was becoming acutely conscious of dropping out of contact with my squadron. They would tell me about training they'd done and I felt I was letting them down by not being there. I started fighting with myself over it. Should I be away with them? Should I give it up and concentrate on being a father and husband? We were trying to have another child. Amid all that, the demands of the Cross increased the pressure. I was being pulled this way and that by too many different commitments.

By Anzac Day, everyone was asking me to go to their parade, a lot of them rural and regional. All I wanted was to be at home. On the day, I walked with the SASR Association in Perth. They put me out the front. I had never walked in an Anzac Day parade. I remember watching it on my pushie in Dorrigo, sitting on the corner watching the old soldiers marching to the monument. Everyone was quiet, so I was too. I remembered the look on the diggers' faces. Now, to be in one, I finally understood how emotional it was. Until then, I just hadn't got it. People were yelling out, 'Hey, here come the SAS boys!' or shouting my name. I never thought the public would be that proud of us. I also felt very exposed, like being on a cliff face or in a firefight, those moments when the big nuts you thought you had turn out to be small nuts.

Afterwards, I went to the Gratto and hung out with the boys. Lee Harden, a graffiti artist, had done a painting of me before Anzac Day. It was only the seventh time he'd done oils, and it was amazing. The CO and RSM unveiled it that day. Everyone was yelling out things like, 'Where's the G-string?' When I was back with the boys, the question of my future was settled. I knew where I had to be.

Within a few days, there was another memorial to mark. It was the eleventh anniversary of the last day Mum had been seen. I went down to the beach, as I had every year, for five minutes on my own to think about her. I took some deep breaths. I remembered who she was, and said thanks to her. It didn't feel like eleven years. It felt like a lot longer, especially after the year I'd just had. I guess I hope she's up there seeing it all. I doubt it, but you never know.

TWENTY-FIVE

It was mid-May before I finally made it back to the troop. There was always the chance the minister for defence might pull my approval at the last minute, so I wasn't able to relax yet – and I still couldn't quite come to terms with the fact that my personal deployment might be on the minister's desk. But for all the importance of the Cross, I was still me, focused on getting on with the job.

We went up to Townsville for some exercises, and I was ecstatic. Everything felt like it was my first time again. We jumped out of helicopters, and I said, 'That was unreal!'

The guys said, 'What are you talking about? It's normal.'

'No, that was awesome!'

'Why are you so excited? Are you on drugs or what?'

I was like a little kid. 'You don't understand how good this job is!'

They rolled their eyes and said, 'All right, calm down, it's fine.'

While in Sydney for some training, I went to Rooty Hill RSL where they made me an honorary life member of the RSL. It was another enormous honour, considering they usually only gave it to those who'd been members for fifty years. But it was protocol to give it to a VC. Again, I had to see myself as a custodian of this great tradition, part soldier, part statesman.

We went to Perth for the usual time off and build-up before going away again. All things considered, Emma was fantastic – she acted normally, not making a big deal of it even though she was concerned about me going. It would have been hard to leave if she hadn't been so tolerant. But the older Kaylee got, the harder it was getting to leave her. I made a couple of videos of me reading stories that she could watch while I was gone. She often complained that I read too fast for her, so now she could control the pace.

When we stepped off the back of the Herc in Afghanistan, I paused on the ramp, almost like I was in a movie. The heat, the noise – again I had that feeling that everything was new again. I shut my eyes and took a deep breath and smelt the Afghanistan air. I was taking a moment for myself to suck it all up – I'd managed to get back there when everyone had told me I wasn't going to be able to do it. I was still a soldier.

'Fucken get the fuck out of the way, Donno!'

In TK, there was the usual garbage smell and constant sound of horns, whistles, sirens and lorries, together with a new sound. The town was being expanded and there was a constant clunking rock-digging machine, generator-powered, with pipes boring down into the earth. The clunk-clunk-clunk sound of the generators was part of the new soundtrack of TK. We had the usual death-by-PowerPoint briefs and handover from 2 Squadron, who had picked up on what we'd been doing in 2008 and taken it further. The big change this time was that we would have helo support from the American Aviation Group, known as Wolfpack, who'd come out of Iraq. They came with Apaches and some gunned-up OH-58 Deltas, modified Kiowa helicopters, like the Australian Army used to have. I liked how the Yanks always thought of ways to use their assets more and for longer. If only we did the same. We could now base our insertions around those helicopters. It was a huge improvement, because it lessened our chances of getting hit by IEDs and also enabled us to surprise the enemy and get hold of them.

Protecting ourselves, it goes without saying, was a high priority after all the casualties of 2007 and 2008. In the old SAS, it was said that the shot you didn't fire was as important as the one you did; if a patrol fired a shot, it failed. But that was the old world. In my time, the Regiment was being used for aggressive purposes, as an attack force, which was the way I liked it, but it led to much greater risks: although Special Forces made up five per cent of the Australian military, we'd suffered 90 per cent of the casualties in Afghanistan.

Another big change in the wind since 2008 was the rules and restrictions that our own side was putting on us. There was always a process to go through before we could go out on jobs. At night-time, we would have to jump through extra governance and legal hoops. It was frustrating enough already, but now the screws had really tightened. The amount of extra work our ops guys had to do to get us out at night was too much, eventually forcing us to do a lot of day jobs, which levelled the playing field. We had now lost our element of surprise by night and had to adapt to fighting the enemy on what was becoming more his own terms.

Our first job was back at the place where we'd blown up the target's house and motorbike. We inserted off the helicopters at first light. Sitting on that chopper at four o'clock in the morning, I was soaking it up, on a high – back on operations to a place I'd been before, with potential for getting a result, on a helicopter so we didn't have to walk. I thought, *It doesn't get much better.*

It was later in the year, and the poppy-field smells were different. After the harvest, once they'd bled and dried out and picked the poppies, they fertilised the paddocks and reseeded them with corn or maize. So the dry poppy smell was giving way to a fresh maize aroma, which is more like the grassy, wheaty smell of wheat belts at home.

We cleared a campsite that the enemy had hastily left. Their sleeping rolls were still warm. I was puffing in the high altitude. The PC gathered us together and said, 'We're going to go up this re-entrant [an indent in the mountain between two spur lines]. Donno, you stay here.'

The guys were dumping some of their gear. I had to hold the spot for other patrols coming up behind.

I said, 'Are you fucken kidding or what?'

'Nup, I need someone to stay here with the gear.'

I couldn't argue with the PC. They took off, and I was walking in circles kicking the dirt, throwing a tantrum. I suspected that he'd left me there because he didn't want to risk me. That probably wasn't why, but I was oversensitive to any change in the way they were using me.

All of a sudden some shots rang out up the valley. I thought, *Fuck it, you fuckers, I'm going!* I ran up the hill towards near where they were. They'd been into it for a while. They had no radios, having dumped them with me. Some rounds were pinging off the rocks. We knew where the enemy were and pinned them down. One of our guys hit a Talib through the neck. We ended up getting three EKIA, including a Taliban commander. The funny thing was, we'd been looking for a suspect codenamed Scalpel, but the one we'd got was a different target, codenamed Tomahawk. It turned out that he was probably the more important of the two, so that was good.

Being the scout, I had to do the SSE (sensitive site exploitation), getting information, taking photos, gathering what intelligence we could. We searched the tents in their camps and the Black Hawks came to take us back home. It wasn't a bad result: three and a half hours from take-off to being back at base. Flying back, we waved to an Australian patrol in the TK bowl. It felt awesome to be back out on the job again.

It wasn't that I was particularly gung-ho or anything, but combat can have an almost addictive quality. It's scary to be shot at, and when we fly out for a mission we don't necessarily want it to be a two-way range, yet it makes it a lot more interesting. When you have done a few jobs without some gunplay, in a weird way you want to be shot at, or at least hope there's some action. It can get worse each time too. When I got to a state where I really wanted action I had to keep checking myself and saying 'Yeah that's great Mark, but you know the consequences when it goes bad, and it only takes one piece of lead to flip those feelings.' Still, if we got out of a contact with no scratches or casualties then it was all the more exciting, and your desire for the next time increased. It's an odd feeling to convey.

One of the junior guys in the team on a later tour said to me he was enjoying his trip and the jobs we had done but was hoping for closer, two-way action. Without saying those dreaded words, 'Be careful what you wish for' I told him: 'I understand. I've been there. But be aware that as fun as it can be, it can change really quick and you could find yourself thinking after it all dies down, maybe that was a bit too much of a close call or, I hope my mate is okay'. But even as I said it to him I'm don't think I wholly believed it.

The strange thing about being in contact is that afterwards you forget about the bad consequences, and that need or hunger to experience it again just rises up. Later, after the day I was shot and some good friends and operators died, he came up to me and said, 'Remember that stuff we spoke about? I know what you mean now.'

*

The tempo was steadily increasing. A few days later, we went after Scalpel again in the Char China Valley, a massive insurgent area where back in 2006 no coalition patrols had dared go. It was the first time we were hitting them in this safe haven. Our tactic was to push them into areas they thought were safe, and make them unsafe. We managed to take out thirteen Taliban on that job, and were very pleased with the result, but from that point the tactical use of SAS patrols took what we thought was a step backwards. The emphasis changed to Castnet operations, or big forces going into large populated areas to 'clear' them of insurgents. These bulk-style standard infantry tasks were a blunt weapon. We were folded into them and lost a lot of our autonomy, which was frustrating when we'd been doing well with specific targeting. The 'good idea' people, usually bored officers, were restricting our actions. They just loved the idea of an SAS major being in overall command of a Commando unit, Incident Response Regiment engineers, a USA Airborne element, a Dutch SF element, and whatever else, because it satisfied their notion of complex top-down coordination, but the truth was that its successes were rare and it was a poor use of SAS assets.

I voiced my opinion to my PC, an older man with leathery skin named Daryll, aka Snakeface. He was only in his forties but we liked having fun with him. 'Hey,

Snakeface, was it like this in Vietnam?' 'Did they have helicopters when you were in World War II?' 'Was it exciting when they invented the steam engine?' To his credit, he was a good sport and also took our complaints on board and promoted them to the officers above him. But the decision had been made to take tactics back to the pre-2006 era, and we had to comply.

On one of the bulk clearance operations, we worked with 1RAR, my old battalion. A mate of mine from infantry days, Walshie, was now a section commander. It was good to see him, and on the Chinook flying in, I said, 'When we hit the deck we're going to run flat out, moving as fast as we can to break into the safety of the green belt.' He was excited to be part of it. The Chinooks are such a big, slow target, like flying cows, and the pilots had been ordered to land us further than planned from the green belt, leaving us a 700-metre run to the nearest cover. This was a good example of the clash in tactics. Having been working in this area for a few years, we thought it was safer to land in the green where we would already have cover. But the 'good idea' people, who'd never been outside the wire, were worried about the Chinooks getting shot at, and said it was safer for us to run 700 metres without cover.

We jumped out and ran, feeling very vulnerable. I looked back and saw Daryll running behind me, with his rifle up and his dick out. He was pissing as he ran, trying to get a last one out. The guys behind him said it looked like he was marking a Christmas tree on the ground, as it waved from side to side.

The threat didn't materialise, which meant we had to round up entire compounds, detaining and screening people. We found some IED-making equipment, but basically the job was very broad, very officer-driven. The idea was to move several hundred local males within a certain age bracket into a 'reception area' and screen them. It took more than a day and a night, and rarely achieved more than picking up two or three suspects on whom we didn't have much evidence.

At one point, a target named Quarterstaff, accompanied by fifty fighters, had been pinpointed in a certain area. We had two and a half hours to clear a valley that was about a kilometre by 300 metres wide, with seventeen to twenty compounds. The whole area turned out to be friendly. About two kilometres away, a camp was found where Quarterstaff and his men had been, but we'd been sent out to chase the area rather than the individual. The intelligence, driven from the top, had only approximated the nearest settlement to where he was, and ordered us to clear it in the hope we'd find him. We were pushing the point that we needed to be more surgical, and to be allowed to drive the intelligence. We had to chase the man, not the infrastructure, a lesson we'd learnt from 2008. This required the higher-ups to trust a sergeant or a corporal to take ownership of that intelligence, which they weren't then prepared to do.

Both sides were unhappy, us and the Afghan civilians. We'd lost our essential advantages: our speed and ability to surprise the enemy. We spent days going in and out of houses, dragging everybody out. Afghan houses have narrow, low doors, even though the people are the same size as us, and we had some tall blokes who were getting the shits with yet another low door to squeeze in and out of, in order to herd out an innocent group of locals. At the end of the day we would move out into the desert to find them straggling back into the village from a reception area where they'd been held for hours. We were cheerfully saying hello, and they were responding with dirty looks. There wasn't much hearts-and-minds benefit in dragging them out of their houses during the middle of the day to screen them in the desert.

The entire operation was very timetable-driven, even down to the helicopters clocking off at specific hours so they could have the scheduled amount of rest. Funnily enough, the hierarchy thought the Castnets were so successful – Canberra heads loved the idea of lots of units working together – that they did it again further up the valley. I was growing disillusioned. What we'd done in 2008 wasn't perfect, but it was much more effective than what we were doing now.

*

The clearance operations ran until August. Meanwhile, I got news that the New South Wales coroner was reopening Mum's case, to revisit the open finding from the 1998 coronial inquest. The cold case police had reassessed the evidence, and this would lead to a new finding, that Mum was deceased and had probably been murdered. The only suspect was Chris Watt. It was good to get a form of closure – especially for Brent, Kenny and Margaret, who were at home and close to the proceedings – but until Mum's remains are found, I guess there's no ultimate resolution. And even then . . .

Once we were able to resume our targeting-style jobs, we were relieved to have our autonomy back. We went into Paygolkar one night, searching for codename Longbow. We went onto the roof of the same compound we'd been up the previous year, and found nine RPG warheads and a landmine. We didn't get Longbow, but three Talibs squirted from the target building just before we were due to take it down. They ran straight into our cordon teams and were killed. One had a very nice chrome-plated, clean AK-47.

He turned out to be Javelin, the target we'd gone after a year earlier in the same area. Further evidence established that he had a job helping high-value individuals coming in from Pakistan. The Taliban leaders, who we suspected were based in Quetta, would come across to run religious 'commissions', basically recruiting exercises where they held *shuras* and whipped up support or coerced local men and boys into fighting. Javelin housed and fed the leaders as they ran their commissions, so taking him out was removing yet another nuisance.

A year to the day after the big ambush, I was itching to mark the anniversary by going out there and giving a bit to the Talibs, but nothing eventuated, despite my best efforts at hanging around the operations centre and making a pest of myself. We did a few small jobs, often taking Rex, one of our two combat assault dogs on this trip, who we called the 'land shark'. Rex was aggressive, going about like he had a rocket on his back. He caused a bit of havoc on our side. On one job, we were clearing a cornfield when he must have picked up my scent. I heard him barrelling through the corn and could see it getting smashed over as he charged towards me – it was like a scene from *Jaws*. He saw me, leapt, and was mid-flight, mid-bite on my arm when I yelled out, 'NO!!!' I was shitting myself. At the last instant he must have realised I was on his side. He closed his mouth and bumped into my shoulder. It was a close-run thing.

Rex's handler was Dute, and they were close. We were always falling into streams and aqueducts as we tried to wade across them, and once Dute had to make it all the way across a river with Rex, first with him hanging on to his leg with his front paws, and then dragging him by the lead. In one house we were clearing, there was a manhole going up into the roof space. Rex didn't like being picked up, and when another trooper tried to hoist him up there, Rex gave him a nip.

We suffered from plenty of frustrations. In one location, where we could see Taliban squirters running everywhere as our helicopter approached, the pilot tried to get the landing perfect and ballsed it up. The three minutes' hesitation had been long enough for several enemy fighters to get away. The next day, we started a two-day special reconnaissance patrol and found a bed-down location for six or seven males who were often coming outside to make phone calls – but nobody acted on the intelligence we'd gathered. We had one job where we went to clear a target house and took the risk of splitting our patrol on some tricky shaley rock; but at the crucial moment the job was called off so that we could go somewhere else to do a massive clearance job. Yet another ridiculous task was going into the Mirabad Valley, where we'd done numerous clearances, to do what was effectively reconnaissance for the infantry's reconnaissance. They sent us on a hellish walk, 13 kilometres on a stinking-hot day, into an area that we already knew was IED city: there were blast holes, battery packs, bits of wire, sangars the enemy had built for overwatch, power cords from phones with the wires cut, all the IED paraphernalia you could think of. We narrowly avoided stepping on two stacked anti-tank mines. All of this was to take photos in preparation for the infantry's reconnaissance, in an area that we could already have told them was very sketchy indeed. That trip, the frustrations never ended. Another day, we had an operation set up and ready to go, but it was called off for UN Peace Day. We were pretty sure the Taliban didn't adhere to UN Peace Day. We're the better men, I suppose.

Otherwise, we coped with boredom and frustration in the time-honoured military way. We had a wind-down room called The Fat Lady's Arms, and set up a slip-and-slide down the hallway, greasing it up with all kinds of fluids and getting a bit rowdy. We had the annual 'Stirrers' celebration, the one day of the year when we could speak frankly and take the piss out of each other and the officers. Sometimes, as you'd expect, military attempts at humour would back-fire. One day, when we'd picked up some detainees to fly by helicopter to the handling centre where they would be questioned, the pilot thought it would be funny to throw the helicopter around, do some hard turns and weave from side to side for about twenty minutes. These captives, who were blindfolded, were freaking out already at being in helicopters. One of them, near the front, started going green. The door gunner was laughing, and then suddenly the detainee power-vomited all over him. You couldn't say it wasn't a kind of justice. The pilot thought it was all very funny until he was ordered to clean the spew out of his helicopter.

As the summer started to cool down and our trip approached its end, we did see some action. Our patrol went into an area where we knew if we stayed long enough, the insurgents would have a crack. They would normally watch us, and if we stayed for more than two days, they would get pissed off. For some reason, these one-shot attacks took place between nine and eleven o'clock in the morning. Like clockwork, at 10.30 am an RPG burst over us, followed by some PK machine gun and AK fire. It was quite a well-vegetated area so they'd been able to come close and run away. We tried to chase and flank them, but they were too quick. It was over before we could do anything.

We had intelligence that there was a suicide bomber in this village. He'd been described to us as a young teenager, dressed in white, with mascara around his eyes. We came to a high cornfield with an aqueduct through it. The whole valley was quiet. I heard someone coming through the corn and got ready. A boy popped out 15 metres from me. He was dressed in brown, had make-up on his eyes and was the age of the suicide bomber. I told him to get his hands up. In our best Pashto, we got him to take everything off. He wasn't the suicide bomber, but that was how edgy things could be. You can be one instant from a serious mistake.

Increasingly, incidents were drawing administrative attention, with our jobs being routinely followed up by Q&As, which became a touchy subject with us. Our rules of engagement were straightforward. If you fear for your life or your mate's life, if civilians are threatened, you can engage. If someone has a hostile intent, you can engage. It's much the same as self-defence law in the civilian world. But judgements of hostile intent have to be made in a split second, and are subjective. What if I'd thought that boy was the suicide bomber? Fifteen metres from me, he could have blown us all up. Would I have been justified in shooting him if I'd seen him make a suspicious movement? I can imagine how, if I had, and had been questioned afterwards, it could look really bad. Sometimes a hostile intent, as you've perceived it, doesn't sound very hostile when you explain it afterwards, under cross-examination from some officer. But from our point of view, we're trained so highly just so that we can be trusted to make such decisions. Year on year, there was far more reach-down into our actions, and it's not an exaggeration to say that the guys resented having their decision-making taken apart by a process that wasn't informed by ground-level experience. It was also potentially dangerous. We had to make split-second decisions in situations where the wrong move might mean death or injury, so if we started second-guessing ourselves in combat we were putting our mates, our allies, the people we were protecting and ourselves in peril.

The enemy knew our ROEs and constantly played on that. The first question they would get asked in the processing centre was 'Have you been abused in any way by the soldiers?' It was a licence for them to make up stories, and the result was that our operation was fast becoming a catch-and-release program. We often likened it to game fishing: we bagged them and tagged them, and the 'good idea' people would let them go.

After a couple of Castnet-type jobs, we went to assist Matiullah Khan's militia on the road between Gizab and Tarin Kowt. MK, as he was known, was a local warlord type who'd been embraced by the coalition, and his militia, the KAU, were incorporated into the Afghan security services. His group was trying to put checkpoints along that road, but had come into a stalemate with the Taliban, who had set up a Dushka heavy machine gun in a high position, stopping the KAU from progressing.

I felt we could have gone in, gridded the suspected enemy positions and called in air support for pre-bombing. Instead, three SAS patrols went in, set up at night and linked up with the KAU commander to take over the fight with two groups of about fifty of their men. It was a more complicated way of doing it, and more confrontational, in my opinion.

We did some initial overwatch and found out that the Dushka was where another SAS patrol was planning to insert. Julian was in that patrol, and I'd made some ill-received jokes about this operation having the potential to repeat Roberts Ridge in Operation Anaconda in 2002, when coalition troops had received some fatalities through flying onto their recce position, cut down out of the sky by Al Qaeda. Julian was understandably unimpressed by my attempts at humour.

We warned our bosses not to insert near the enemy gun, and moved up to join some KAU fighters, who were quite exposed on the spur of a low bald hill and very happy to see us. They were living on bread and water, operating on very little pay and weaponry – an oily rag, basically. Through a mixture of broken Pashto and English, we understood that there was potential, in that position, to get completely surrounded. There was no vegetation or any built structures, and all they had for cover was a small rock wall they'd constructed themselves; it was so flimsy it would barely survive a minute in a firefight.

During the night, we moved them into better positions to set up by first light. We were all more spread out than usual, and sure enough, before long the KAU mistook an SAS patrol for enemy and opened up on them. Immediately, the actual enemy joined in. With our mates hunkered down, getting shot at by both friendlies and the enemy, we put suppressive fire on the Talibs and frantically radioed the KAU to stop firing. So there was a loose, three-way fight going on: the KAU shooting at an SAS patrol, the enemy also shooting at that patrol, and us shooting at the enemy. When we finally got the KAU to stop, so did the enemy.

It was nearly sunrise when we heard we'd got a friendly WIA (wounded in action). The team Julian was in had inserted into a relatively protected part of the ridge line compared to the original HLZ (helo landing zone). Julian was moving up the ridge line within his patrol, and as he stepped between two rocks the Taliban machine gun opened up from a high point of the feature Julian's patrol was attempting to establish a foothold on. A round hit him through the arm, shattered his ulna, and came out the other side. Luckily for him, it hit the butt stock of his rifle. If he hadn't been carrying his rifle correctly, the bullet would have gone into his stomach.

As JTAC, Julian called in some Apache air support, which suppressed the enemy fire. The air strikes continued while a medevac helicopter came in to winch him out. The amazing thing was, Julian was on the radio, still calling in the Apaches and coordinating his own evacuation while he was being winched up. The Americans in the helicopter were astonished by his courage and persistence.

Things calmed down after some jets came in with 500-pound (225-kilogram) bombs and multiple gun runs. The main KAU push went forward from lower in the valley, and the Talibs were firing back at them, but we were too far away to provide effective fire, instead acting as the eyes to direct more air support. One of our patrols was still pinned behind a rock. Another of our guys had torn his groin muscle and was radioing his medic for pain relief, but the medic said tersely, 'I can't really make it right now, I'm pinned down behind a rock.'

When the bombs had suppressed the enemy firing, we saw an unusual sight. The twenty or so KAU on the high ground dropped their weapons and sprinted forward to take the next Taliban position. It was weird that they dropped their weapons; they said they had to get there as quickly as possible. They were rough and untrained, recruited for a few dollars a day. They would be given a rifle and webbing, which they knew how to use – they grew up with AKs the way we grow up with cricket bats and footballs – but fought on a strictly casual basis, only working for a few hours a day before knocking off. Their methods were often unorthodox and, as that night had shown, it could be pretty sketchy working alongside them.

It was a long day; the moments of fighting were interspersed with extended lulls. Between times of being shot at, I actually fell asleep once. We reconsolidated with our patrols in the valley late the next afternoon. We heard through the ICOM that more enemy fighters were going to shoot at us, and when we went looking for them we found a staging area they'd used – cooking, tents, supplies, beds, Dushka ammunition, mortars, paperwork, sixty days' worth of naan bread, palm oil, water. It could have supplied enemy forces on the hills for weeks. We found lots of hidey-holes in the rocks where they were even safe from the Hellfire missiles, but the Talibs themselves had squirted.

The final result was sixteen to twenty EKIA and, most importantly, a cleared road. We'd helped the KAU break the stalemate and travel freely through that part of the road, so it had been a success, albeit an unorthodox one.

*

For one of our last jobs on that trip, we were moved to the Helmand Valley, near Kandahar, our first job as Special Operations Task Group (SOTG) in a province other than Uruzgan. In Helmand, a traditional Taliban stronghold, the Brits had taken a lot of casualties. The bureaucratic restrictions were so complex that our theatre commander didn't even have the power to authorise us; it had to go a long way up the chain for approval. It seemed strange to me.

Even in a new province, the frustration continued. The job we were doing was in concert with the 4RAR Commandos. From experience, we'd told them in our briefings that if there was no immediate threat when clearing a village, it was counterproductive to 'blow in' – that is, to use explosives to enter the first target house. It would wake up the whole village and alert all the enemy fighters in the area. The Commandos agreed, but when the moment came, they blew in. We thought they would have enough professionalism to do what they'd said. When they set their explosion off, our terp's radio went bananas with all the enemy fighters waking up. They knew where we were and what was going on. The Commandos' blow-in had enabled them to get their network of fighters ready. As a result, we were involved in sporadic contacts all through the day.

As each trip to Afghanistan approached its end, my mood changed. I slowed down and grew more reflective. I'd compare it (although it's obviously a lot different) with a session in the surf. At the beginning, you're frothing to get as many waves as possible and go about your business frenetically; once you've achieved that, and turned it into a good session, you stop and take a look around. I would want to soak up every detail and remember it all, in case it never happened again. Even though the 2009 trip had fallen short of expectations, it was still successful because we didn't lose anyone. I still loved the job and wanted to make sure I didn't forget it.

Our last job was to fly into a bazaar in Uruzgan in a helicopter and take out a particular target. As we descended, we saw him jump on a motorbike and take off. We shot at him but missed; he crashed but got up and ran. A crowd of children had gathered around, we couldn't shoot, and he got away. We hooned around on his bike afterwards, dressing up Daryll in an old Russian fur cap and giving him a local name and character. It's the type of thing you do when the trip is ending and the mood is lightening. When we finished fooling around, we blew up the bike.

TWENTY-SIX

A feeling that assailed me towards the end of the trip was how much I was missing Emma and Kaylee. There were phones set up at the base at Tarin Kowt, so throughout the trip I'd been able to phone whenever I was back there, usually every second or third day. Communication tended to find its own rhythm when I was away. There would be a lot of calls at the beginning, but once we both got into our routines it was more a matter of monitoring things. There isn't a lot to talk about when you can't say in detail what you've been up to, and nothing else happens in Afghanistan that makes very interesting small talk. I wanted to hear about what was happening at home, but Emma knew not to drag me through the fine details of problems I couldn't help with. Towards the end of the trip, though, the phone calls picked up more, as we got excited about being together again. On 1 October Kaylee had her third birthday party and sounded so happy on the phone after going to an animal farm to play with rabbits and ride on ponies. She made me laugh every time I heard her voice.

Our reunion would be especially exciting this time, as it would be taking place in London, where I was to go for a private reception with the Queen. I had to leave a week before the rest of the squadron, and was fairly crook flying out after a big last night. I emptied my guts before the Dash 8 flight from Tarin Kowt to Kandahar, and then, not having eaten that morning or the night before, I was starving. Using my SAS resourcefulness, I purloined a blueberry pie that had been cooking in a microwave oven, and ate it on my way to the bus stop, shooting a filthy glare at anyone who looked at me as if it might not be my pie.

There was a Canadian general aboard the Hercules flight from Kandahar to Dubai, and the pilots decided to show off, as they do, throwing the plane about. I get motion sickness at the best of times, and now, feeling as I was, I had my body armour and helmet off and was tearing down the back of the plane before it had even levelled off. I managed to keep the blueberry pie down until the end, when the pilots decided to weave and duck and dive again, and it all went into my helmet. Fortunately, the liaison officer sent to pick me up in Dubai suffered from air sickness too. He said, 'You poor bastard,' and emptied my helmet into the bin.

On 6 November I landed in London and met Emma and Kaylee, as well as Barry from my patrol, who I'd been allowed to invite over. He was off crutches but still struggling with his legs. We did some tourist stuff and went to Hereford to see the 22 SAS base – the original model for the Australian SAS. I was impressed with the whole thing, but strangely, while I was sipping a whisky in the RHQ building, what hit me hardest was a poster of an American soldier who'd lost a leg to an IED in Iraq. The picture showed him in his multi-cams, back in Iraq, with one pants leg rolled up and his prosthetic leg showing. The text read: 'What's your excuse?' Having Barry there, barely able to walk, it was pretty emotional for me. He was one man who didn't need to offer any excuses.

The next day was raw and rainy, and I was taken in my service dress to Windsor Castle. Barry and my mentor Patto came with Emma, Kaylee and me. Outside, in the rain, soldiers were selling wristbands for Help for Heroes, a charity for wounded soldiers. They were about to deploy to Afghanistan for the first time and were really keen. Five guys from their unit had already come home after IED blasts. They wanted to be over there to look after their mates. Although their background was very different from ours, their inner drive was the same.

A stuffy army colonel came to meet us. Formality, as I've explained, was not my strength as a soldier. I had to learn to adapt again. This colonel turned to Barry and said, 'Look at Mark's service dress. Does that look right?'

Barry took a look and said, 'Yep, he looks fine.'

The colonel persisted: 'Look at my tie, and look at Mark's. It's not straight, is it?'

Barry said, 'Still looks all right to me.'

Having just come out of country, it was hard to adjust to this type of thing. I was still getting used to having people around me. A few days earlier we'd been sleeping with the dogs, like dogs, on whatever scraps of cardboard we could find in a village in Afghanistan. A few days out of that, Windsor Castle was a bit of an adjustment, and nobody had really briefed me on what I was expected to do.

Leaving the others outside, Emma and I were shown through some rooms. The Green Room was green with gold trim. The Crimson Room was crimson with gold trim. You never anticipate that a place is going to be just as over-the-top and ostentatious as on television, but it was. Everything was covered in gold.

I sat on a couch with Emma. The Australian defence attaché was there, and a Canadian general who was reporting to the Queen on the state of the Canadian forces. He said, 'You're going in before me. I've been relegated.'

I apologised.

He said, 'I'll be relegated for a VC winner any day.'

We heard a distant barking, and paws scratching the floor: the corgis were coming. Ushers and minions were rushing about. I was told to stand in front of a pair of white doors. I said to the usher, 'What's the protocol? What am I supposed to do?'

'Nobody's told you yet?'

This was seconds before Her Majesty was ready to receive me. He quickly said, 'Bow when you go through the doors and move towards her and then bow again, don't speak until you're spoken to,' and a lot of other Don'ts that I immediately forgot. He said, 'There will be camera crews and journalists to photograph the meeting, and then it'll be you and the Queen alone for fifteen or twenty minutes.'

I said, 'Is it Ma'am as in jam?'

He said, 'Yes. Bow and take three steps forward.'

We met in the White Room, which was, funnily enough, white with gold trim. I bowed, took three steps forward, and bowed again.

'G'day, Ma'am. Mark Donaldson.'

The photographers snapped and left, and we stood and chatted for fifteen minutes about Afghanistan, where I'd grown up in Australia, and my family. She was talking about her grandchildren running around destroying the place, and we exchanged stories about the willpower of three-year-old girls. I just found her an extremely warm, down-to-earth lady, more like a favourite grandma than a queen. We stayed standing up the whole time. She was shuffling in her shoes, as if they were making her uncomfortable, and I was so relaxed with her I was going to say, 'Do you want to take a seat, Ma'am?' I later heard that that would have been a definite no-no, so it was just as well I didn't say it.

Then she said, 'At this event tomorrow night, just remember to pause before you lay the wreath so that I can touch it.'

The next night, the evening of Remembrance Day, there would be a wreath-laying ceremony in Westminster Abbey for the passing of the last of the World War I generation. All I'd been told was that I had to go to it.

I said, 'Are you going to be there, Ma'am?'

She looked at me funnily and said, 'Yes, at the wreath-laying, I'll be there.'

We talked about Windsor Castle and she said, 'I had an American here in this room, and we were sitting here, and he said, "This is a lovely place, Ma'am, but I don't understand why you built it so close to the airport."'

I laughed and said, 'You should have said, "The land was going cheap."'

She had genuine concerns about Afghanistan, and was very inquisitive. I asked her about the VC. She said, 'I remember signing off on it on Christmas Eve. I read through it twice with all the family around. I was so amazed.'

I said, 'Sorry, Ma'am, did you say Christmas Eve?'

She said she remembered it well. Interesting – when the chief of army had met me in January, he'd said that it still needed to be sent to the Queen for confirmation. It was good to know from the source how it all really happened! But maybe General Gillespie had been given the wrong information.

It was awe-inspiring to talk with her about the Cross. She'd given Keith Payne his VC, and Ray Simpson too.

It was her great-great-grandmother who conceived the award back during the Crimean War. The medal is older than Australia as a country. To be attached to that is a huge honour and being in England, seeing how much they respect it, brought that sense of history home to me. To meet the Queen, who was related to the person who instigated its inception, was incredible.

We shook hands again, and I was ushered away through the big doors. Outside, crowds were already cheering and clapping and saying, 'Well done, Mark!' The pictures taken by the photographers less than half an hour earlier had already gone around the world. It humbled me to see how much it meant to a crowd of Brits outside Windsor Castle.

I went to the Abbey for the rehearsal for the wreath-laying, and was shown how it would run. The Queen and all the heads of the Commonwealth or their representatives would be there. I said, 'Cheers for the heads up! I've just made myself look like a dick in front of the Queen!'

Sergeant Johnson Beharry, the British soldier awarded a VC for his actions in Iraq in 2004, was going to lay the wreath with me. He was a really nice guy. As we did a walk-through, a British Defence Ministry staffer told me how they had gone through my VC recommendation and compared it with the 1300 others who had received the award, checking through the criteria. I'd never known it went through such a strenuous process, but I was always learning new things about the importance of the Cross.

While Emma and Kaylee wandered off to do a self-guided tour of the most secluded parts of the Abbey, Johnson and I had a laugh while a tenor was practising for the ceremony and hitting some high notes. Johnson said, 'They must be grabbing his balls to get him that high. I'm not going to be able to look at him tomorrow without laughing.'

I said, 'I'll look after you.'

'The Queen'll be sitting right there watching us from the throne.'

During the ceremony, the feeling when the Queen arrived couldn't have been more different from when I'd met her the day before. The whole place bowed. She wore a royal robe and a crown, and had an entirely different demeanour – she was large and powerful, not a favourite grandma but The Queen. As everyone was bowing and scraping, I was just taking it all in and found myself looking at her. She caught my eye. I thought, *Fuck!* and ducked my head. We weren't there as people any more. She was Queen Elizabeth and I was a subject.

The tenor came out to sing. Johnson was daydreaming, and I nudged him. He got the giggles. I was saying, 'There's nothing to laugh about, mate!' He couldn't stop. Then we both looked up and the Queen was staring at the pair of us. Johnson put his head down. I looked away.

Johnson and I walked up some steps in unison, picked up the wreath, which was the size of a truck tyre, and walked it down through the abbey with the Queen behind us. We walked to the grave of the Unknown Soldier. The Queen put down her card and touched the poppies, and we laid the wreath on the tomb and stepped back. I was thinking, *I'm just an Aussie country kid from Dorrigo, laying a wreath with the Queen for the passing of the World War I generation.* Sometimes there's a chasm between who you are and what you find yourself doing. I was thinking to myself that you can become something bigger and better than you ever imagined.

Outside, I found Emma and did a couple of interviews. We went to a pub with Barry and Patto for a feed. British people were coming up, hugging and thanking me. A man said, 'I'm from 3 Para in the Falklands. I just want to shake your hand.' It was full-on, getting this treatment in England, and brought home again how important that award was to them.

Over the next few days, we were privileged to see some unforgettable sights and people in London and across the Channel. At the House of Lords, we met Viscount Slim, who had been an important mover in creating an Australian SAS back in the 1950s. His father had been Australia's governor-general. Their family crest has wattle in it, to show the link to Australia. He looked, acted and talked like a lord. In his eighties, he still had the movements of a forty-year-old. He congratulated us on what we'd done, and hit me over the head with a roll of paper and said, 'Don't let it fucking go to your head!'

'I'll try my best, sir.'

He said, 'I like you guys,' and took us on a private tour of the House. He said, 'Don't listen to what they're saying or else you'll go to sleep like everyone else.' Sure enough, one of the lords was racking out in the middle of parliament. We took a look around before he bought us a drink at the bar and showed us where Charles I lost his head.

In France, we saw another side of the historic links between Australia and our allies. In Paris I participated in the nightly lighting of the flame at the tomb in the Arc de Triomphe, where among other things they thank the forces that came to save their country. We toured the Western Front, visiting Fromelles when they were excavating the World War I graves, and were allowed to handle precious artefacts, such as Rising Sun badges, a morphine vial, a lucky charm and a button that had been dug up. At Menin Gate in Ypres, Belgium, I spoke the Ode at the nightly service. It was as if they had Remembrance Day, or Anzac Day, every single night. They truly never have forgotten. On the walls there were 55,000 names of those who died in battle. About a hundred British schoolkids were at the ceremony, and some French services personnel, and the kids mobbed us, wanting photos with Australian soldiers. Later, sitting in a pub in dress uniform felt very comfortable and natural and honourable, perhaps more so in Belgium than it ever could in Australia.

We went through the battlefields heading south back to Paris: Pozières, where there's a memorial to the Australians who won VCs; and Villers-Bretonneux, to see the Victoria school and the Commonwealth War Graves Commission cemetery. Earlier that year, back in Australia, I'd met some kids who'd won a prize to go to the trenches at Pozières. They'd won an essay competition in which they'd written about someone from their town who'd died over there. 'Just remember,' I said, 'when you see his grave, you'll be sur-prised how emotional you're going to be.' One of the kids later wrote back to me, 'You were right.' It's indescribable, the emotions that come over you in that setting, knowing what happened. As a group we always took the appropriate time at each site to say thanks and pay our respects for those Australians, New Zealanders, Canadians and others who did not make it back.

In Villers-Bretonneux I was given a paperweight inscribed with the Victoria Cross, made of the same stone as the gravestones. Nearly a hundred years after World War I, people were still coming up and expressing thanks to Barry and me, just because we were Australian. Even though I didn't do it consciously, I was trying to be a good ambassador for Australia.

At Le Hamel, we were shown the battlefield where Sir John Monash had led the integration of forms of warfare in a decisive battle, in which two Australians had won VCs in ten minutes. I still carry around a small piece of rock from one of the bunkers at Le Hamel, along with mementos from throughout that trip. If ever I'm getting overwhelmed, I pick up that piece of rock and think, 'This is nothing compared to what they went through. Stop whingeing.'

TWENTY-SEVEN

Before I'd left Afghanistan in 2009, Ken Gillespie had contacted me in country to tell me I had been nominated and chosen as Young Australian of the Year for Western Australia, and was therefore up for the award of Young Australian of the Year, which would be announced on Australia Day 2010. Having just returned to being a soldier once more after all the attention around the Victoria Cross, I told him again that I was hesitant. I don't know if he saw this as my (laudable, I hope) commitment to my profession, or just thought that I was a pain in the neck, but he said it would be a good thing if I accepted. I said, 'Okay, I'll accept it, but if it later turns out to mean a lot of extra time away from my family and the job, I hope you'll understand if I back off and decide to turn it down.'

When we were in Fromelles, the Chief of Staff of Army Headquarters, Brigadier David Mulhall, called to ask if I would accept the Young Australian of the Year honour if it came to me. I took my counsel from Emma and Brent, who had gone to Perth to accept the state award on my behalf. Brent said, 'There's two ways of looking at it. You might not do it, and that's fine because you want to spend that time with Emma and Kaylee. But on the other hand, no private soldier has been awarded the Young Australian of the Year. A trooper's the lowest rank, and to be awarded this is a pretty big deal. Don't think of it as yourself, think of it as representing all those other soldiers you're working with. You're getting the word out to younger people about the job you're doing.'

Emma said much the same thing, and the two of them swung me around. In January, after we'd got home from France, I had a chat with Adam Gilchrist, the great former Test cricketer and chairman of the Australia Day Council. When I told him I was worried about travelling the country again for public appearances, Gilly said, 'We didn't choose you because of the amount of time you'd put in. We chose you because you're an inspiration.' It was a nice thing to say, and lifted a lot of the pressure I'd been putting on myself. The award ceremony was great to be a part of. I was impressed to be able to meet so many amazing people. Many of them were completely selfless in what they endeavoured to do with their lives.

In the end it was a great honour, although sometimes I felt I was disappointing people because I couldn't answer all their questions about what we were doing in Afghanistan, which was a hot topic of course. There was always this tension between us wanting to tell our story about all the things we were achieving over there, and the restrictions on what we could say. And I'm not exactly the world's smoothest salesman. I hoped that my own story could inspire people all the same.

Back at work, I spent 2010 in a 'recovery' role in Perth, meaning I had to be prepared and ready to go at a moment's notice. I did my promotion courses for corporal, a stage I'd missed out on due to my commitments in 2009. I definitely wanted to step up and begin the path to leadership. The truth is, you can lead from any position. They call Afghanistan the war of the 'strategic private'. Your attitude, leadership style and the way you do business shows leadership at any level. But gaining promotion is the normal progression, and you won't have much longevity in the Regiment if you don't want to be a PC or TL (team leader). Guys often say they want to stay a trooper and stick to the simple life, but they find that their mates progress, more junior people go past them, and eventually a bloke who's been a trooper for seven or eight years will be operating beneath a corporal who's much less experienced. That can create instability and distrust in a team environment. And besides, the Regiment is always looking for leadership qualities from the very outset, and I'd found that the longer I was in it, and the more action I saw in Afghanistan, the more interested I was in seeing the bigger picture and influencing events where I could.

I went to Adelaide to do one of my courses with the regular army. Once again, my shyness about being the centre of attention got the better of me. Within the Regiment, I was treated as Donno. In fact, when the VC came up, which was every day, it was often because of Bruce's unyielding belief that what I did was stupid. We still laugh about it. He would give orders, and sometimes finish with, 'Unless you want to do something stupid like Donno.' Those who understand, they like to take the piss out of each other. By contrast, on the promotion course with people from the wider army, which are almost like corporate training days, I was treated as 'the VC guy', with everyone wanting to hear about Afghanistan, which was a little unsettling when I was trying to blend in with the crowd doing a course for one of the lowest ranks. I didn't mind too much, but I was still adapting to what I had to accept was now my normal life.

The course put me into an agitated state. It was dragging on for eight weeks, which was a long time away on top of operations and training. It added a huge burden to my home life, and I was beginning to think that the point of the course was not much more than a tick in a box to say we had passed the army's corporate governance standards for junior leaders. It was also eight weeks when I could have been giving back to the Regiment, sharing knowledge on our own training. In the mood I was in, I talked myself into thinking the course was counterproductive, detracting from our own capability. My frame of mind was also typical of how a combat soldier can feel when away from the action: impatient and critical with the slow pace of things when they're used to a high tempo, excitement and the satisfaction of achieving results.

I became a corporal, but soon I had something much more important to worry about. Late in 2009 Emma had fallen pregnant, but halfway through my promotion course she called up, quite upset, to tell me there was something wrong. Two weeks earlier, she'd had an accident on her bicycle that had resulted in Kaylee breaking her arm, and Emma hadn't felt right ever since.

When I called her doctor, he said, 'She's okay. Just calm her down.'

I said, 'She knows her own body. She knows if something's wrong.'

The next day, she went to hospital with pain and bleeding. I flew home and went straight there, where they told me that Emma had been pregnant with twins but had lost both of them. The operation they performed had damaged her tubes. When I got to see her, she was very upset because it might mean she couldn't have any more babies.

Over the next weeks and months, she and I started discussing IVF. We decided to commit to it, but it was harder than usual. I was often away on courses or doing representative duties when Emma was ovulating, so they had to freeze my samples, which apparently wasn't as good for the process as having me on the spot. Time after time we tried it, and when nothing was happening the anxiety and disappointment began to wear away at Emma. The constant cycle of having to do it all herself without me there to help would have been extremely hard for her and I really don't know how she managed. We really wanted to increase our small tribe by one and it was depressing both of us that it wasn't working as easy as we'd hoped.

In fact that year, when we were supposed to be back in Australia spending time at home, I actually spent more time away from it than I would have if I was involved in a full tour in Afghanistan. After two promotional courses, a skydiving course, a two-week surge into Afghanistan, VC duties and other time away with general SAS training, Emma and I figured out how long I'd been away. By the 38-week mark of the year, I had been away from home for 28 weeks. There were still 14 weeks left and a lot of work to come.

Meanwhile, work was taking an interesting new turn. Ever since childhood, I'd loved dogs. Angie had been a favourite, and my own dog, Lister, had definitely been my best friend when things were at their lowest. The opportunity to combine my love of dogs with work came up in 2010, when the Regiment was stepping up its use of combat assault dogs. In Afghanistan, we were now working much more during the daytime, and the dogs could act as a force-multiplier. Having an early warning system of a dog running into abandoned buildings, through thick vegetation or high-risk compounds would give us a buffer before we contacted the enemy. The Talibs hated and feared dogs.

They did have dogs themselves, but tended to treat them like . . . dogs, keeping them in a filthy state and feeding them badly. Properly trained combat dogs could transform the way the Regiment contacted the enemy at close quarters. So, rather than become a patrol 2IC, the normal role for a corporal, I put my hand up to be a dog handler.

In August, my mate Blue and I went to visit a dog breeder in the western suburbs of Sydney. There was a Belgian malinois that had a different quality from the ones I'd been training with. He was aggressive but highly obedient. There was just something about him. I thought, 'If I had a dog to work with, I'd love this one.' I'd been having trouble developing an ex-RAAF dog, and this one had an X-factor. His name was Devil, and he was eighteen months old. Blue decided to take him and put him through our selection process.

Back at Swanbourne, the boys were sceptical because Devil was small and self-contained. The typical dogs we used were big, hard-hitting and menacing. But I could see his potential. We were pushing a dual role for the dogs, in which they could both attack armed fighters and also sniff out explosives. Speed, flexibility and adaptability are always key to what we do, and having dogs that could combine multiple jobs would be part of our light, fast-moving work patterns.

I began working with Devil every day, coming into work early, walking him and training him. There was one day early in our partnership when he tested who was in charge. The other handlers had warned me about this but I didn't think he would try it, not my dog. It was afternoon feed time and I was prepping his meal. I had it in a dish on the counter and he was patiently sitting behind me on the floor. I moved away to wash my hands and when I turned back he was two paws up on the counter helping himself to a free feed. I scolded him and went to pull him away from it. I had a hold of his collar when he turned and snapped and snarled at me, trying to bite my arm. I quickly grabbed him by the scruff of the tail and lifted him off the ground, but he managed to sink a few teeth into my arm. I carried him to his kennel and threw him in with a kick up the bum mid-flight. I didn't give him his food that night and after that there was never an issue with who was in control, at dinner time anyway. It was a steep learning curve for both of us. We had some US Special Forces personnel visit for a few days to do some training with us, and one of them said the quality of your dog would result directly from the amount of work you put into him. The key, as the others were always telling me, was: 'Trust your dog, trust your dog.' The dog knows what he's doing. It's you that second-guesses and plays mind games. But it takes a while before you realise that in most situations you, the human, are the weaker link.

Training Devil was almost like going back to the beginning and relearning how to be an operator, this time with him as my other half. Urban combat was especially important; as a team, we went down ropes, jumped out of planes, did low-light and night work, live-fire contact skills and fighting house to house. It was in a training exercise at Swanbourne that we had our breakthrough moment. I sent Devil to scout in thick bush where someone was hiding to ambush us. Devil's job was to find him and attack him before he got us. I thought the guy was in a certain spot, and Devil kept going the other way. He was off-lead, 100 metres or more in front of me, working his nose on the enemy's scent. He turned and, through some bushes, gave me a look. I was trying to point him in another direction with hand gestures. He paid me off, as if to say, 'Mate, you don't know what you're talking about.' Five seconds later, he found the bloke hiding in the bush. Devil 1, Mark 0. I had to learn to trust him.

*

Late in the year, I was finally in Perth at the right time to contribute to the IVF process (to give a live sample). The heartache, pain and worry that Emma went through was really hard and almost pushed us to the brink. We had tried so many times, and the emotional changes came upon her in big wrenching swells. Though it was difficult, I had enormous love and respect for how much effort and heart she put in, all for the chance to increase our family by one.

Shortly after that attempt, we were invited to England for a reunion of the VCGC (Victoria Cross and George Cross) Association. Emma would get to meet the Queen this time, and we took her mother to look after Kaylee while we went to events. It was exciting for Emma to be able to do more with me, though there was something missing. I really felt like I had left someone behind. I said, 'I can't stop thinking about what's happening to Devil.' Emma just rolled her eyes.

There were only eight or nine VCs and twenty-odd GCs, so the reception with the Queen and Prince Phillip in Buckingham Palace was quite intimate. We were at the end of the line waiting to meet Her Majesty and were having the pleasure of meeting Prince Edward and Sophie, Countess of Wessex, as well as other members of the royal family, when Emma started getting extremely emotional.

She began this high-pitched whisper: 'That's the Queen – she's right there!'

I tried to calm her down. 'Yep, don't worry, she's just the Queen.'

'That's what I mean! She's almost here!'

We got through it, but Emma's emotions were at a peak. And there was a reason for it. Later that day, she called the hospital in Australia and they said she was pregnant. We were absolutely stoked.

The next day we met Prince Charles and Camilla, Duchess of Cornwall, at Clarence House for lunch, a tour and a photograph. I found them extremely knowledge-able and approachable, but as usual I didn't have a clue about the protocol. I was chatting with Prince Charles and Camilla while we were waiting to go into lunch, and then a reporter sidled up to ask me some questions. I got caught up in the conversation and suddenly there was a tug at my elbow.

'Mark!' It was Emma. 'Get the hell in here. Everyone's waiting for you to come inside the hall! No one can sit down!'

I went in, and stood between my chair and the table. My embarrassment wasn't quite finished. Camilla stood next to me, and I was in the process of sitting down when Emma, on my other side, grabbed my arm.

'Mark! Don't sit down yet! They sit down first!'

As I tried to stop myself from sitting, I managed to knock my chair over. It went down with a great clatter and as I was fixing it up, Camilla sat next to me and said with a wry smile, 'You've got to watch those chairs, they can be tricky sometimes.'

We had more official functions, which I probably enjoyed even more than the previous year because I was ready for them. I met Princess Anne at the opening of a VCGC exhibition at the Imperial War Museum. I was extremely surprised by how much she knew of not only me and Emma, but also my actions and the number of times I had been to Afghanistan. She was impressive and straight down the line. I spoke the Ode of Remembrance at St Martins in the Field on 11 November. Giving the Ode and hear-ing my voice echo around the church was a very powerful, emotional moment. I chatted with Charles and Camilla, Viscount Slim and others who'd been there in 2009, and we did another ceremony at the Remembrance Monument. Weirdly, it almost felt like a reunion. These people were as foreign to my upbringing and experience as can be imagined, but I was comfortable, as if among old friends.

TWENTY-EIGHT

The first months of 2011 were about gearing up to go back to Afghanistan, and I was building a real bond with Devil. Craig was the senior dog handler in the squadron. He was extremely helpful, passing his knowledge on to me when I was learning all the basics. He had been doing it for a few years so his advice was sound. His commitment to his dogs was a testament to how well they performed, so much so he has received recognition for his efforts in the form of an award. Craig and I had two dogs for the whole squadron, and our plan was to float between the patrols and attach ourselves wherever we could be most useful. It was a hard sell to say to these super-professional, brave and keen operators, 'Stop and we'll send the dogs out in front.' It wasn't natural for them to accept that a dog might be smarter and faster in finding the enemy. But we demonstrated it in exercises. We'd jump out of helicopters with the dogs, looking for suspects hidden in the bush, and suddenly the dogs would get a scent of them on the wind and take off. Or, the boys would clear a room and the dogs would find someone hidden in a cupboard who'd been overlooked. Once our guys saw it happen, they understood what a force-multiplier the dogs could be.

We would have to adapt the dogs' training to what we learnt in combat situations. Initially, in training our 'enemies' would carry on with a great noise. But we learnt that the insurgents in Afghanistan actually just froze. So we had to train our dogs to react correctly regardless of the targets' actions or reactions, and whether they were moving or not. There were many ways of training the dogs to tell the difference between friendly and enemy forces. Eventually their ability to do so was amazing, and enabled them to weave around and among operators to engage an enemy threat.

It was February when we arrived in country; there was still snow in the mountains. The whole country smelt crisper and harsher at that time of year than in late summer, when I'd last been there. New grass, new growth, new year, new fighting season. Devil proved his worth on one of our first jobs. We were clearing a house, and some armed Talibs had hidden deep inside a room. If we'd walked in, one of us may well have been shot. Instead, I sent Devil in first and he got the fighter with the weapon and broke his arm. I was elated for Devil, and my mates became total converts. You can do all the training in the world, but you never know how a dog will react until you're in the real thing. Just like a soldier. And Devil knew exactly what he was doing.

On the first few jobs, Craig and I and our dogs were switching between the ground assault force and the AFS (aerial fire support) birds to assist in catching squirters. Soon, we were proving ourselves so useful that we were asked to go on the first lift. Troopers were being cut out to fit us in. In the helicopter you get a five-, a three- and a one-minute call before landing. Devil lay under my feet. Eventually he learnt that the precise change of the engine's pitch before the one-minute call was his signal to sit up and be ready. He really understood and liked his role. And the squadron's attitude changed from 'We're not sure' to 'We're not going out unless we have a dog with us'.

Added to that was the morale boost the dogs gave us. When I was having a bad day, just giving Devil a pat and telling him my thoughts, or tickling him behind the ear, improved my outlook. As for my mates, when I brought Devil into the lines, it was no longer, 'Hey, Donno.' It was, 'Hey, Devil! How are you, mate?' I might as well not have been there. I couldn't let him over-socialise, though, because he'd start to lose his edge. The guys were always trying to pat him or sneak him something to eat. We had a rule that if they got caught, they had to come training with us and take an attack from Devil.

After a hard day, or waiting for extraction from the helicopters, I'd let Devil just be a dog and sniff around. My rule was, if I can rest, he can rest. I saw on the guys' faces how he took them back home, to their own dogs. It was such a simple thing, to pat a dog and see him wag his tail. Then he'd come back to me, put his head in my lap and rack out until the chopper came. I knew he'd be my mate, no matter what.

The tempo of work was accelerating. In our first thirty days, we did twenty-two or twenty-three jobs. Our OC had us on the front foot, capturing and killing the Taliban leadership. He said he was going to work us to the bone for three months. 'We're going to kick the arse out of them. We're not here for a holiday. Let's do our job as effectively as we can.' Being told that upfront, we were keen to work for him. It was good to know where he stood and what was expected of us. The other bonus for this trip was our SSM (squadron sergeant major) was Deano, my troop sergeant from 2008. As well, our troop sergeant was Daryll. So that meant we had experienced 'ground up' soldiers in those influential positions.

Even though the enemy leaders replaced themselves quickly, the effect of losing them gave the regular Australian Army and ANA enough time to get in and set up the legitimate governance the people were wanting. Our targeting was helped by the higher quality of intelligence we were getting compared with previous years. It was better organised, so we could fuse that information with what we'd picked up on the ground. For instance, intel might have been telling us that Taliban leaders were coming from Quetta to Tarin Kowt, and giving us a few days to get them. But with our experience, we knew that Quetta to TK is like Sydney to Dubbo, and they could be in and out in a day. So the mission was launched more speedily. The war was definitely turning our way, due to the coherence and accuracy of the intelligence we were getting. We were also being assisted by divisions among the enemy. The Talibs were surprisingly quick to rat each other out. Some of the informants were very close to our targets, and were keen to have them knocked off.

A lot has been alleged about us being used by the part-nering force intelligence to settle personal feuds; there were suggestions that they would lead us to target individuals not because they were part of the insurgency but because they were someone's old enemy. I'm not saying this never happened, but the reports of it were exaggerations. The fact was, we would never take one man or one group's informa-tion as the last word on targeting. We took our intelligence from a number of different sources, crosschecked and cor-roborated it, and only went after someone if we were sure he was an enemy. If the Afghans said, 'Get this bad guy in this house,' we wouldn't just roll out and prosecute. We'd get a lot more information through our own intelligence systems. It's a bit of a myth that coalition forces are easily used by locals to go after their personal enemies.

*

The excitement of going out on a job is a feeling that will never leave me. In my life I like to bring out the boy, the sense of adventure and the unknown. I think your excitement needs to come out no matter what it is you are doing. If you don't then you just become a cranky, grumpy person.

I still get excited going out on missions. It's hard to curb that enthusiasm sometimes and not hoot, yahoo and show that excitement. I'm jumping out of my skin on the inside, but I try to remain calm and focused on the outside. I used to get really bummed out when there was a possibility of a job on and it looked like a go but then for whatever reason it was turned off. It takes a while to learn how to deal with that and realise that you sometimes need to be patient. Within half an hour of getting the word, we would be on the helicopter. I sat with Devil at my feet, the blades turning, lifting off into the unknown. It is almost euphoric when you have that confidence. You are excited, but also retaining control of your emotions. Even now, if I shut my eyes, I can be back there.

We did a lot of jobs where the dogs were beneficial. We went up to Char China, where we'd taken out those thirteen Talibs on the dry riverbed a couple of years earlier. As we landed, the helicopter's rotors kicked up a big cloud of dust that smelt like goat shit and fur. I was running from the landing zone to link up with a patrol in the green belt. Devil's lead was clipped to my belt. It was a hot morning and beside the track, a strong radiant heat was coming off the compounds we went past. As I was running, I noticed an Afghan paralleling me, darting from building to building. I couldn't get a good read on what he was doing, but his demeanour was suspicious. Innocent people usually just stood and stared at us. He was moving in a tactical way.

Devil and I made it to the centre of the village, and came into a tight alleyway. The residents had been burning rubbish, and there was a strong smell of scorched plastic. Right beside us was a pile of smouldering ashes. All of a sudden, a big local mongrel came tearing down towards us. Our dogs are trained to be neutral towards other animals. We don't want them to be distracted by animals and potentially miss a threat. But this dog was frothing and hell-bent on charging at Devil. At the last moment, as it leapt, I shot it three times. The last shot was very close to Devil's face. The dog dropped dead, and Devil just stood looking at it, no doubt wondering what that was all about. My heart was racing.

Having heard the shots, one of our guys came over, and I explained what had happened. I mentioned the suspicious man who'd been paralleling us. There had also been a lot of Talibs squirting from the target area to get weapons and set up an ambush or to get away. While we were talking, we heard some shots from a poppy field where another patrol was. It was a dangerous spot.

Just then, my mate saw the man who'd been tracking me. He was moving between two mud walls behind a house. Just as he snuck towards us and raised his rifle, my mate shot him.

Soon after, we had to clear the area and join the other patrols. I sent Devil into a house in front of me. He had a camera mounted on his back, and I could watch the picture on a screen on my chest. He went into a dark bedroom and began sniffing a bed.

I poked my head in and said, 'What is it, mate?'

I could see someone under there. Strangely, Devil wasn't attacking them. My mate and I went in, and I called Devil back and clipped him up. In the bed were two kids, aged about four and seven, sound asleep. Devil had known not to engage them. Under all the pressure of the noise and danger around us, he made that distinction. I was very pleased that he was smart enough to tell the difference.

We went outside the village, where our patrols had already swept the poppy fields twice, looking for the squirters. A river ran past the village, with a steep bank dropping from the fields to the water. The river was running fast, cutting away the bank with fresh, deep snowmelt. A footpad of hard-packed earth ran along the top of the bank, cutting in between each field. These were high-traffic areas and vulnerable for IEDs, as the enemy knew we'd be walking along the footpads. If they hid in the fields or down the riverbank, they could have the drop on us.

Typically for early in the poppy season, the day was thick with pollen, and the fields, which had been drenched with water, had a cabbagy smell. I was struggling with my breathing and a runny nose from hay fever. I sent Devil 50 metres ahead of me, let him search, and waited. Then I went up and joined him. At one point, when he picked up something on the wind, he gave a head-flick. As a handler, you're looking for those indications. His hair started standing up, his tail was upright, his ears forward, all the mannerisms of excitement. My mate and I paused. Devil followed the scent, and we pushed up behind him. He stopped. He'd found a pair of shoes on the top of the riverbank, and down below on a sandy patch were some footprints.

We looked further up river, where Devil was now headed. My mate, a New Zealander, saw a couple of broken branches and some markings on the riverbank. Fifty metres ahead of us, Devil did a double head-flick and dived head first into a hole in a tree stump overhanging the riverbank. His tail was going like mad. His battle jacket was catching, stopping him getting into the trunk. We patrolled up to his position. I pushed him with my foot. He got in and grabbed onto something he'd scented. It was an elbow. Devil was pulling back on it, dragging someone out. I saw the tip of a weapon and shot the Talib as he emerged. He fell into the river. Devil was still attached to his arm, and the water began pulling them both down. I was yelling commands to Devil to let go, but the current was taking him and I was thinking, *Fuck, I've lost my dog.*

Next minute, Devil popped up and swam back over, all excited and spinning around. He'd done his job all right, probably saving our lives. That insurgent in the log was a real danger to us, and would have got us if we'd walked another 50 metres. It just showed what Devil brought to the patrol.

The river had cut a little island in the next bend, and the bank fell away. Devil now ploughed in and swam across to the island, having smelt someone on the opposite bank. If any enemy fighters were there, we were in a tricky spot, vulnerable from the high ground across the water. I lost sight of Devil. Again, I had that sinking feeling that I'd lost my mate. I was genuinely concerned for him and ran down looking for something that suddenly seemed impossible: a tan dog in a brown jacket in a brown river.

I yelled to my mate, 'Have you seen him?'

He hadn't. Just as I was feeling panicky, I looked down into an eddy, and there was Devil, paddling on the spot, fighting the current. I jumped in, waded across and dragged him out. I couldn't be angry with him for doing his job. As we got out of the water, he wanted to tear across again and go after whatever it was he'd scented. As we were being extracted on the helicopters, the enemy across the river ended up having a crack at us: a few bursts of PKM fire and RPGs, just to remind us they were still there.

It was a satisfying day for Devil and me. We, as a troop, ended up getting all eight of the enemy we'd targeted, and came back to base exhilarated. Devil had saved my life, and my mate's. We were busy and right where we wanted to be.

*

Changes in the Mirabad Valley, an area very close to Tarin Kowt district centre, indicated how well the war was progressing for us. In April, after my birthday, we did a couple of successful jobs there. On the first job, our intelligence was so good that we just about landed on top of the target, a fully rigged-up senior Taliban fighter, and got him trying to escape across a river. Then we went after an insurgent who had been intimidating and murdering civilians since the previous year at least, and had escaped from 1 Squadron on their trip. As we flew in, we saw men squirting everywhere, darting between trees and trying to blend in with the farmers. I was on the AFS for this mission. It's like police work: good guys don't run away. I remembered my own actions in the Coffs Harbour mall. If I'd done nothing wrong, why would I be running from the police?

We identified a secondary target and fired smoke markers at him to pinpoint his whereabouts for the ground force. He went into a building and tried to make another run for it. We were going to land in a paddock, but I let the TL know that if he dropped me in with Devil, we could pick him up while they talked us on. But at the last moment he ran into another building and the TL aborted.

As patrols on the ground began to close in on the building, we watched from above. A few minutes after going in, the target came out, dressed in a woman's green shawl, leading a cow. It was a pathetic disguise and fooled nobody. Suddenly he let go of the cow, ran down the riverbank and then doubled back into a compound. We finally landed and followed, and the women and girls were out the front pointing into a room. He was not from there, they said, and they didn't want him in their place. We found him hiding behind some cushions and got him out.

We took our captured ringleader and some other suspects to our extraction point that was near a police checkpoint. What happened then illustrates the low price of life in a country that has been at war for decades. The Afghan police commander had our earlier target under guard. He knew him well. The suspect had killed the family of a friend of the police commander's, and had tried to kill him too. He had been a really nasty piece of work in that valley, and the police commander was not about to let us have him. We wanted to take him with us, but the police commander stated that we would only release him again in a few days. What he did next was too fast for us to react. The police commander settled the matter by walking over to the insurgent, taking out his AK and shooting the man dead. As can happen in Afghanistan, a three-year-old boy was with some other people milling around, watching it all. He started crying at the loud noise of the gun. One of our terps gave him a fruit juice. He began sucking on it quite happily.

There were serious repercussions from the episode. A coalition eye in the sky had been watching the whole thing, and the drone operator in Kandahar rang his bosses in Dubai and said he'd seen an execution of a captive. We had to answer some interrogatories to explain how that wasn't the case at all. It was a very quick and uncontrolled action by the police commander, his way of settling a dispute. As a group, we had no real qualms about a really bad guy being taken out of the area by the responsible Afghan. He was, all in all, a strong and effective presence, running his area with very little coalition help. He was so effective that the Taliban launched a yearlong campaign to assassinate him. Unfortunately, after many attempts, they were successful, getting him with an IED. He was one of the few local authorities I encountered who was true to helping the people and fixing the place up, undeterred by threats. It was a real shame that he paid the ultimate price.

But this was the cost of success. The Mirabad Valley became very quiet, and the local government was able to establish itself. The Talibs stopped going into the valley, saying it was too dangerous, whereas up until 2008 it had been the reverse, with us having been wary of going into a non-permissive area. In these small but significant ways, village by village, valley by valley, we were making progress.

*

My bond with Devil was growing exponentially. I knew now that if I didn't trust him, I would get myself killed.

On one job, he found some enemy fighters with rifles and RPGs hiding in thick vegetation only five metres from where my mates were. On another, we were in the backyard of a house and he was staring at the dirt. I said, 'What are you staring at? There's nothing there.' I went over and had a scratch. Devil was insistent and I chose to trust him. I sat him down and called an engineer with a metal detector, who found a big buried bag of machine gun rounds. I was amazed that Devil had sniffed it out. To him it was no different from a training run, while to me it was the best thing in the world. Our methods and training – all the hard work – were paying off. On yet another job, Devil went up to a normal-looking rock wall and stopped. I thought he was giving me a 'falsie', or false indication, trying to trick me into giving him a reward such as a tennis ball to chew on or a pat. In our early days he'd been a shocker for trying to outsmart me with falsies. I thought he was doing it again. But he'd found the wind pooling with a scent in an indentation in the wall, and lo and behold there was a stashed-away AK and chest rig, all bombed up and ready to go. Just like that, a weapon that could have been used to kill one of us or intimidate the local populace had been taken out of circulation.

Even though 2011 was a very successful trip for our squadron, there were always moments of frustration. I was used to them, but sometimes they tested us to the limit. One early morning in May, we got word that an Australian had been shot in the Chora Valley, in what was the first green-on-blue attack on one of us. These attacks – where a uniformed Afghan serviceman turned on coalition soldiers – had been getting progressively worse in 2011, but until now they hadn't involved Australians. We asked to be sent up to Chora to find the perpetrator. It was a matter of honour and urgency. An Australian soldier had been killed; we thought there should be no debate. We had good intel, and thought we could lock up one part of that valley and force him to show his hand.

The hierarchy outside of our squadron were toing and froing for eighteen hours before finally allowing us to do something about it. We were agitated. In those eighteen hours, he could have got to the other side of Afghanistan.

Intelligence came up that he was near the Pakistan border in another province, near his family. The insurgency had facilitated his movement up there. Two SAS teams, a headquarters element and Devil and I were put together to go. The Americans were fully behind us, treating our morale issues very seriously. They gave us three helicopters and full logistical support, plus a place to stay with some of their Special Forces. We were going to get a C-130 Hercules up there. But at the crucial moment, the RAAF had reservations about the dirt airstrip we were to land on: dirt strips they were supposed to be able to land on, unseen, all the time. The US were landing C-17 aircraft, twice as big as a Herc, on that strip every day. But apparently that wasn't good enough for the RAAF. Go figure. We were wild with frustration. We thought showing people what would happen if they treated us like that should override whatever managerial and political issues were going on. But in the end our mission petered out, and we handed it off to American Special Forces. They ended up finding and killing the target, but we were feeling let down, extremely disappointed, that we hadn't been able to take care of a matter that involved one of our own.

*

Towards the end of our 2011 trip, Devil and I were involved in a big day of fighting that gave conclusive proof of his value as a lifesaver. I wouldn't be here now if not for that dog.

We were going after an insurgent leader who helped supply a stream of enemy fighters into the western edge of Uruzgan. I'd had a bad sleep the night before, and was grumpy at the 6 am update. It was mid-June and getting hot. I sat down and the briefers said, 'There's nothing going on today.' We were going back to our lines when the word came through: 'We've got a hit on this guy; we're off.' Within twenty minutes we were flying out.

I slept through most of the forty- to fifty-minute flight. At the five-minute call I woke up, and woke Devil. When his one-minute call came – that change in the machine's sound – Devil sat up, ready to go.

It was an unusually hot, steamy morning. We were going into an area full of flat, yellow wheatfields with a river winding through. We had an action-packed start to the job. I had to shoot a mongrel dog that charged out of an aqueduct to attack Devil, and then Devil ran down the riverbank and caught a bloke trying to squirt. Soon after, rounds were cracking over our heads – friendly fire, thankfully. We moved into position to see what they were shooting at. I caught sight of an enemy fighter in a paddock less than 50 metres from us. He was lying face-down, possibly dead. But the insurgents had developed a technique of lying on a grenade if they were wounded, so as to turn themselves into a bomb when we rolled them over. If they had to go, they were highly motivated to take one of us with them. I sent Devil out in front to turn him over. It's a gut-wrenching but necessary exercise. I obviously didn't want Devil getting hurt, but it was the alternative to one of us taking the risk. Fortunately, it turned out all right: the dead fighter had an AK, grenades and ammunition, but had not booby-trapped himself. Devil had done his job well, as had my mates by picking the enemy off over my head, but I hated the feeling of putting Devil at risk.

The heat intensified through the morning. A mate and I pushed off towards where that fighter had come from. We could see a village, separate from the main green belt, with about fifty compounds and some visible insurgents talking on their ICOMs. We took a few shots at them, and they manoeuvred out of sight. When we linked up with the rest of the teams, Daryll, who was now my troop sergeant, said he'd seen some local men acting erratically at another building further down the valley. Devil and I went where he indicated, and saw two men ducking in and out of a dry yellow unharvested wheatfield. These types of vegetation are dangerous areas; you can almost step on an enemy before you know he's there. I sent Devil in front, and he launched himself in and got them. The insurgents didn't yell or scream when attacked; instead, they fell silent, whether out of fear or courage it was impossible to tell.

In a nearby compound, we found and destroyed a lot of weapons, ammunition and IED material. Daryll and two others went onto a bare hill overlooking the fifty-compound village, and within minutes we heard them getting smashed by PKM machine gun fire. The team I was with and another team pushed up quickly through some dead ground, out of the enemy's sight, to assist and return fire, and we were eventually able to get a different angle on the insurgents. From about 300 metres, we returned fire, and the JTAC called in some Apaches to help identify the enemy locations and, we hoped, drop some ordnance.

The insurgents lay low when an Apache came over them, and then opened up again when it flew away. Our JTAC tricked them, pushing the helicopters off target. Thinking they'd flown away, the insurgents bobbed up again. They fired a few fruitless rounds at Daryll's group and, as usual, were shouting over their radios, 'We've had a great day, we've killed hundreds of them!' and more of the usual bullshit about the magnificent victories they were hav-ing. Then the Apaches swooped back in, fast. A couple of rounds from those amazing machines and the targets had no hope of survival. The Apaches left a distinct smell on the earth, where rocks had been literally cooked. They were still smoking, with that cordite-charred smell, long after the helicopters had flown off.

After that had settled down, we had to clear the village. There were only twelve of us available, and we split into three teams of four. Each team picked a compound to break into and started the clearance. Daryll gave us overwatch of the initial front. We left the JTAC with one other operator on another small bare knoll to watch and provide cut-off to the rear of the village. The place must have had some kind of tactical importance to them, because it was completely deserted, more like a fighting location than an ordinary village. No civilians, minimal animals, few signs of life. There weren't even any trees or bushes. It was unusually desolate. We were clearing one deserted compound after another, watching every step for IEDs or barricaded insurgents. We'd seen some suspects still hanging around in there, and I was sending Devil ahead of me into each house, each room, one at a time. As usual in these situations, he was wearing a video camera mounted on his back in a rectangular metal frame, and I received the pictures instantly on a screen that I wore on my body armour. It was extremely tense work. Every alarm bell was ringing, especially for IEDs. Mentally we were ticking off each compound as we cleared it.

Devil and I came to a room and saw what looked like one of the plastic tubes they used as containers for RPG warheads. It was left there almost too obviously, and we were concerned it was a 'come on', or a trick to draw us in, with an IED trip set on it. We stood a fair way back and I cast Devil near the room to see if he would pick up any scent of explosives. Luckily he didn't. The tube was just left behind from the initial contact. You had to be able to think ahead and see all these potential threats.

Not long after, Daryll reported seeing enemy moving around the village not far in front of us. The JTAC, who was still on the hill, has just called in an Apache for a gun run on some suspected fighters outside the village. The shells of the 30-millimetre cannon were pinging and bouncing around us. Devil and I pushed in to clear the next compound with another operator. Suddenly we heard some shooting and grenades. Devil and I went onto the roof and saw a firefight in a house about 70 metres away. Two SAS troopers were pinned down in a courtyard, and rounds were coming at them out of a doorway. I put some fire into the doorway over our guys' heads to try to suppress the shooter. On the roof of the building above the shooter's head, two of our guys moved along and dropped some grenades down a small chimney hole. There was a dull thud as the grenades inside the closed space went off. The percussion from the blast created a small dust plume that puffed out of the building.

But the Talib continued to fire; the grenades had apparently not been effective. We started to move down to help. Devil and I jumped a wall to get into the compound. The enemy was holed up in a warren of small rooms in this mudbrick structure. We moved in behind an adjoining wall. Our guys were continuing to drop grenades through smoke holes in the roof, and rounds were punching back through the roof at them. Even after five grenades had gone into the little room, whoever was in there was still firing back out.

On the other side of the wall, they were only a couple of metres from Devil and me. We could hear them shouting. Their resilience was truly amazing. A fighter came out blazing with his gun and the boys shot him. He was down to his last three rounds when he made his suicide dash. The call was made to use anti-structural grenades now. Normal 'frag' grenades work by exploding a packet of shrapnel in all directions. Anti-structural grenades don't have shrapnel, but cause overpressure that will collapse a structure from the inside. Outdoors, they create nothing but a bang, a shockwave and a brief ball of flame. Inside, they can bring down a house.

Our guys threw one of these grenades into the room. *Boom!* – it collapsed. We let the smoke clear. The grenade had ruptured the wall we'd just been standing on.

I sent Devil in, but the smoke was still obscuring the picture on my screen. I followed, with Blake behind me. Blake was the 2IC of the team I had flown in on. He is a good friend and we had served together on a few operations by this time. He is a solid operator. He saw a PKM set up at the back of the room among the blankets under a shelf, its muzzle pointed at the opening we'd just walked through. Devil was carrying on among the blankets, his tail wagging. We could hear a low groaning. Not knowing what state the wounded Talib was in, or whether he was armed, we fired into the blankets, killing him. When we ripped off the blankets, Devil found the fighter, all bombed up with guns and chest rig.

I hadn't noticed the clouds massing overhead. Most days in Afghanistan in summer are clear and blue, but this day was more like Melbourne. After the initial heat, there had been a smell of rain in the air and that electric pre-storm feel, and now a thunderstorm was gathering. There were still plenty of fighters scattered through the other buildings, and plenty more compounds to clear. On the radio, their leader was bragging about what a great day they'd had. But the fighters in the village were screaming with panic, telling their commander they were trapped. Our assault had caught them completely off guard. Their commander said, 'Allah is with you.' From the tone of his voice, he was nowhere near the village. They were telling him they were scared. His response was, 'Take one of them with you when you go. Farewell.'

Knowing how desperate and suicidal they were, we cleared the buildings with caution. In one, we found three women with maybe fifteen kids. 'Close the doors,' we said in Pashto, 'and don't open them or come out until the morning.'

The building beside them was fairly small. Three of us went into the entrance point. I turned left with Devil to sort a couple of rooms out. My mate pushed in to the right to clear a few smaller rooms, more like animal pens. As he pushed a wooden door, his light caught and reflected two eyeballs and a gun. Shots rang out and he nearly caught a bullet under his arm. As he pulled back from the room, another gun opened up from his left, no more than half a metre away. Two of us scrambled into place and gave him cover fire, shooting into the room to keep them in there. Two grenades went in, but the enemy was still returning fire. It was an extremely dangerous and intense confrontation.

Devil was meant to stay by my side during a gunfight, but he'd kept wandering off to a room less than three metres to my right. While shooting, I called, 'Devil!' He came over, but then disappeared again into another room behind me, against my orders. We threw more grenades at the enemy in the first room, before I heard a commotion behind me. Devil was dragging out an insurgent who'd been hiding on a firewood ledge with a gun. If one of us had gone in, he would have had a clear shot at our head. Even now, as he was wrestling with Devil, he was trying to get control of his gun. I shot him.

In that situation, all I was thinking was, *Protect yourself, get a good sight picture, squeeze.* This insurgent had a gun. You don't have time to analyse it. In war, you're aware that somewhere out there is a bullet that might be coming at you. You don't know where it's going to come from, but everything you do is to stop that happening. All your tactics are to stop that. It's not a thug's game; it's tactical and clear-headed. But it is life and death. In this building, Devil had saved me. Again.

I let the boys know I had another EKIA. More grenades were going into the room in front of me. How were we going to get them out? We'd put five grenades in by now. Did we run into the room and risk ourselves, knowing they would have a gun trained on the doorway? Not likely.

We dropped in a red phosphorus grenade to suffocate him out, but didn't know what effect it had. With smoke everywhere, it was impossible to tell.

Then I had to make a hard decision. There was really only one way to clear the room without taking an unacceptable risk. I sent Devil in. He was half a body length through the doorway when a gunshot came from inside. My heart jumped into my throat. I yelled out, 'Heel!'

Devil re-emerged, and we shot over the top of him. He managed to back out. Rounds were kicking up around his head.

'Heel! HEEL!!!'

I was freaking out, thinking he was going to get shot.

As he came out, he looked at me warily and kept his distance. He wasn't going to come near me. I was too angry. I had to calm down.

'Heel,' I said, more calmly, and grabbed him. I dragged him around a corner and checked him. I couldn't believe he hadn't got hit. The mounting of the camera on his back, the little black metal rectangle, had a bullet hole straight through it. A round had missed his spine by a couple of centimetres. I grabbed his head and rubbed it and said, 'Sorry, buddy, I shouldn't have done that to you.'

Up to that point, we hadn't known where in this room the fighter was. I checked the angle from which the bullet had hit Devil's camera mounting, and deduced where he must have been hiding. Another team showed up with an explosive charge, and we decided to blow the whole room up. Mud and rocks flew everywhere. There had been two Taliban inside, one had been killed in the initial firefight and the other was killed instantly by the blast. Devil having got out without being hit was pure luck.

The thunderstorm came and went, and the weather turned fine again. We cleared out the rest of the village, and pushed back to consolidate. We had to continue towards the green belt to clear out the escape route they'd tried to use earlier in the day, and came across a Talib who'd been hit by the Apaches. The high-calibre rounds had basically dismembered him, a reminder of why the gunships were so feared. We still had to get photos and conduct a search of his gear for intel purposes, and the state he was in was stomach-turning. When we searched the dead enemy fighter, one of his pockets had some paper in it. When removed it flittered away like confetti.

I followed Devil and Rex, the other combat assault dog, through a wheatfield, and we found another cache of weapons and money. Once we reached our limit of exploitation we moved back to the village to collect all the gear, and then linked up with the team that was still at the original target building before our extraction.

Devil and I had a long, exhausted sleep that night. Our group had killed thirty enemy fighters in a full day's fight-ing. A few of my patrolmates had come close to catching bullets, and so had Devil. As dangerous as it was, it was a day that proved the value the dogs provided in heavy fighting. Devil had made a crucial difference, I think, in saving our lives and helping us achieve our objectives.

The 2011 trip was the most successful, at that time, of any SAS squadron, if measured by the number of senior enemy leaders taken out. Without suffering one casualty, we had killed eighty or ninety enemy fighters, among them twenty-three or twenty-four commanders, each running substantial networks. It was a brutal business, but any feelings of com-passion towards the dead were suppressed by our knowledge of what they'd been doing – and would have kept doing if left unchecked. We'd set them back by months, if not longer. The next squadron would tell us there was nothing going on in that western area of Uruzgan for their entire trip.

But there are always swings and roundabouts when you're fighting anything less than a total war. The Q&As and other interrogatories about how we'd operated were putting a dent in morale. Some time after that big fight, I was training with Devil. A senior officer was asking me why, that day, so many people had had to die. I had a simple answer.

'Sir, they were trying to kill us.' I explained in detail about being in that house, at close quarters, with those guns firing at us out of rooms. I explained what Devil had done, and how I'd shot the man who was fighting with Devil while trying to get his gun aimed at me.

The officer said, 'Did you try to detain him?'

I was dumbfounded. The question showed a complete lack of understanding. We were in a war situation, not a policing situation. There's often a lot of exaggerated talk about 'Kill or be killed', but this time, that was what it was. If I, or others that day, had not killed, then we wouldn't be here today and my children would not have a dad.

Back on deck in Afghanistan in 2009. The Chief was true to his word and I was not wrapped in cotton wool. I was happy to be able to do my job once more after the whirlwind of the Victoria Cross experience.

Insurgent supply and resting tent. We denied them that option. Although the operation was successful we had one wounded in action. Guyena, east of Kush Kadir, Uruzgan, 2009.

Daryll at the helm with Rex doing his best to be in the shot in eastern Uruzgan, 2009. There were often valleys of marijuana as far as the eye could see. A dream to some of the people I used to hang around.

Some of the local militia guys we were working with in north Uruzgan, 2009. Pretty hard to tell these guys and the Taliban apart. They were working for a pittance and had their own funny ways of doing business. Sleeping and fighting alongside these guys was a very different experience.

Opposite: Dust plume left by a Chinook helicopter insertion in north Uruzgan, 2009. Our patrol was split, three guys each side of this valley to provide overwatch for the rest of the troop. Boring job but had to be done.

JOHN STILLWELL-WPA POOL/GETTY IMAGES

A reception with the Queen at Windsor Castle in 2009. She was absolutely amazing. We shared some stories and even a few laughs. I never thought I would end up standing in Windsor Castle talking to Her Majesty Queen Elizabeth II.

RICHARD POHLE/WPA POOL/GETTY IMAGES

The passing of the British WWI Generation ceremony on Remembrance Day, Westminster Abbey, 11 November 2009. Turns out it was a bigger wreath than I first thought. What an honour to be a part of – just days out of Afghanistan. Also, it was broadcast to millions across the Commonwealth.

Young Australian of the Year 2010 ceremony, Canberra, 2010. Another amazing honour. Presented to me by Prime Minister Kevin Rudd and Adam Gilchrist, ex-cricketer and good bloke.

The kids from Austinmer Public School had all sent me letters, many wanting to know different things for a project they were doing about me. I felt it best to visit them personally so I did in February 2011. Kids always ask the best questions and I also get a lot out of it. These types of events are as good as all the official ones if not better when you take out the formalities and add in the raw enthusiasm of youth.

Sometimes the beauty of Afghanistan is striking and almost a contrast to the destruction all those years of war has done to the place. Looking towards Baluchi from inside Tarin Kowt Bowl, 2011.

New job: dog handler as well as operator. Devil would become my best and most trusted friend. He would save my life and many others. 2011.

Devil and I in 2011 taking the walk to the choppers for yet another mission.

Under-slung dog. Suspended Extraction training for the four-legged boys. 2011.

The camera on Devil's back. The bullet hole shows how close it came to his spine. I had nearly lost my best mate, near the western edge of Uruzgan, June 2011.

One of the boys and some of the hardware we discovered on the day I nearly lost Devil. We ended up with nearly 30 enemy killed in action that day. The place was very bare, minimal vegetation.

Devil cooling off in an aqueduct, 2012. He was with his new handler by this stage but thoughtfully always came up and said hello when nearby.

RIP Devil, 2 July 2012. You were unconditional and will be sorely missed.

Consoling a mate and farewelling another. RIP Quake, 2012. A few days later we would find ourselves in the same position.

Ramp ceremony for one of our four-legged operators. We treated them like one of us and showed the same courtesy when saying goodbye. 2012.

BOOM! Explosion set off to destroy the biggest cache find of arms and ammunition in Uruzgan since 2005. In excess of 450 rocket-propelled grenades were found here. Also surface to air missiles and scores of weapons were hidden and buried. The blast was huge! You can see all the dust escaping from the house to the left of the flame. 2012.

Right: Some of the boys getting amongst it with a tenacious insurgent shooting at them from inside a water well. It took a few goes but the boys got the upper hand in the end. Eastern Uruzgan somewhere, 2012.

Moments before wheels up. Everyone had a different ritual before going out on a job. The US crews were good to us and would always try to get us in to wherever we asked. 2012.

About to drop an anti-structural grenade through a hole in the roof of an enemy hut in western Uruzgan, 2012. Paddy in the foreground moving out of the way. Unfortunately on the ground behind me was the body of one of the Afghan partners who had been shot by the enemy in the doorway of this hut.

The first stage of my anti-structural grenade.

The end stage of the grenade. I love these things, they work so well.

Cleaning out the small mud igloo after the contact. Just one of six weapons we got off the enemy that were in this hut.

Returning from another successful job. 2012.

Local women and children leaving the area was always a sign that a contact was imminent.

A selfie moments before extraction from Tarin Kowt Bowl, 2012. The hay fever was killing me this day, identifiable from my red eyes. The poppy season was in full swing and it shows how thick it can be in the greenbelt.

Safe and sound spending some quality time with Kaylee and Hamish. It's a rare photo when one of us is not pulling a stupid face. They always bring me back to earth after being away. September 2013.

TWENTY-NINE

Because of Emma's pregnancy, I came home from Afghanistan at the beginning of July, a week before the rest of my squadron. Our squadron leaders were very understanding and flexible in that way. Earlier in the trip, when I'd rung Emma for her birthday, she'd said, 'Are you sitting down? Right. The house has burnt down.' Our place in Fremantle had gone up in smoke after an electrical fire. It can be hard sometimes when you're away doing the job and catastrophes, like a house fire, happen back home. You want to be home to help out, organise it all and tell them everything will be all right. The normal things you would do as a husband and father. When you can't, it can be stressful. Emma and Kaylee weren't living there at the time, having moved to a house near Campbell Barracks, but her father had been in the Fremantle place. Fortunately he was all right. Nevertheless, my troop sergeant, Daryll, had asked me if I wanted to go home for seven days. I hadn't needed to, but it was considerate of him to make the offer.

I got home on 5 July and was staying up late each night to watch the Tour de France, which Cadel Evans won that year. Settling into home life and the Australian time zone, it can be hard to re-establish your sleep patterns. I was also wondering what the boys were up to back in Afghanistan. Just like when I was a little kid running around after Brent and the others, I had a phobia about being sent to bed early and missing out on the fun.

On the night of 9 July, Emma came out of the bedroom and said she thought she was going into labour. We weren't sure, and I crashed out on the couch, but just before dawn she got up and said it was time to go. We dropped Kaylee with Taylor's wife on the next street across – he was flying in from Afghanistan that morning – and went to the hospital, where Hamish was born a few hours later. Emma had done a great job of keeping the sex of the new addition a secret while I was away. She had found out but I wanted it to be a surprise. The labour was a lot quicker than Kaylee's, and the thrill of seeing my son wiped away all thoughts of the war I'd been fighting in just a few days earlier. We gave him a good Scottish name that Dad would have loved. Most importantly, if I'd come home with the rest of the squadron, I would have missed his birth by two or three hours. If that had been the case, I might have needed Devil to protect me from Emma.

She and Hamish stayed in the hospital for five days, and he was easy with feeding and sleeping from the get-go. Over the next six months, family life with a newborn and a five-year-old was bliss. We went to Thailand for ten days, splashing out on a resort near Phuket. It took me seven days to wind down and stop wanting to race around sight-seeing, seeing Buddhas, riding an elephant, going to town, checking out the nightlife. Emma kept saying, 'Stay here and enjoy it.' By day seven I was listening to her.

*

The 2012 trip to Afghanistan, which would start in February, would see another transition for me. I was going to hook up with Bruce's team as his patrol 2IC. That meant handing Devil over, which was hard. I was convinced he wouldn't take easily to Nick, his new handler, but they just clicked. Devil was pretty unsentimental! He made the transfer easy for me by going off and training Nick, getting his job done. It gave me a chance to reflect on how I'd contributed something to the Regiment's practices through the dog program. Bringing Devil into the team was one of the most satisfying things I've ever done. Seeing someone else have success with him was massively gratifying. And, as I've said, Devil might have been the difference between me coming home and not coming home in 2011.

In January 2012, Bruce was knitting us into a tight team. I'd always admired his professionalism and his skill in pushing hard to achieve an objective, and it was a privilege to work under him. Being 2IC was a new adventure for me. As a corporal in a patrol, you take charge of admin, ammo, food and water, which are basic tasks for an SAS operator, but they still have to be done, so your mind can be switched on to the task ahead. The 2IC is also an intermediary between the PC and the men. You can explain to them in greater detail why they're doing something. The PC isn't always able to do that, whereas the 2IC can back him up by explaining it in terms they understand. I don't know if anyone would have seen me as a leader earlier in my life, but it was another sign of how the Regiment had brought out the best in me.

We had a late-night departure on a C-17 to Diego Garcia, and then went straight in to Afghanistan, avoiding the 'fobbits' (a derogatory but common nickname for FOB staffers) and other obstacles in Dubai. The weather was cold and squally when we arrived, and the trip had a fairly slow start. We had to 'martac' the relatively new American helicopter crews we were using – basically sweet-talk them into doing things our way – but there was a large mixture of force elements as well as an SAS squadron competing for the same helicopters, same intelligence and so on. Sometimes the easiest part of the mission is when you've finally stepped out of the helicopter to engage with the enemy.

After a few small tasks around Tarin Kowt, we were sent out west near Deh Rahwod, to an area that was a big highway for the enemy smuggling weapons and drugs to their fighters in Helmand, where they were giving the Brits a hard time. The roads out there had all been tarred since I'd first come to Afghanistan, a sign of progress in infrastructure, but not a reason for us to get complacent. The IED threat was still high, as the insurgents had discovered that they could wait for the tarred roads to heat up in the day and then dig them up at night and bury a device. They tended to do this in late summer, leaving them in there with the wires unattached through the winter. Then, when the fighting season was about to start again, they would go around attaching battery packs to the IEDs to get them ready. Also, the better infrastructure gave them opportunities: the roads now had a lot of drains running beneath them, which the insurgents saw as handy places to plant IEDs.

We were after a middleman who was linking this traffic through some big bazaars, cashing up through drug-selling and distributing arms. It was interesting to see how, as we decimated the Taliban as a fighting force, the big picture was changing. Whereas we used to target the commanders, by 2012 they weren't around. They were sending orders across to the lower fighters who were living out in the caves and holes in the ground in Afghanistan. We couldn't go after the leaders because they were in a different country, but we could still ruin their networks by taking out their minions.

As we came in to land, some enemy fighters, including the target, were squirting from the village towards a river. The farmers stood by and watched as we hared off across their fields after the Talibs. The target ditched his pistol, personal effects and some IED materials into a blackberry bush, which we set fire to. Quake, the dog handled by my mate Craig, jumped into the river and swam after the target. We watched the Talib bob down the river. A dozen of us were within our rights to shoot at him, but we left it for the moment. Bruce called in the helicopters and we flew downstream with another patrol to get him a bit later.

The job had sent out an important message. This target had only been in Afghanistan for two days, and we'd been right onto him. We received a document off our intel that came from the head of the Taliban. It summed up the situation for them and showed us the results of the hard work we'd put in as a Regiment. '2011 was a terrible season for us,' it said. 'The Australians with the red beards are very good fighters. Do not fight the Australians. We will lose every time.' There was a bit more to it, but the document was virtually saying they'd lost Uruzgan. That was pretty good, hearing that from their top man.

On our next task, our intelligence was so good that the target had only been in Afghanistan for one day before one of our patrols landed pretty much on top of him. The Talib leaders, panicking that their men weren't able to make a move before getting hit, put out communications to the lower-downs saying he was still there, but was uncontactable because he was busy fighting. Then they tried to tell them he'd gone back to Pakistan to get more money and fighters. But the insurgents on the ground were freaking out; they knew he was gone and that their leaders were lying to them.

Personally, I was excited to be back in battle rhythm, working in Bruce's team. It was harder to be leaving my family, since Hamish was just beginning to crawl and Kaylee had a better understanding of how long I'd be away. But professionally, this was a pay-off time, when we were drawing the benefits from several years' hard work. Fighting is more enjoyable when you sense that your enemy is on the run.

The outside political situation was changing again, and we understood that the coalition was planning to steadily withdraw its forces. After coming here six times in seven years, I realised I might be in Afghanistan for the last time. Knowing this experience was coming to an end, I would look around the helicopter as we went into a job and take time to reflect. Soldiers had different rituals and routines for getting ready – some wore lucky undies, some listened to music, some cracked jokes, some got very talkative and others went quiet. The differences were especially noticeable when we knew we were going to get into a gunfight. For my own preparation, I was still into the same music as when I was young: the metal and then Nirvana, Pearl Jam, Foo Fighters, Red Hot Chili Peppers. High-stress situations brought me back to that music, and through it I could reach down and find the same feelings as when I was going for a surf or a snowboard. I found that music could not only calm me, but sort of knit my whole self together. Once I had my body armour on, helmet in hand and rifle ready to go, walking out the door heading to the helicopter was the time to focus. It is about a mental preparation and being at peace with what you are about to do. We all have our jobs to do out there and I focused on what mine was.

We hadn't lost a man for nearly two years by April, when we went out on a job in a wide-open area, all rocky plains and small bald hills in a dry riverbed near Deh Rahwod.

Our target was an IED maker who had attacked an Afghan police checkpoint and was a link between those in charge and those fighting. The helicopters dropped us 400 metres further from the target than we'd planned. The fine powdery dust got into my nostrils and throat. It's not a neutral desert smell, but is kind of gamy, the dust mixed with centuries of goat shit, goat fur, sheep shit, sheep's wool, an animal smell that gets everywhere and never goes away. We sped off across this bare moonscape to link up with a team led by my mate Paddy, who had four Australians and three Afghans with him. We called him Paddy because he could be a bit loose like the crazy Irishman from the *Braveheart* movie. These locals were good soldiers, well educated and easy to train. They were not Pashtun, and didn't work for Matiullah Khan. It was an advantage having armed operatives who were not from the area, because they wouldn't let tribal ties cloud their judgement.

Paddy's team was moving towards an abandoned nomad settlement of *kutchi* huts, low mud igloos held up by sticks. Some of them had been abandoned for the season; they would only be occupied by shepherds during the winter. We paused on higher ground to watch. Paddy's group approached one hut and discussed who would search it. He was encouraging the Afghans to have a go. One of them, Rahul, went around the doorway. We'd trained them to do the same as us, which was to swap the gun to whichever shoulder was nearer the opening, so as not to expose half the body. For whatever reason, Rahul didn't swap his gun, and ducked his face towards the opening. There was a burst of fire and he dropped to the ground. As he lay there, more volleys of bullets were fired out of the hut into his body.

A lot of us rushed down to help Paddy. He chucked a frag grenade into the hut while I covered him.

'Get out of the way!' he said.

I said, 'I'm here to cover you.'

He threw an anti-structural grenade in, but it bounced back outside. In the open air, it went off but did no damage, aside from knocking one of our guys onto his arse with the shockwave.

Paddy threw another frag grenade into the doorway. Others from the team were charging in to help and JTACs were suggesting calling in an Apache and hitting the hut with a Hellfire missile. Craig wanted to send Quake in. All the guys were wanting to get in on the action. I didn't blame their enthusiasm, but it was causing a bit of havoc. Paddy and Bruce told them to back off and let them deal with it.

As I covered him, Paddy pumped a full magazine into the doorway of the hut. There was a small air hole at the top, and I dropped in an anti-structural grenade, which blew the hut apart. As the wind cleared the dust away, Paddy put in another burst of fire, as did some others. When the dust settled, we saw two Talibs who could still have fired at us, and shot them.

We got a medevac for Rahul, but he'd been shot through the head twice and several more times through his body. He was gone, but it was important to show the Afghan partner force, who were pretty shaken up, that we would treat him the same way as any of us.

Digging through the rubble, we found four AK-47s, chest rigs, grenades, a PKM machine gun, a G3 automatic rifle and a lot of ammo. It was quite a heavy set-up for a small faction living in a mud hut. They also had some IED material and componentry for suicide bombs. The EKIA included the target plus three younger boys, most likely sui-cide bombers who'd come straight out of a training camp in Pakistan, we guessed. Everything we found fit in with the intel picture we'd been given.

It's a sad fact that the younger fighters were generally much more fanatical than their commanders, more motivated by religious ideas of death and glory, and so more dangerous. It's also possible that the Taliban leaders were reaching down to younger warriors because they were easier to influence. There were similarities to the Hitler Youth in 1945. Running out of experienced fighters, the Taliban leaders could gee up kids who wanted to make a name for themselves as the boys who'd taken out a local police officer, government official or coalition soldier. Their status would rise if they could get away with it, and the leaders would offer their parents money and houses if their children would undertake these missions. Then these kids would get pushed around like pawns, and live literally the life of a dog in these isolated huts in the middle of the desert or in the mountains. If they were in villages or towns, they had to move from house to house every night to avoid capture. And throughout, they were waiting for someone to tell them to go and blow themselves up at a police checkpoint. If you live in the West, it's hard to fathom.

That April, we heard there were suicide bombers newly arrived in Tarin Kowt. Our intelligence was that three of them, kids around fifteen or sixteen years old, had been sent to a Taliban handler. The first one went into a team of Americans and Afghans, in downtown TK, and blew himself up. Two Americans and two Afghans were killed. Our priority became to focus on this suicide bomber network, and we picked up four or five heavily involved individuals. The other two suicide bombers were out there still, but the brainwashing had worn off after they'd seen what had happened to the first one. The organisers we'd grabbed had links to the Afghan Government, playing both sides. It wasn't easy to prosecute them, but our arrests meant the network fell apart and the boss running it from Pakistan apparently abandoned his aim of sending more suicide bombers into Tarin Kowt. We were pleased to have achieved that, and the Americans were grateful. But seeing such young children being used as cannon fodder was a sobering reminder of the types of people we were up against. As they grew more desperate, their tactics were getting uglier.

THIRTY

As the weather warmed up and the enemy increased its activity, recruiting boys and men for the fighting season, I was given more responsibility as 2IC. Essentially the PC runs each job, but Bruce always asked for my opinion. We were directed to do some strike to develop (STD) jobs, which are deliberate actions to make the enemy do something that will expose them and bring them above the 'threshold', to allow us to target them more easily. Bruce wanted to hit a couple of areas to create disruptions, which we could follow up. In the first, we got four Talibs and plenty of arms and intelligence, and in the second we hit a bazaar early one morning.

Our plan was to get into the bazaar before dawn, surprise the enemy and squeeze them up the green belt to the end of the valley where we had people to put fire on them. Bruce delegated control of the team to me for a short period so he could organise the rest of the assault. We had Nick and Devil with us. I said, 'Let's go super-quiet.' We hid in the long grass outside some houses where we suspected the enemy had been sleeping. They were sending young kids out to spot us, some as young as four, five, six years old. They'd know if a single blade of grass was out of shape. It was their backyard and they looked at it every day – no video games or TVs for these kids. They eventually saw us and scuttled back inside. Then some old women were sent out to have a look for us. Lying low, we crept to new positions. One of the little children was searching for me as I moved around in the high grass. Behind a building, I could see a man sneaking around, an enemy fighter. He was about 100 metres away. I got a bead on him. With a suppressor on my rifle, I took a shot but missed him. He stopped, looked around, and made another call on his radio. Paddy was only 25 metres from him, but hadn't seen him. I calmed down, in a crouch position, making fine adjustments, and then shot him three times in the chest. We sent Devil to check him out, with Nick and a couple of others following. The most surprised person was Paddy, who'd never known the threat was so close to him. Compared with back in the 2006–08 period, I wasn't now having moments of curiosity or speculation about who these men were, or what they had left to come and fight; as far as we were concerned, the purpose of my action was simply to save my mate's life.

People were rushing from building to building, and we picked up another three enemy fighters in the bazaar. Throughout the day we were flushing the bulk of them out at the other end of the green. Barry, my good mate who'd been injured during the big ambush in 2008, was finally back with us after three years of rehab. He'd passed all the tests, even though he still had a limp. Barry was on a hill over two kilometres away. He had a 7.62-calibre machine gun, or what's known as a MAG 58. He was providing cut-off by fire to the northern end of the village so the insurgent

squirters could not escape. Crackles of gunshot were ringing out through the valley, and we picked up more enemy
fighters trying to escape by swimming across the river.

That night, the main target in the area had risen above
the 'threshold' and we knew where he was. The STD had
worked, by prompting him to act. Within the following
days, Bruce wanted me to run the team, which not a lot
of patrol commanders will do. It was a big step. It took me
back to the days when I'd be following Dad and Brent
through the bush or across a river. It's easier being number
two, watching your big brother make mistakes and finding
a better way for yourself, but a lot harder to be number one.
I couldn't do anything until guys were feeding information
up to me, being my eyes and ears. It's a real two-way street.

I was nervous but focused when we flew in. When I
compare the feeling of being in combat in 2012 with my
early trips to Afghanistan, there's a big difference. This time
I had a much better awareness of what was happening on a
larger scale. When I was still a scout, I was focused on minute
details that I had to take care of for the patrol. My heart rate
would tend to go up, and this affected my fine motor skills,
so I would have to place all my attention on doing the little
things correctly. By 2012, when I was a lot calmer, these fine
motor skills were automatic. I could do more tasks without
thinking about them. In a way, I could sort of filter them
out. My mind, now, was on piecing together information
to get a picture of the entire battle space. And if that led to
better decisions, it would increase my survivability and my
team's. I guess that's what experience is all about.

We went across the river to where those insurgents had
been swimming the previous days. As we came in to land
the layout of compounds and other teams' positions was
clear; once we dropped below the tree line, however, the
vegetation was thick and it was almost like being in a

jungle. Trying to spot other teams and potential enemy is a difficult task. A fighter stuck his head around a corner. I took a shot at him and he ran. We fired a couple of shots. He made it around the edge of the building. When Nick saw that he had a weapon, he shot him. We made it to the house we were targeting, and found a hidden cellar full of guns, chest rigs and ammunition. The occupants complained that they'd done nothing wrong, but we explained that the deal was pretty clear: 'The helicopters and soldiers will stop coming when you stop working with the Taliban.'

It was a straightforward job, and we were back at camp by lunch. Bruce and the squadron sergeant major congratulated me for the patrol's conduct. Compared with being a trooper in someone else's patrol, I felt great satisfaction for not only having done the job as a soldier but having looked after the men I was responsible for.

Soon after, I was given another job. This time it was because Bruce had tweaked his knee and decided to give it a few days' rest. I had to organise thirty-four blokes to go on three helicopters – initially four, but one had broken down, giving me a last-minute challenge – and target a couple of Taliban go-betweens in the remote north-west of Uruzgan. These men were running drugs and weapons with some Iranians who visited them a lot. I felt calmer for the previous experience of leading a team, and we picked up nine armed insurgents, a PKM machine gun with hundreds of rounds, and a fully assembled IED. Devil picked up a target on his own, and intelligence showed us a few days later that we got the one we were after. Again, Bruce was complimentary about my leadership. But after we'd been on the front foot for most of the trip, every aspect of our soldiering was about to be put to the test.

*

We were getting into late June, the last few weeks of our 2012 trip. Bruce was often awake early, looking at pictures from the Predators, supplementing his own knowledge from the intelligence network he'd developed over the years. One early morning I stopped by the command centre to see what potential targets were up for the day. As I walked in Bruce was up the front, tracking five or six different televisions all with different images on them. The radio chatter between the JTAC and the unmanned drones was intermittently breaking up the morning greetings. Within moments Bruce's hard work had paid off and he got a good picture of a target we were after in the north-west. He said, 'We're rolling.'

The insurgents were situated in a steep-sided valley, more like a gorge. The satellite and Predator footage hadn't revealed how near-vertical the walls were, and as we landed we were taken by surprise by several Talibs shooting at us from positions hidden in the rocks. Our patrols were dropped off at several points around the valley, and we leapt off and ran for the nearest cover. In one of the other patrols, there was a comical moment when a young bloke was racing away from the gunfire with Blaine 'Didds' Diddams, another PC. Didds had bad hearing and a great laconic sense of humour. The young guy kept yelling, 'We're getting shot at!'

'Eh?'

'We're getting *shot* at!'

'Eh?'

'WE'RE GETTING SHOT AT!'

'Yeah, right,' Didds said. 'Good thing we're running, then.'

One enemy machine gunner was above us on cliffs that were like an escarpment in the Blue Mountains. The echo from his gunfire was making it even harder to work out where he was. One of our guys kept exposing himself to attract shooting, but aside from knowing the machine gunner was about 100 metres away and high above us, we couldn't pinpoint him and couldn't assault him without taking too much of a risk. The JTAC couldn't safely talk-on a helicopter, as we were below the shooter and the helos could easily miss him and hit us. Meanwhile, we were hearing the excited chatter of enemy fighters closer to us. I told our patrol to watch a footpad leading out from the escarpment below us and shoot anyone who ran out.

Another patrol, led by a PC named Brock, tried to get around the machine gunner and take him from higher than where we were, but he turned his gun and started shooting at them, nearly hitting them. They threw a grenade that bounced near him, but it didn't do anything. A decision was made to call in two helicopters, so they dropped some purple smoke for the Apaches to target. The first Apache came blasting into the area. As per their usual operation, Apache 1 came in first, with Apache 2 protecting it. They did two gun runs. The rocks were exploding from the 30-millimetre rounds, not far away at all, chips of rock flying past us. Then Apache 2 came in, having been told to hit the same target. But instead of shooting at the base of the smoke, it shot at the top, which had drifted away from the target and very close to Brock's team. My throat swelled up with dread. I could see the exact spot Brock was and that is where all the Apache's ordnance was pounding into. I said to Bruce, 'They're fucken dead, they're getting hit.' I could hear the urgency in Brock's voice on the radio: 'Call them off! *Call them off!*' Then it went silent.

Bruce tried to contact Brock. I wasn't expecting to hear anything. I thought they were done. Thankfully, he got through. They were lucky to have been behind a boulder. Later on he told me that it was one of the scariest things that has happened to him. I told him it was one of the worst things I had seen. One of Brock's team members got some shrapnel in the leg, but still, we were super-lucky. It was beyond fortunate. The Apaches were told to fuck off back to Tarin Kowt.

We now had a better understanding of what we were up against. This gorge was an incredibly dangerous area with the enemy already in position. Not only was it steep and craggy, but there was an unusual amount of vegetation and nooks and crannies. The air was thicker than up on the plateau, and strongly scented with the straggly pines that grew in the gorge and gave the enemy cover.

It looked like we had to take them on without air support. The enemy had a clear view from high up, almost all the way to TK – in summer, the mornings were still and clear and the afternoon heat haze hadn't yet fallen over the land – so they could see any choppers coming long before they arrived. The Talibs who were up high had a lot of advantages over us.

Brock's team, settling down after nearly being taken out by the Apaches, went to an overwatch position. The enemy machine gunner hadn't fired for a while now, so we crept up towards him, darting from rock to rock. Then he opened up on Nick and Devil and their team, lower down. I moved to another big bunch of rocks with two of our newer guys, recently off their Reo cycles. Rounds whizzed over our heads. That machine gunner had us dialled in.

We got ourselves better positioned, but the situation was so hairy that it was decided to call the Apaches back again. They'd done some damage to us, but if we could talk them in they still looked like the best way of dislodging that machine gunner. Apache 1 did another gun run, but again had trouble identifying the spot. Bruce told us to put some rounds up there to mark his position, which we did, kicking up some dirt and rocks in plumes around where we thought he was. The Apaches went in and dropped their last ordnance on him, including a Hellfire missile. Rocks were whizzing everywhere. He went quiet. Finally, it seemed like we'd got him.

He'd been holding us up from our main objective, which was to flush the other fighters out of the gorge and ambush them on their way out. But they were well dug in and concealed. The other tactical issue was that while we were dealing with this machine gun it had given the other fighters in the gorge plenty of time to establish defensive measures against us.

I was with Bruce, halfway down the side of the valley trying to identify the enemy positions, when we heard Craig on the radio.

'Has anyone seen my dog?'

It's one of the worst questions you can hear. One of the young guys said he'd seen Quake, but then some AK rounds went off. Craig said again, 'Has anyone seen Quake?'

I didn't see it, but Quake had gone around some rocks and found two enemy fighters in an ambush position. He latched onto the first one, but the other had shot him through the chest. He'd spoilt their ambush and showed us where they were, but had paid the highest price.

Most of the patrols didn't know that yet. We were busy establishing an ambush position. I moved to a little ledge on the steep slope of the gorge that was covered in a lot of scree. Down below I could see what was effectively a big, naturally occurring rock tent, almost like a bunker, big slabs of rock leaning against each other. From inside, AK fire and grenades were coming out. Bruce and I saw a bloke, who had been startled by Quake and the advancing patrol, run from the area and we started shooting at him. He wore a white robe with a chest rig, and carried an AK. He stopped behind a rock. Bruce and I shuffled along the cliff to get a better angle, and waited till he came out. Our aim was to hit him as soon as he broke out, but when he emerged we missed him again.

'I'm going,' I said. I climbed over a rock, Bruce behind me. The Talib in the white robe broke out along a path. I shot at him and he stopped behind a big bush, which I pointed out to Bruce when he caught up. We each fired twenty rounds rapid. I could have sworn I saw him go down. We were elevated, but only 30 metres away. Another enemy fighter then broke out, and we shot at him until he went down. A third, wearing blue and black, barrelled out towards a big cubic rock and set himself up to ambush our guys who were lower down. He didn't know we were there, and we shot him from above. The other team members were in position to assist at this stage. Two more enemy fighters came into the same position and also got shot. We thought we had five EKIA down there.

There were still insurgents scattered through the valley. I saw a head pop out from behind the scree, and shot at him but just missed. *Shit*, I thought. As I took my next shot he ducked away towards a little concealed cave. Blue was standing on top of it, and a burst of machine gun fire came out. I was annoyed; I was pretty sure it had come from the fighter I'd just missed. We went down to clear the insurgents we'd shot already, and had a search of the places where they'd been hiding. We stayed as quiet as possible, as we knew there was still at least one of them at large.

Blue threw a grenade into the cave. A second later, it came flying back out. Blue ran for cover, but the shrapnel nipped him in the ear. The man in the cave was obviously willing to fight to the death and was well hidden and armed. He was firing sporadically out of his position. He hadn't been picked up by any of the Predators' cameras, which were still roaming high above. We discussed how to get him, and it was decided that one group would assault the cave while we would provide support.

We pushed back up to the cube-shaped rock. I was looking towards the cave, and thought if I climbed a bit higher up the slope and got behind some thin curtains of vertical rock for cover, I could get a good angle on the small opening he was firing from. Bruce agreed. I only had to climb up about 15 metres of open ground on the loose scree. As I crept up, I heard two shots and felt a hard slap at the top of my left thigh. Instantly it went numb. The second shot hit the ground right next to my foot. If it had hit, it would have done a lot of damage to my foot, so I was lucky.

The force of the bullet that hit me spun me around on the spot. I grabbed my thigh, moved back down the hill to the nearest rock, took cover and got on my radio.

'He got me.'

One of the boys heard this and, thinking I'd been seriously hit, shouted some expletives over the radio network.

I'd never been hit in battle before, so this was a new experience. My thigh wasn't too badly hurt, but the emotions rose up, the red mist. I was consumed by a wave of anger. I rushed back down towards Bruce and yelled, 'Someone fucken shoot that cunt!' I wanted to run into the cave myself and get him. 'I'm gunna fucken shoot this prick in the face!' I was taking it personally – this was the same fighter I'd missed shooting before, and part of me was angry with myself. I completely lost my cool.

Bruce calmly told me to get back behind some rocks for cover. As I got down, he steadily talked me back into normality. My leg had a dull pain throughout, with pins and needles, but once I settled down I thought it couldn't have been too bad because I could still move about.

Bruce let the boys know I'd been hit, and they were putting more fire into the cave. Our patrol medic came up and told me to roll over. Bruce looked and said it was just a hole, no problem.

'I'm fine,' I said.

'Let me do my job,' the medic said.

Later, we laughed at my reaction to getting hit. You were always learning something new about yourself.

At this point, we'd lost a dog and two of us had been clipped. We weren't prepared to take more risks just to get one Talib. Bruce decided to call in fast air, which would be one of the first times the Regiment had asked for that option in two years.

It was late in the afternoon by then, and our team leaders decided we would stay the night and get whatever enemy were left in the valley. We pulled back up the hill and received our 24-hour packs, water and ammo from a helicopter drop. I fell on my arse a few times, and the medic said I should think about going out with the resup that was due to arrive a short time later with some water, ammo and our packs.

'It's not that bad,' I said.

'It's not worth losing your leg over, if you get an infection.'

Probably unwisely, I ignored his advice and stayed with the team, but my arse was throbbing and my leg was stiffening up. I didn't want to show the others that I was struggling, and pushed through the pain, telling myself it wasn't a bad wound, just a foreign body in my leg.

The jet came and bombed my old mate in the cave. I rediscovered that sense of assurance you get from fast air. That screeching approach, tearing the sky, and then the crack as it broke the sound barrier. I could feel the explosion of the bomb right through me – it's physical more than auditory, like being next to the bass at a big concert but deeper and more menacing, rocking your whole body with its effect. Smoke, shrapnel and rock flew out from the impact site. Our blokes checked it out, and then called for another. 'Clear hot.' Another bomb came in and finished the job.

By then it was 5.30 pm and getting dark. We decided to lock down both ends of the gorge and leave it till morning to check the contact site. We set up on the edge of the gorge, with the other patrols readying to ambush them if they tried to walk out. None of us was sleeping, and we weren't talking. At about 10 pm, one of the teams heard some enemy talking and the sound of rocks crunching nearby. Two insurgents with weapons were trying to sneak past.

One of them let out a yelp, and then there was a metallic bouncing noise. He'd dropped his gun down the gorge. At that point, the other patrol shot him and his mate. Didds's crew then got another trying to sneak out further down the valley.

By morning, they were all gone. We'd got nine EKIA in a fight that had started in mid-morning and gone on for more than twelve hours. The bombs from the jet had cleaned up the guy who shot me. I went down to his cave and looked up to where I'd been climbing the slope. He'd had an absolutely clear line at me. I was really lucky.

We found a lot of weaponry and ammunition, as well as a pair of state-of-the-art American NVGs. In that tent-like rock formation we found a cache of IEDs, rockets, mines, guns and launchers. The IEDs, we noticed, had been modified so they carried hard graphite rather than metal shrapnel – so they wouldn't be picked up by a metal detector. There was also some evidence of the Iranian connection our prior intelligence had told us about.

Even though it seems like it was just about numbers and getting as many insurgents as possible there were many,

many jobs when we would have to spend a lot of time sifting through individuals trying to determine who was who to pick out the guys we were after. Sometimes it took a lot of gumshoe work by our operators. Sometimes the body language when being asked questions would be enough to bring an insurgent back to base and start the detainee process. There were times when guys were well within rights to engage an insurgent, but decided not to and they were detained and trialled instead. It can be a tough call on whether or not to take a shot and one that has to be made in milliseconds.

Frustratingly, the guys we would bring back and get locked up generally got let out not long after, or had friends in the jails already so they could continue their insurgent business as usual, albeit in a somewhat limited way.

*

That afternoon, having been flown back to our lines, I had my leg checked. It was stinking.

The squadron sergeant major came in and said, 'Holy fuck, when did that happen?' It hadn't been reported correctly that I'd been shot. I'd said it was just a scratch, and that was what had been passed up to the boss.

Eventually the process started where I could call Emma and let her know what had happened. She was picking Kaylee up from school. She sounded happy to hear my voice.

I asked her if she remembered the underpants she had bought me before the trip that I said would be my lucky ones. She was confused but said she did. I said to her, 'Well they have a hole in them.' Again she thought this was strange as she didn't really know what she could do about it especially during school pickup.

'Yeah, what about it?' she said.

'I've been shot in the leg but I'm okay.'

Silence for a few seconds . . . 'Hello . . . Emma?'

'Yeah I'm here. Are you okay though?'

'Yeah, I'm okay and everyone else is too. Except for Quakey: he was killed. But everything is okay and I will call you again soon.'

They took me to the Tarin Kowt Role 2 hospital. After an X-ray, the surgeon said to leave the bullet there and treat the possibility of infection with antibiotics. The round is still there now, about two centimetres long, and sits between my sciatic nerve and hamstring, near the femur. A souvenir from Afghanistan.

THIRTY-ONE

As intense as it was, occurring just a few days before we were due to leave, that fight was not the last major episode of the 2012 trip.

Four days before our scheduled departure, my thigh was still sore but I was mobile – and determined – enough to stay with my patrol. We received information about an insurgent group in the Chora Valley that had been attacking US Navy SEALs and Australians. We didn't go then, but on our last day, following new intelligence, we flew up there.

It was a hot spot. They were shooting at our helicopters as we came into the green belt, and we hit the deck fast, moving into our blocking position as quickly as possible. It's a dangerous moment straight after you jump off the helos. The thud of the blades cracking the air made it hard to hear, and a cloud of dust, grass and foliage got kicked up around us. In those critical moments, we were deprived of sight and hearing. We had to move at full pace onto a hostile target, where, it being the middle of the day, the enemy could see us clearly. It took great trust in our mates to be there and cover us; we also had to have complete trust in our own ability to do the job for them.

Once we made it into position, I caught a glimpse of some enemy fighters moving hard off the target area. They were heading straight towards another of our teams. I shot at a Talib who was running with a PKM machine gun, but missed. Fortunately he was taken out by another team, led by Paddy, with his three attached Afghan soldiers.

A few rounds from the target building were flying over our heads. We held a position on the corner of the building and tried to neutralise enemy fighters as they squirted. We could hear a close and fairly heavy battle not far from us, in the direction of another team commanded by Blaine Diddams. Didds came on the radio and said, 'Frag out,' meaning grenades were going off. A few more bursts of fire went back and forth from both sides. Then he said, 'Devil's down.'

I heard it but refused to compute its meaning. I jumped on the radio and said, 'Say again?'

'Devil's down. Dog's down.'

I was hoping he was just wounded, but the amount of gunfire coming from around their position told me to expect the worst.

There was no time to think about what might have happened. Bruce said, 'Let's flank these guys,' and we started to manoeuvre into position. Bruce coordinated with the two teams in contact, one being Didds's. There were more bursts of gunfire from both sides. Then someone came on the radio saying, 'Didds is hit, he's down.' We didn't know any more than what we could hear. A few more frags and some more covering fire went in, and it came over the comms that our boys had got Didds out.

The fight was very much on. We pushed down into the aqueduct where the enemy fighters were shooting from.

Bruce said, 'Do you want to take one of the other guys and split up and give us some covering fire while we clear through this aqueduct?'

Taking another team member with me, I moved up on a flank to the enemy firing position. Two rounds pinged against the wall above our heads. We put in covering fire while Bruce and the rest of the team put some frags in. I could see someone lying behind a tree and shot him. There was a break in the wall and I told my mate, one of the young fellows, 'Cover down in that direction so someone doesn't hit us from behind.' It was a tight little area with conceal-ment from mud walls and thick vegetation, a great spot for these fighters to scurry around unseen so they could counterattack our positions. I got on my guts and crawled towards the aqueduct. Bruce had thrown another frag. I saw Devil down there, slumped onto his side with his tongue hanging out. There was no doubt now. He was dead.

We cleared the immediate area and found two fighters with AKs and PKMs. For such a small force, they'd done some terrible damage. Later, after talking with the guys who'd been in contact with them, we pieced together what had happened. These two insurgents had been in a shootout with Didds and his team, plus Devil and Nick. They were no more than 10 metres away, but the walls and vegetation had given them protection. Devil had identified their posi-tion, run at them and taken one by the arm. Devil knew his job, which was to protect our soldiers. The team were trying to shoot the insurgent without hitting Devil, and Nick was trying to recall Devil. Then the insurgent shot Devil through the back of the neck. In the same passage of fighting, Didds had been hit by a round that passed through his clavicle and hit his aorta. Even immediate medical care wouldn't have saved him, though Barry was working on him, under fire, trying everything possible to keep him alive.

In the aftermath, an AME helicopter came in and took Didds out. More rounds were shot at the bird as it flew away, and we got the culprits, eventually. Once that part of the village was cleared and we could rest, I was sitting beside Nick. We had Devil on a stretcher. Nick went off to clear out an area while I sat there, patting Devil on the head, spending those last couple of minutes with him.

We killed twelve enemy fighters that day. They'd been setting up an ambush for an American–Afghan patrol, and we'd landed right on top of them. But foiling their ambush meant little to us. We all had an empty feeling. That was the last day of what might have been our last trip to Afghanistan. It was a shit way to end what had been a really successful trip.

When we got back to base, we took Devil to the vet and put him on the table. We found out where he'd been hit and got his vest off him. It was tough seeing him lying on the stainless steel table. Nick and I each knew what the other was going through, and just hung around to be there for one another.

Back in Dorrigo, when I was a kid, our dog Angie walked off to die alone in the bush. She was old and blind and deaf by then, and just walked off the acreage, never to be found. Dad spent three days walking around the bush looking for her. Seeing how upset he was, I was quite shocked. It was the first time I was hit with a realisation of how sad life can be for adults. I remembered this now, when I was saying goodbye to Devil. Nick and I had been through so much with him, the sense of loss was extremely deep. Our relationship with the dog was completely unconditional. I felt like I'd lost my best mate, my brother. I think that's how I would feel if I did lose my brother. I was just gutted. This must have been how Dad was feeling in those days when he was searching for Angie.

I was dirty at fate that I hadn't been with Devil. I had no bitterness towards Nick, who'd done a fantastic job with Devil and was feeling as devastated as I was, but I couldn't help wondering how I might have been able to protect him. I think about that in every situation – Devil, each of the boys who died in Afghanistan, going all the way back to Mum. *What could I have done if I'd been there? Could I have changed it?* I couldn't help feeling that way.

Devil got his own ramp ceremony, as had Quake a week earlier. He was put in a casket with the Australian flag and his collar on top, before he was sent down to Kandahar to be cremated. I'm still devastated about him to this day. In June 2013 we had a ceremony honouring the dogs who'd been killed in Afghanistan – a sculpture of a dog with his work vest on and a roll of honour made of rock from the same quarry as the rock used for the roll of honour of the men who've died there. Devil's name is honoured alongside those of the men.

As a squadron, we were adamant about escorting Didds home. That afternoon, once we returned to base, the guys lined up to say goodbye to him before he was fully wrapped up. We travelled home with him to Perth, to give him to his family. It was the only way to do it right.

There's a saying that you're never a good bloke until you're dead. But Didds really was a great guy: larger than life, very generous, a lover of fun. To unwind, he would rope the boys into a poker game. I'm not a big gambler but I enjoy the social side, so I was often the dealer. We always got a laugh when Didds started losing his money. He was such a hustler. One game, he pulled out a flush first go. He'd never done that before, and was so excited he had photos taken of himself with his hand of cards. It's a memory we all cherish.

A country boy, he loved his motorbikes, leather jackets, blue jeans and cowboy boots. Not long before he died,

I was talking with him about getting a good set of cowboy boots back in Perth. He helped me search the internet for the proper ones that come just below your knees. I said, 'Mate, out of thanks, whenever I wear denim jeans I'm going to wear these boots.' He said, 'I'll hold you to that.' It didn't matter if it was midsummer in Afghanistan, he held me to it.

And he still does. When I wear jeans, I always wear my boots.

EPILOGUE: Rewriting History

As I write this, it's increasingly likely that that 2012 trip to Afghanistan will have been my last. Losing both Didds and Devil on the last day of fighting left more than a bad taste. There's a gap in our lives that will never be filled. It makes me angry, but it's also a permanent reminder of the risks we faced. No matter how well we were achieving our aims, we were at war, and lives could be taken at any moment.

The coalition plans to pull out its major military forces from the country before the end of 2014. That doesn't mean training and mentoring personnel won't still be there, and the need for Special Forces operators can arise at any time. I may still be sent back there. But the withdrawal opens the question of what we achieved, what we've left behind for that country's future, and whether our participation and the sacrifices we made were worthwhile.

I'm definitely proud of what we achieved since we first got there. From a Regimental perspective and from the perspective of a soldier, we travelled a massive distance in those six years from 2006. Our combat experience increased by many multiples. We now have better techniques, tactics and procedures, smarter ways of doing things, and, in all the intangibles that strengthen a regiment, we've grown. If not for those seven years, we wouldn't understand fighting as we do now and wouldn't be as effective a defence force for Australia. We've tested our TTPs in the most challenging reality. I'm full of pride in what we've done.

The question of what we left behind will take years to be answered. Certainly the Taliban was decimated as a fighting body by 2013, but there are many forces undermining the Afghan Government and security forces. I'm not qualified to talk about the broader political picture, but I did see a lot of the transition towards indigenous control of the people's security.

Before 2011, we worked mainly with Afghan National Army (ANA) personnel. Since 2009, there had been increasing involvement with the Provincial Response Company – Uruzgan (PRC-U). We'd been reluctant about working with the PRC-U, because we had some easily trained, capable ANA soldiers, and were concerned that these PRC-U personnel might just be thugs off the street with tribal connections and beliefs. Initially, these fears were confirmed. They didn't want to do the work the way we did. It was hard to train them. They were always claiming some- one was being offended. 'This is my sister-in-law's father's cousin. He's a good bloke,' they'd say, when we knew full well the suspect wasn't a good bloke. Or we'd go somewhere and find guns in a house, and instead of arresting the owner, the PRC-U would come out and say, 'He won't do it any more. Don't arrest him. He's a friend of ours.'

We understood that it would take time for them to trust us. But they needed to understand that real trust has to be earnt, and until their loyalty was to the job, not to their old mates and relatives, trust would be hard to come by. They had to *want* to make the place better, *want* to go to villages and make them safer. Some of these guys, if they didn't live in that particular village, they didn't see it as their problem. They worked hard in short bursts, but then wanted to sit around under a tree for the rest of the day. Or, we'd be clearing a village in a high-threat situation and they'd put their weapons down, have a wash and prepare to pray. We couldn't believe they would want to stop and pray in front of a building that might be filled with people wanting to shoot them.

From above, we were constantly getting pressure about making allowances for their culture. But sometimes their culture included smoking drugs or shooting smack before coming to work. We didn't want to compromise our standards or risk our lives just because they were fucked up on drugs. We wouldn't allow it in our army. They had to come up to our standards. When the pressure to allow their practices became too insistent, one of my mates said no. 'I won't go out the gate with them if they're stoned, even if it causes the operation to be cancelled.' The trainers said, 'You've got to understand, it's their culture. They're good guys.' He said, 'No, *you*'ve got to understand, I'm the one going outside the wire with them.'

No issue highlights the question of trust as much as the green-on-blue murders. We were worried for a long while before they began. The more PRC-U we had to work with, the fewer screening processes were in place to see where they'd come from, who they hung out with outside work, where their loyalties lay. We tried to bio-enrol them – fingerprint them and see if they had insurgent allegiances – but this process was limited to a few. When we were going on jobs with them, they would ring their mates and say, 'The green eyes [naming us after the glow cast by our NVGs] are walking up your valley now.' By the time we got there, the targets had disappeared. We had to start taking their phones off them.

Green-on-blues became a constant anxiety. In 2011, at the height of the insider attack events, we developed an early warning system of code words that we could rapidly transmit among ourselves if an Afghan shot one of us. We couldn't take the risk that there was a level of coordination among them and that others were preparing to shoot us in the back. It's a measure of how low the trust was. Once, after we'd finished an assault, the PCs came in to talk to the troop sergeant and the captain about the next step. One of the terps saw a PRC-U guy sweeping his weapon across that little group. He didn't pull the trigger, but was making that gesture. Only he knew what was going through his head, but we weren't going to cop it. We said, 'You're gone, mate. We're not taking that risk.'

It's hard to know how widespread untrustworthy people are, how far they've infiltrated the government forces. We found scores of Afghans who were great workers and wanted to fix their country. They were sick of the Taliban. The SAS was in a lucky position, because we could scour the place for the best soldiers and train them up. Within reason. It wasn't so easy for the regular army. What's more, it could be hard to train them as a collective. They might be willing, but if the man commanding them was a religious zealot or was corrupt, they would follow his influence and act differently when he was watching them.

For the future, if the coalition's intervention in Afghanistan is going to leave a legacy of stability, I think what they need is the numbers and resources to have a large footprint on the ground. I think the best Afghan personnel are well enough trained to do high-threat prosecutions as a tactical unit — to do the kinds of things we've done as Special Forces. What they don't have is reach into tribal and rural areas, where strongholds develop and the insurgents move in. I think the Afghan authorities have the district centres under control. For the outlying regions, it's going to come down to numbers and assets.

When I think about whether it was all worth it, however, I don't think about the future politics and stability of Afghanistan. These are enormous matters way beyond my control – beyond anyone's control other than the Afghan people themselves.

Was it worth losing all those fantastic soldiers, from Andrew Russell in 2002 through to Didds in 2012? And possibly more? When you go to war, there's a chance someone's going to get hurt, whether that's physically wounded, psychologically wounded, or losing their life and never coming back to their family. That's who we are. We sign up for that. That's why we train and work so hard, to minimise that threat. If we weren't smart and weren't adapting our TTPs, we would have lost a lot more people. I'm proud of our efforts in pitting good training and smart operations against a ruthless insurgency and the ever-present demon of bad luck.

As far as job satisfaction goes, and personal pride in working with the best people I've ever had the privilege of being around, working in a brotherhood, my time in the Regiment has been far ahead of anything I could imagine. The best soldiers I have ever seen and worked with are all from the Regiment. It is such an honour to have been able to serve and fight alongside them. Words can't do it justice, that sense of achievement in having completed a mission successfully. Just as words can't describe it if you lose someone. For me, as a soldier, it's all been worth it. But that's more my gut feeling than something measurable.

Was it worth it, geopolitically? Was World War I worth it? World War II? Korea? Vietnam? You can argue that about any war. Would the Al Qaeda terrorists have flown into more buildings if we'd left them alone in Afghanistan? Would there have been another Bali bomb produced by people trained in Afghanistan? We can never know for certain. But does not knowing mean we shouldn't have tried to reduce that threat? Protecting our country doesn't just mean battening down the hatches and staying on our island and hoping the threat won't come our way. It can mean going somewhere else, going to war to uproot the threat at its source. Ultimately, you just don't know, you can't know, if it's worth it. But as a soldier, you can look at your own role. I wanted to go because that was what I had trained for. If your country wants you to go somewhere, 99 per cent of soldiers will say yes. This is what they've dedicated their lives to.

And it's not just so we can fulfil our training. Potentially the threat can reach out and touch anyone at home. I guess for people who've already made their mind up that going to Afghanistan wasn't worth it, I would ask what they would say if there was an attack on Australia. If it happened to their family, and they were directly affected, what would they then want their country to do? Until it directly happens to them, a lot of people don't care. When it does happen to them, they care with all their heart. Our leaders had to make that judgement on behalf of the country, and when we were sent, we soldiers had to carry out our tasks to the best of our ability.

One question I've been asked, as our involvement comes to an end, is whether I respect the enemy fighters and can ever see myself making the personal kind of peace with them that soldiers were able to make after the World Wars and Vietnam. As far as respect as fighters goes ...

Yes I do respect them. They live a difficult life and do know how to fight hard. As far as making a personal kind of peace . . . It's too early to say. While I like the idea, I don't know if we have that level of mutual respect that soldiers would have had in a traditional war. The dirty tactics the insurgents employ are hard to get over. A lot of the Talibs we came across were pieces of shit, to put it politely, and I don't feel any remorse whatsoever for what happened to them. If you saw how they treated their women and their families and how they barged into communities that didn't want them but weren't strong enough to kick them out, how they threatened and intimidated kids into fighting for them, how they beheaded and mutilated people – no, it didn't worry me if they died. I didn't hate them, but over time I worried less and less if I had to kill one of them. It's a nice thought that one day we could sit down over a cup of tea, but to be honest I'll be surprised if it ever happens. I don't know if I respect them as peers. You might have that conversation over that cup of tea, but this was not an old-fashioned war.

*

Which brings us back to the question I was asking myself at the very beginning of this. I was bestowed a Victoria Cross for my actions on one day, but I've come to see that as a recognition of what we all did over a long period of time. I'm just the one who happened to be singled out to represent my regiment. I accept that I acted bravely, as we all acted bravely every day. But the question remains, when I unknowingly arrived at that crossroad, when I could (some would say should) have chosen a different path, when that voice in my head told me to go back to that terp, where did that voice come from?

I've thought a lot about whether I would be so driven if not for what happened to Mum. If whatever it was that happened to her never took place, I don't know where I'd be. More than likely, this drive was always within me and would have come out with some focus. I might have been in the firies or the police if circumstances were different.

If Mum was still around, I might have pursued something like this, but would I have been fuelled to drive myself through those two years in the infantry, through SAS selection, through Reo, through all the things we did overseas, through the hardship of being away from Emma and the kids? I just don't know. What I do know is that what happened to Mum turned me into a very driven individual. Anything like that is going to shape a young man and what he does with his life. There was the period after it when I had to find my own way, but looking back, I do think that what happened to Mum was an accelerant for me to become the type of person I am, deep down. It did happen and it did spark me. I see what's happened since as the best outcome I could have achieved, and a way to honour her memory.

As for Dad, I said at one point that he might have been angry with me for joining an army he'd spent a lot of his life resenting. But I doubt it. I reckon he'd probably be pretty happy with what I've done. In my twenties, I found it difficult, when I was having my adventures overseas, not to be able to send him photos, knowing he would have been right into the things I was up to. Still now, I really miss that. Everyone who loses a parent misses out on that. It's still hard not being able to share my experiences with him. One big thing has changed, though. The whole time I had him, and for years after he died, I felt like I had to prove myself to him all the time. I'm not so much like that now. Whatever point I felt I needed to prove, I must have made it. If I could say anything to the old man now, me in my cams and him in his slouch hat and green Vietnam shirt, it would be that imitation is an awesome form of flattery.

Would it have been worth it if I hadn't come home? If I'd caught a bullet in that valley near Anaconda on 2 September 2008, or in any other of the contacts I was in? Would it have been worth it if that second bullet on those last few days had shattered my foot instead of just missing? If you ask Emma, she would say no. This is the burden a soldier's partner carries. Every act of valour is potentially an act leading to widowhood. Whether it's worth it depends a lot on who you ask, and when.

Was it worth not seeing three years of my daughter growing up? Probably not. But at least now I'm more confident that Kaylee will grow up in a safer and more secure world than if we hadn't gone to Afghanistan. At least I know there's less threat coming from that part of the world. And I'll be around to see the rest of her life, and Hamish's as well.

I guess it all begs a question about the future: Where do you go after spending nearly ten years in one of the world's most elite military units? What job could possibly be as exciting and unpredictable as that one?

I have options in the military to move forward and reach higher ranks, but that lends itself to more time behind a desk. Maybe it is time for that. I am not sure. Perhaps, like when I was young, it's time for something completely left-field and different from the Special Air Service Regiment. Who knows? I could quite happily manage a resort that overlooked a world-class surf break. Better yet, Emma could manage it and I could go find unridden and uncrowded waves, if that ever became an option.

Before I left on my last trip, in February 2012, it was harder than ever to go. Hamish was almost crawling. I was rocking him back and forth in the days before I left, egging him on. Then Kaylee and I had a conversation. I sat her down and said, 'You know Daddy's got to go away for work.'

'Yeah, just up the hill,' she said, thinking of my day job at Swanbourne.

'No, for a long time.'

'Like last year?'

'Like last year.'

I took off my wedding ring and asked her to look after it. She put it in a little box and could focus on taking care of it: her little piece of responsibility.

'But why do you have to go away?'

'It's my job.'

'What do you do when you go away?'

I've never lied to her or brushed it off. I may as well let her know what I do – in her terms. And so I gave her a five-year-old's version of the war on terror. 'Dad's in the army, and we fight for the country so you and Mummy can be nice and safe at home and bad people don't come into the country to try to hurt you.'

'Where do you go?'

'To another country far away.'

'Who are you fighting?'

'I have to fight bad people. Sometimes there are not very nice people in the world, and we go over there to make sure they don't come here.'

'But Dad. Are they fighting for land? What are they fighting for?'

'That's a good question. Sometimes for land, sometimes because they don't like each other, sometimes because they grow up fighting each other. My job is to go over there and help out.'

She seemed pretty much at ease with that. She'd been able to ask her questions, and was satisfied with the answers.

She gave me a hug and said, 'Thanks, Daddy.'

Acknowledgements

My acknowledgments could go on forever. I have no last and no least. I have always found inspiration from the less obvious sources, so here goes:

Big thanks first up to Emma (the rock), Kaylee and Hamish. You guys are the reason I come home every day; thank you for reminding me we are human. We have missed some time together, but I am looking forward to enjoying all the time from here on and growing older together.

Thanks to Malcolm Knox for his professionalism, understanding and friendship. We will get that wave one day. Tom Gilliatt and the team at Pan Mac, your patience is outstanding.

Thanks to my brother Brent, you were and will be my hero forever. Also to Kate, Taylor, Abbi and Charlize. I promise we will come and have a family holiday again soon.

Thanks to my extended family: Auntie Margaret and Uncle Ken, Val and Ross, Kenny and Julie – you were always there when we needed you the most. Thanks also for letting me show up unannounced, eat your fridge dry and sleep.

Thanks especially to Jo Beaumont. Not only for basically being my second mum and treating me like one of her own children, but for those critical hours, days and years after Dad and Mum were no longer around. Thanks again and again and again. Words do not do your heart and nature justice. You as well, Gaz.

Thanks to my old friends Murray, Bleaks, Vaughan and Melissa. Good times and good memories.

Thanks to Kelvin for introducing me to surfing but also for teaching me surf etiquette. As well as how to constantly have fun no matter how old you get.

Thanks to the Dorrigo RSL Sub-branch and Bob Denner for his help with Legacy.

Thanks to the people of Dorrigo for coming together and supporting us at one of our hardest times. You truly are a great example of an Australian community.

Thanks to Mike and Misty. Your friendship is straight and true. Thanks for all the good times through Canada and America. One day we will get those Steelheads, Mikey. Thanks to all the amazing friends and people for the great times we had throughout Canada – you will know who you are.

Chris 'Camel' Tulloch: Thanks for the long nights, big laughs, pints of Guinness and snowmaking adventures. Snowboarding still beats skiing, sorry mate! Thanks to all the blokes I ever worked with while making snow. Both here in Australia and also in the US. Hope the snow is dumping and blue skies are forecast for the next day, wherever you are.

Thanks to Dom Freestone for all those parties, hard work days and fun waves around Newcastle.

Thank you Dad. For showing and instilling in me a sense of adventure, tenacity, good work values and how to be a man.

Thanks Mum. I am still yet to meet someone in the world who has a kinder and more pure nature. Thanks for showing me understanding, compassion and how to fight for what you believe in. You were taken from this world earlier than you should've been. Thank you for telling me that there was nothing in this world I could not achieve if I truly wanted it.

To all my cousins: Kay, Tony, Chrissy (Jindabyne was special), Christine, Fiona and Brodie. The times we shared and fun we had should be experienced by every family. Family by blood but friends by choice.

Thanks to Mark Occhilupo for your advice and showing that people can turn their lives around.

Thanks to the following: Steve Paterson – cheers for being the asshole! Dave Harris, Nish Miles – you are amazing at what you do and thank you for the sounding board; Dave and Michelle Mulhall, sorry to do that to you on your first week on the job. Didy Grahame, Peter Harvey, Tony Sanftl, Kathy Sweeney – always be ready! Gary Murphy, Drew P, Willie Apiata VC, Bruce Lee, Johnny Chimpston – you have the funniest way of looking at the world and I have never laughed so hard as I have with you.

Thanks to Hollywood Hospital for looking after two of the three most important people in my life.

To anyone I have ever met, or forgotten, that has made me laugh or made my time on this planet all the richer.

To all those who have served, both here and around the world, who have been wounded in the line of duty. Your journey is an inspiration that reminds me every day: 'What's my excuse?'

Devil . . . Thank you. You were unconditional and saved my life and others. Thank you also to Quake, Kuga and Fax for doing the same.

To all those I have ever served with – it has been a pleasure. To all of you in the Special Air Service Regiment from the beginning to the present – it has been an absolute honour and nothing short of the most unforgettable times of my life. It is an unbelievable job and lifestyle. For those of you I have fought alongside, I hope these words have done us justice. You are the best soldiers in the world and fighting with you has made my soldiering above and beyond what I ever thought it could be. If nothing else, at least I have given plenty of ammo for stirrers!